MARIAN DEVOTION IN THIRTEENTH-CENTURY FRENCH LYRIC

T0335078

Texts centred on the mother of Jesus abound in religious traditions the world over, but thirteenth-century Old French lyric stands apart, both because of the enormous size of the Marian cult in thirteenth-century France and the lack of critical attention the genre has garnered from scholars.

As hybrid texts, Old French Marian songs combine motifs from several genres and registers to articulate a devotional message. In this comprehensive and illuminating study, Daniel E. O'Sullivan examines the movement between secular and religious traditions in medieval culture embodied by Old French religious song. He demonstrates that Marian lyric was far more than a simple, mindless imitation of secular love song. On the contrary, Marian lyric participated in a dynamic interplay with the secular tradition that different composers shaped and reshaped in light of particular doctrinal and aesthetic concerns. It is a corpus that reveals itself to be far more malleable and supple than past readers have admitted.

With an extensive index of musical and textual editions of dozens of songs, *Marian Devotion in Thirteenth-Century French Lyric* brings a heretofore neglected genre to light.

DANIEL E. O'SULLIVAN is an assistant professor in the Department of Modern Languages at the University of Mississippi.

Marian Devotion
in Thirteenth-Century French Lyric

DANIEL E. O'SULLIVAN

UNIVERSITY OF TORONTO PRESS
Toronto Buffalo London

Reprinted in paperback 2021

ISBN 978-0-8020-3885-9 (cloth)
ISBN 978-1-4875-2623-8 (paper)

Library and Archives Canada Cataloguing in Publication

Title: Marian devotion in thirteenth-century French lyric / Daniel E. O'Sullivan.

Other titles: Marian devotion in 13th century French lyric
Names: O'Sullivan, Daniel E., author.

Description: Previously published: Toronto ; Buffalo ; London : University of
Toronto Press, © 2005. | Includes index.

Identifiers: Canadiana 20210167270 | ISBN 9781487526238 (softcover

Subjects: LCSH: Mary, Blessed Virgin, Saint – In literature. | LCSH: Mary,
Blessed Virgin, Saint – Songs and music – History and criticism. | LCSH:
Mary, Blessed Virgin, Saint – Devotion to – France – History – To 1500. |
LCSH: French poetry – To 1500 – History and criticism. | LCSH: Songs,
Old French – 500–1400 – History and criticism. | LCSH: Christian poetry,
French – History and criticism. | LCSH: Church music – France – 500–1400.
| LCSH: Religion and culture – France – History – To 1500.

Classification: LCC PQ155.M3 O88 2021 | DDC 841/.1093823291–DC23

University of Toronto Press acknowledges the financial assistance to its publish-
ing program of the Canada Council for the Arts and the Ontario Arts Council,
an agency of the Government of Ontario.

Canada Council
for the Arts

Conseil des Arts
du Canada

ONTARIO ARTS COUNCIL
CONSEIL DES ARTS DE L'ONTARIO
an Ontario government agency
un organisme du gouvernement de l'Ontario

Funded by the
Government
of Canada

Financé par le
gouvernement
du Canada

Canadä

For my family

Mout a en li cortoizie et valour;
Bien et bontei et charitei i a.
Rutebeuf

Contents

ACKNOWLEDGMENTS   ix

Introduction: Secular and Religious in Medieval Culture   3

Chapter 1: Gautier de Coinci's Marian Poetics of Familiar Strangeness   11
The Human and Divine in Harmony   14
'Amours, qui bien set enchanter' (I Ch 3/RS 851)   20
'Roÿne celestre' (I Ch 5/RS 956, 1903)   24
'D'une amour quoie et serie' (II Ch 5/RS 1212)   27

Chapter 2: Thibaut de Champagne, Genre, and the Medieval Taste for Hybrids   33
Thibaut in the Line of Gautier   36
Thibaut's Hybridized Marian Songs   39
'Commencerai a fere un lai': Genre and Aesthetic Play   49

Chapter 3: Voicing Marian Devotion in Women's Devotional Song   54
Songs in the Voice of Everywoman   57
Religious Women Voicing Marian Devotion   63
Mary's Voice: 'Lasse, que devendrai gié'   68

Chapter 4: Jacques de Cambrai, Distinctive Traditionalism, and Kaleidoscopic Contrafacta   74
Choices of Motif, Theme, and Model: The Case for Distinctive Traditionalism   75

Towards a Generative Model of Kaleidoscopic Contrafacture   79
Traditionalism, Innovation, and 'Retrowange novelle'   87
The Future of Old French Marian Song   90

Chapter 5: Rutebeuf: Beyond the World of Marian Song   93
Rutebeuf's Polemical Marian Poetry   94
Marian Devotion Dramatized   98
When Mary Intercedes: 'Un dist de Nostre Dame'   108

Conclusion: Contrafacture and Cultural Exchange   114

APPENDIX OF TEXTUAL AND MUSICAL EDITIONS OF SONGS
AND POEMS   117
NOTES   221
BIBLIOGRAPHY   239
INDEX   259

Acknowledgments

I wish to thank a number of people for their aid while hastening to add that any remaining errors are mine, not theirs. The first is my mentor, colleague, and friend, Matilda Tomaryn Bruckner: her dedication to patient and thoughtful scholarship is an inspiration to me. Second only to her comes Samuel N. Rosenberg, who generously provided detailed comments and invaluable help in translating Old French. For their insights into earlier drafts, I wish to thank H. Wayne Storey, Laurie Shepard, Kevin Newmark, and Dwayne Carpenter. I offer special thanks to Karen Duys for the many conversations about Gautier de Coinci, and to Joan Tasker Grimbert for her thoughts on women's songs. For their assistance in matters musicological, I am indebted to Thomas J. Mathiesen, Warren Steel, and to Andrew Fox, who steered me through the complexities of musical notation software. I would like to acknowledge the assistance of Shari Grove of Boston College Libraries; Nancy Boerner of Indiana University Libraries; Michelle Emanuel of the University of Mississippi Libraries; and Monique Cohen and her staff at the manuscript room of the Bibliothèque Nationale de France in Paris. Thanks also to the departments of Romance Languages at Boston College, French and Italian at Indiana University, and Modern Languages at the University of Mississippi. The College of Liberal Arts and Office of Research and Special Programs at the University of Mississippi provided essential financial support, for which I am grateful. For their editorial acumen and professionalism, I would like to thank Suzanne Rancourt, Miriam Skey, and Barbara Porter of the University of Toronto Press. I also thank Stephen Monroe for his aid in compiling the index. Finally, I offer thanks to my parents, Carol and Daniel, my sister, Megan, for their loving encouragement, and to my own family – my children, Marion and Colm, and especially my wife, Patti. I dedicate this work to them for their uncompromising support, even as their father and husband spent Saturday reading in the library instead of playing in the park.

MARIAN DEVOTION IN THIRTEENTH-CENTURY FRENCH LYRIC

Introduction:
Secular and Religious in
Medieval Culture

This is a book about expressions of devotion to a unique woman: the Virgin Mary. Texts centred on the mother of Jesus abound in religious traditions the world over. I have chosen to study only a small part of this panegyric tradition, Old French lyric poems of the thirteenth centry, for two reasons. First, the cult of the Virgin showed signs of unprecedented growth in thirteenth-century France: the building of cathedrals dedicated to Mary, like Notre-Dame de Paris and Chartres; the promulgation of Latin liturgical materials in the form of masses and offices; the foundation of lay confraternities of artisans devoted to Mary; a rich theological tradition that continued debates begun in the previous century on the Virgin birth, the Assumption, and Mary's role as the coredemptrix of humanity; and, finally, the proliferation of hagiographical and pious literature in both Latin and the vernaculars. My second reason is inversely related to the first: in spite of the rich context afforded by this art, theology, and literature, the over one hundred extant Old French lyrics praising Mary have garnered little critical attention from scholars over the last two hundred years. Indeed, in trouvère bibliography, work on secular love song easily eclipses the scattered studies on religious songs.

By and large, the prevailing approach to Marian song, when scholars have studied it, has been anchored in Pierre Bec's now familiar typology of medieval genres that locates individual texts along the axes of *aristocratisant* and *popularisant*. Bec characterizes medieval literature as one of 'interférences registrales' where any given text displays traits of both register X and Y (*La Lyrique française* 1:40–3). The medieval text is fluid – less a work than a work in progress. Unfortunately, the judicious nature of these theoretical considerations is not always apparent in Bec's treatment of particular texts, especially devotional ones, ascribing these to the 'registre pieux' which he calls a 'registre parasite' for its reuse of forms, melodies, and motifs from secular song (*La Lyrique française* 1:149). Anna Drzewicka's two-part article, 'La fonction des emprunts à la poésie profane dans les chansons mariales de Gautier de Coinci,' illustrates the arbitrary nature of Bec's characterization of devotional works: each and every medieval song, whether secular or religious, no matter its national tradition, relies fundamentally on motifs and forms that preceded it.[1] Devotional song is no more parasitical than the *grant chant courtois* that countless scholars have esteemed for well over a century.

It is true, nevertheless, that devotional song is formally indistinguishable from secular song: the two repertoires share melodies as well as rhyme and metrical schemes. Consequently, Marcia Jenneth Epstein derives five thematic categories among the devotional songs she anthologizes: courtly, laudatory, political, catechetic, and personal (21–2).[2] Courtly songs are closely modelled upon the secular *chanson d'amour*; laudatory texts praise Mary; political songs comment upon the state; catechetic songs emphasize doctrine or paraphrase scripture; and personal songs offer personal prayers for forgiveness or salvation (22). Although admirable in its attempt to describe devotional song in and of itself, Epstein's approach fails to account for the fact that individual texts overlap her categories. For instance, in Gautier de Coinci's 'Mere Dieu, virge senee' (II Ch 3/RS 556), the singer praises Mary in the first stanza (laudatory), speaks of Adam and Eve in stanzas three and four and of the Incarnation in stanza five (catechetic), and then offers a final plea for personal and collective salvation (personal).[3] Into which category should we place the song? Even individual stanzas may intermix these categories: for example, Thibaut de Champagne's 'De chanter ne me puis tenir' (RS 1475) contains a stanza that simultaneously praises Mary's beauty, discusses the Incarnation, and alludes to salvation. When faced with songs made up of such stanzas, how is it possible to discern discreet generic categories?

Old French Marian songs are, above all, hybrid texts in which forms and vocabularies common to more than one literary tradition are utilized. However, hybridity does not obviate generic categories. When motifs from different genres are introduced into a song, it is precisely there that the audience becomes conscious of the text's generic status, mixed as it may be.[4] Marian song combines motifs from several genres and registers to articulate its devotional message, not because of some impossiblity, as Bec contends, 'd'arriver à créer des genres spirituels autonomes' (*La Lyrique française* 1:149), but because, as we shall see, it makes the message clearer, easier to disseminate, and, perhaps just as important, aesthetically pleasing. In order to understand this, we must venture beyond simply recognizing that the devotional repertoire shares poetic and musical material with the secular tradition. We need to contemplate the meaning of the to-and-fro movement between secular and religious traditions in medieval culture that Old French religious song embodies. Doing so demonstrates that Marian lyric was far more than a simple, mindless imitation of secular love song. On the contrary, as I hope to show in my study of lyrics representative of the whole corpus, Marian song participated in a dynamic interplay with the secular tradition that different composers shaped and reshaped in light of particular doctrinal and aesthetic concerns. Consequently, the corpus reveals itself, in spite of its inevitable thematic continuity, to be far more malleable and supple than past readers have admitted.

Even if the religious interacts dynamically with the secular, the poetry is still devotional in intent, and so it behooves us to consider the peculiarity of religious poetry. Does one have to believe to understand religious poetry or, to pose the question differently, do believers understand religious poetry 'better' than nonbelievers? For poets like Gautier de Coinci, the answer is clearly yes: to do otherwise means that one misunderstood the text. Gautier urges us – he commands us, in fact – to convert ourselves to Marian devotion and, in so doing, he converts secular motifs to religious purposes in the hermeneutic tradition of Augustine's *De Doctrina Christiana*.[5] In this tradition, the text matters little in one sense: any and every text means the same thing; yet, in another, each and every text acquires value as a cipher of God's transcendence if the reader knows how to read properly. Consequently, for Gautier, religious language conveys unequivocal Truth. The secular poetic sign's overdeterminacy, its ambiguity, renders secular poetry both a foolish waste of time and a dangerous activity:

As mos ou n'a point *d'efficace*
Ne be je mie. Fi! qu'a ce
Ne doit baer hom qui riens vaille.
Mielz vaut li grains ne fait la paille.   (II Pr 1: 83–6, my emphasis)

[For words that are not efficacious
I care not at all. Hmph! a man who is
worth anything should not care at all about this.
The grain is worth more than the chaff.]

Like wheat used for an end different from itself, namely, flour, the religious sign is used only as a means to an end; it always points beyond itself and towards God. Something lies beyond the sign itself. However, there is no 'going beyond' secular poetic speech: the chaff has no use after the harvest: the poetic event, once over, fades into nothingness. Secular poetic speech is merely speech for its own sake; religious poetry, by contrast, lives on in the life of the listener, because she is moved – Gautier uses the word 'esciter' (II Pr 2: 109) – to Marian devotion.

For other poets, like Thibaut de Champage and Jacques de Cambrai, not to mention those of us living on this side of the Reformation, such distinctions are less clear. Hans-Georg Gadamer and Paul Riceour have posited that the transcendent quality formerly ascribed to only religious language belongs to all language. Gadamer concludes that understanding a text, any text, means that we have applied (*appliziert*) it to our own historical situation.[6] One can disagree with a text's message and refuse to apply it to one's life – promising devotion to Mary, for example – but doing so means that application has already taken place: only a person who has applied the text to his or her historical situation has understood it. The promise to love Mary occurs in a secondary world, that of the text. Paul Ricoeur refines this idea in the concept of 'appropriation': the hermeneutical gesture by which the text appropriates us – not vice versa – and projects a world of possible self-understandings. The theological implication of this is, asserts Ricoeur, considerable:

> The primary task of a hermeneutics is not to bring about a decision in the reader but first to allow the world of being that is the 'thing' of the biblical text to unfold. In this way, above feelings, dispositions, belief or unbelief is placed the proposal of a world. ('Philosophical Hermeneutics and Biblical Hermeneutics,' 95–6)

Affirmations or denials of belief or faith therefore follow, not precede, appropriation, resulting less in a desacralization of religious language than a sacralization of all language, and transcendence becomes an experience of all texts, not just religious ones. Religious poetry moves each and every reader, regardless of personal belief, at some fundamental level. Do believers understand religious poetry differently? Surely, but they do not necessarily understand it 'better' than nonbelievers.

Reading, analysing, and understanding the dynamic relationships among the devotional and secular lyric and literary traditions studied in these pages means being conscious of context – not only the literary, philosophical, and theological implications briefly sketched above, but also two other important contexts. The first is the primary texts' manuscript context. When we think of trouvère song, we understandably think first of compendious chansonniers such as Paris, BnF fr. 844, the *Chansonnier du roi*; Paris, Arsenal 5198; or of Oxford, Bodleian, Douce 308. Just as often as devotional lyric comes down in these collections, however, it is transmitted in fragments, miracle compilations, collections of devotional tales, and more heterogeneous anthologies of spoken didactic, satiric, and devotional verse. As modern critics too often divorce these religious works (or secular ones, for that matter) from their manuscript context for the purposes of both interpretation and editions, it is all too easy to lose sight of their place in medieval culture and their relationship – or lack thereof – with other products of culture, be they secular or religious. Consideration of these texts' material context will, therefore, prove crucial.

The second significant context regards the songs' mode of performance: most of these texts were sung. Concentrating solely on words would bracket off an essential part of these works, that is, their musical properties. Like language, melody is a system of signification that creates meaning through differences, especially when considered along with syntax, prosody, and rhetoric. Large- and small-scale repetitions of melody, musical rhyme, motivic development, contrafacture, and other techniques give shape to a song, thereby enhancing the meaning of words. In turn, poetic techniques – rhyme, metre, enjambement, rhetorical figures – as well as syntactical arrangements enhance the experience of music. It is to this dialectical relationship between words and music that I devote considerable space in the following pages.[7]

The technique of contrafacture – the setting of an existing melody to new words – deserves special comment for both its importance to the devotional corpus and its reception by modern critics. For the purpose of my discussion, I use the term 'contrafacture' for the process of putting new texts to existing melodies. I call the resulting song a 'contrafactum' (pl. 'contrafacta'). Critics like Pierre Bec point to the widespread use of contrafacture in the religious tradition to conclude that devotional lyric was derivative, parasitical, and secondary to the secular tradition. Such a conclusion misses the point entirely of many contrafacta: their composers use existing melodies not because they deem their religious compositions unworthy of a new melody, but rather, as we shall see, because doing so furthers their devotional aim. The discursive relationship between secular model and devotional contrafactum often prove polemical, not neutral, as one might conclude when perusing indexes of metrical or musical form such as those by István Frank for troubadour lyric or Ulrich Mölk and Friedrich Wolfzettel for trouvère song. I call mine a generative approach to contrafacture: the reuse of melody generates associations in the minds of the audience, resulting in a highly allusive texture in performance that enhances rather than detracts from the experience of devotional song in performance. Not every song analysed is a contrafactum, and not every song invites an explicit musico-poetic analysis; neverthless, even when considerations of music are not at the forefront of the discussions surrounding these songs, melody should never be entirely absent from our minds. Indeed, when discussing Rutebeuf's largely nonmusical corpus, melody, in light of its absence, proves equally significant.

With these considerations of context in mind, I begin my study with Gautier de Coinci, who became the first significant composer of medi-eval French Marian lyric by inserting vernacular Marian songs into his *Miracles de Nostre Dame*. The place of lyric in this large devotional project proves helpful in outlining the first interpretive frame for reading ver-nacular religious lyric. When focusing on the lyrics themselves within this context, I move dialectically between tradition and individual song and between words and music to show how Gautier combines various elements to articulate a cogent religious argument, one calling for our conversion to Marian devotion. I will first look at these elements more abstractly before considering individual songs. These songs articulate a message that is both familiar and strange to the initiated listener as they utilize components that are also strangely familiar to an audience initi-ated into the Latin religious and vernacular secular traditions.

In moving to the religious songs by Thibaut de Champagne we extend the conclusions of the first chapter: Gautier mixes motifs from both reli-gious and secular registers for his religious literary project, but Thibaut pushes the hybrid nature of vernacular religious song to new limits. This extreme hybridization seemingly complicates the task of interpretation, but I conclude from my analysis that many of Thibaut's songs may be read simultaneously as Marian lyrics or as examples of other genres. This kind of pluralistic reading strategy allows for a highly enriched encounter with Thibaut's lyric corpus. Where Gautier attempts to funnel interpretation in the direction of conversion and dogmatism, Thibaut restores herme-neutical freedom to the listener.

Devotional songs were neither the exclusive purview of male authors nor sung only in the male voice. In my third chapter, I demonstrate how songs in the female voice offer us an interesting counterpoint to those in the male voice. When read in context, these songs, especially those that survive in the so-called *Rosarius* (Paris, BnF fr. 12483), demonstrate how the female voice addresses concerns both common to all humanity and specific to women's issues. Moreover, the female voices heard are highly varied among themselves: we hear those of Everywoman, of female religious, and even of Mary herself. Women's devotional songs, neither identical to nor mere inversions of songs in the male voice, provide distinctive, unique voicings of Marian devotion.

Chapter 4 on Jacques de Cambrai considers the meaning of participation in the Marian devotional tradition once it had become well established. By the time this northern trouvère was active, an abundance of motifs, types, and images were available, but through his particular choices among textual and melodic motifs, his production proves distinctive, and so I name this quality 'distinctive traditionalism.' Our understanding of contrafacture must also be nuanced. When motifs are shared among several repertoires and melodies reused among several songs, as was the case when Jacques was composing, it becomes difficult to posit a simple, linear model of influence. The associations created when melodies or motifs are reused repeatedly in several texts over time produce what I call kaleidoscopic contrafacta, offering us a rich glimpse into the reception of these songs. From that question, we will consider the question of Jacques's influence upon the following generation of composers of vernacular Marian songs. It may indeed be more important than past work has suggested.

With my final chapter on Rutebeuf, I venture, strictly speaking, beyond the world of lyric: whereas the work of the composers of chapters 1 through 4 was sung, Rutebeuf's poetry was spoken. In the past, several scholars have attempted to define Rutebeuf's 'lyric' or 'lyrical' works, pointing out that many of his poems express a subjective, personal viewpoint characteristic of lyric poetry (Frappier, Spencer) or are nonnarrative or nondramatic in form and mode and therefore lyric. In the hands of Rutebeuf, the vernacular Marian tradition proves most malleable and supple. In many ways, in fact, Rutebeuf's poetry represents the culmination of the tradition by combining many of the salient characteristics of the poets that preceded him in a different mode of performance and thereby taking the tradition a step further, a step beyond the world of lyric song and into the wider vernacular literary tradition.

Note on Textual and Musical Editions and on Translations

Many songs are examined closely in this study, and I have given ample citations, both textual and musical, in the text itself. For the convenience of the reader, I have provided an appendix of melodic editions of the first stanza of each song together with complete editions of texts with translations. Songs that do not appear in the appendix are translated along with the original citation in the text.

chapter one

Gautier de Coinci's Marian Poetics of Familiar Strangeness

Gautier de Coinci (c.1177–1236), prior of Vic-sur-Aisne from 1214 to 1233, was the first important composer of Old French songs to the Virgin. These come incorporated into his *Miracles de Nostre Dame*, a vast collection of vernacular Marian narrative miracles and lyric songs. In order to understand the beginnings of Marian lyric, we need to understand the place of the lyrics in the larger project of the *Miracles* and their relation to the work's prologues, narratives, and prayers. In so doing, we realize that the communicative speech act at the core of Old French Marian lyric works to bring humanity in contact with divinity, and so it follows that Gautier's preferred tropes help accomplish that goal. These come from the Latin liturgical and paraliturgical services as well as from the secular trouvère lyric traditions. Finally, as a reading of every song in the *Miracles* would be both unwieldy and repetitive, I offer readings of three songs in order to show how Gautier's efforts to bring the divine in line with the human results in a poetics of familiar strangeness: Gautier's new vernacular devotional poetics is both familiar and strange to us, much as the Virgin herself occupies a liminal space between humanity and divinity.

The textual architecture of Gautier's *Miracles* is sophisticated.[1] The first of the two books of the *Miracles* begins with a general prologue followed by a prologue to a seven-song lyric cycle. Thirty-four miracles ensue, followed by a lyrico-narrative sequence that relates a miracle that Gautier personally experienced, first in narrative and then in song. The second book opens with only one prologue and a second seven-song cycle. After the prologue, we encounter the miracles of the second book, twenty-three in all, with a sermon on chastity inserted after the first miracle. After the miracles, the reader finds the epilogue, a sermon on fearing death, a prologue to a Marian psalter, the Marian psalter itself, and a song that summarizes the Marian psalter.[2] Finally, Gautier closes out the *Miracles'* structure with three prayers to the Virgin and one prayer to God. The songs form, therefore, a small but, as we shall see, important part of the *Miracles'* devotional aim.

At first glance, the placement of the songs in the *Miracles* seems to relegate them to the subservient role of frame for the miracle stories, even though there is also a frame in the work's prologues. In fact, the absence of a prologue to introduce the seven-song cycle of the second book might also prompt us to think that because he did not bother to write a separate prologue for the second cycle, Gautier deemed his songs to be less important. However, a comparison of the beginning of the second prologue of the first book – the one that introduces the first song cycle – and the end of the prologue to the second book, that is, the one that precedes the second song cycle, leads to different conclusions.

> *Ainz qu'*ouvrir welle le grant livre
> Qui mout me done et mout me livre
> Grant matere longe et prolipse
> De la pucele qui l'eclipse
> ...
> Canter vos veil deus chançonnetes.
> ...
> Un *petitet,* s'il ne vos grieve
> *Ainz que* plus lise, *veil chanter.*   (I Pr 2: 1–4, 7, 16–17, my emphasis)

> [Before opening the long book
> that gives me and provides me
> with long and lengthy matter
> about the Virgin who eclipses it,
> ...
> I wish to sing two little songs.
>
> If it does not bother you,
> before I read any more, I wish to sing a little bit.]

> Leü en ai tant que ma teste
> Bien me tesmoigne et bien m'ateste
> Que toz sui vains et toz lassez,

Mais j'ere ja toz repassez
S'un *petitet* chanter, par m'ame,
Puis des doz chans la douce dame.
Ainçoys que dou livre secont
Riens vos die ne riens vos cont,
Talens me prent que de li chant.   (II Pr 1: 387–95, my emphasis)

[I have read so much that my head
tells me and attests indeed
that I am spent and weary,
but I will get entirely past this,
by my soul, if I can sing for a while
some of the sweet lady's sweet songs.
Before I tell you or recount to you
anything of the second book,
a desire to sing of her seizes me.]

The use of similar subordinating conjunctions – 'ainz que' and 'ainçoys que' – and the reuse of 'petitet,' as well as the synonymous expressions of desire in both prologues to sing before reading more miracles suggest that a general prologue to the second song cycle has been subsumed into this single prologue. The fusion of a general prologue with a prologue to the second song cycle suggests that narrative and lyric work in tandem to accomplish an overriding religious and rhetorical goal.

This conclusion is supported by the nature and placement of the lyrico-narrative Leocadia sequence, found between books I and II and that recounts the miracle that Gautier allegedly experienced personally. According to the text, in 1219 the relics of Saint Leocadia and a statue of the Virgin where stolen and then recovered through the intervention of Mary. These events are first recounted in narrative verse and then in three lyrics. Gautier is both protagonist and lyric subject, performing the communicative act that occurs between the human and divine in Marian literature. That speech act has always the same illocutionary function: the speaker surrenders his or her will to the divine, bringing the two realms into contact. Gautier's modelling of this speech act places the Leocadia miracle and lyric cycle in a position of hermeneutic centrality: at this crucial moment, Gautier models the hermeneutical attitude that he sees as proper to his *Miracles*, conflating, in turn, third-person narration, i.e., 'Theophilus called out to Mary,' with first-person lyric enunciation, i.e., 'I call upon Mary,' and fusing them both with the homiletic 'we.' The narrative subject becomes a '(s)he/we,' and the lyric subject, an 'I/we.' Furthermore, since the differing circumstances of performance have no impact upon a narrative protagonist's situation a miracle functions illustratively as an *exemplum*. On the other hand, Marian song creates a more direct relationship between the lyric 'I' and the listener: the listener understands Marian song in the context of his own life, substituting his unique circumstances for the protagonist's narrativized circumstances at the moment of performance. The salvific discourse of Marian song becomes both universally applicable and infinitely specific as it bears directly upon each and every believer's own life situation.[3] Moreover, as the Leocadia sequence comes between the first and second books, it constitutes not only the *Miracles'* hermeneutic centre but also its textual centre.[4] The *Miracles* revolves around the application of Marian devotion by the persona of Gautier and his appropriation by Marian discourse, which in turn intimates that the reader is supposed to do the same when experiencing his songs.

The Human and Divine in Harmony

The wish to reconcile humanity with divinity pervades the *Miracles*. The individual semantic, formal, and rhetorical components of Gautier's lyrics in the seven-song cycles, Leocadia lyrics, and songs that come at the end of the second book evoke this desire. On the semantic level, Gautier derives his material from the intense contemporary interest shown in Mary and the flowering of secular *fin'amors*.[5] In regard to the former, highly sophisticated discussions concerning dogmas such as the Assumption of Mary continued to rage, but the prior of Vic-sur-Aisne shies away from theological subtleties in his poetry to focus primarily upon popular, accepted teachings.[6] In II Ch 2, 'Pour la pucele en chantant me deport' (RS 1930, 1600), II Ch 3, 'Mere Dieu, virge senee' (RS 556), and II Ch 36, 'Entendez tuit ensemble et li clerc et li lai' (RS 83), Gautier uses a play on words that proved popular from Justinian onward: the juxtaposition of 'Ave' – the first word of the 'Ave Maria' – to 'Eva' as a way of demonstrating how Mary, the second Eve, reverses the fate of the human race after the Fall.[7] In II Ch 7, Gautier employs the Old Testament typologies of Isaiah's prophesy of the virgin birth (Isaiah 7:14) and Jesse's rod (Isaiah 11:1, 10). He often calls Mary the 'queen' but alternates between the words 'reine' and 'fierce,' the Old French word for the queen on a chessboard.[8]

Gautier dwells most extensively on the themes of the Incarnation,

Mary's maternity, and marriage to Mary. The first, both historical event and timeless mystery, is treated variously. Gautier sometimes uses the word 'incarnation' without explanation: 'Pucele en cui Jhesus/ Prinst incarnation' (II Ch 4/RS 1546: 45–6). In other instances, he adapts the vocabulary from the dogma's primary source – 'Spiritus Sanctus superveniet in te, et virtus Altissimi obumbravit tibi' [The Holy Spirit will overtake you, and the power of the High One will overshadow you.] (Luke 1:35) – and meditates on the mysterious image of God overshadowing Mary:

Entor li si bon umbre a
Et si tres sain
Que Diex en li s'aümbra
Et jut dedens son saim.   (I Ch 6/RS 1845: 29–32)

[Around her this is such a good
and wholesome shadow
that God shaded himself
and lay in her bosom.]

Although contemplating a most sacred mystery, Gautier plays freely on key words: 'Amons la rose espanie/ Ou Diex prist *aombrement*' [Let us love the blooming rose/ In whom God took shelter (lit. shadow)] (II Ch 5/RS 1212: 34–5, my emphasis). Although these passages are far from hermetic, it is difficult to discern to what extent Gautier's public would have understood them.[9]

Gautier introduces more concrete imagery when he explicitly treats Mary's maternity, a theme already implicit in the Incarnation. For example, in I Ch 7, 'Esforcier m'estuet ma voiz' (RS 1836), he begins nearly every stanza plus the refrain with 'Mere Dieu.' The frequency with which a performer would utter the motif makes the theme significant. In other songs, Gautier mixes lofty vocabulary with concrete imagery of motherhood. In I Ch 8, 'Quant ces floretes florir voy, (RS 1677), Gautier brings together the naturalistic metaphor of Jesus as the 'dous fruit' [sweet fruit] (I Ch 8: 20) with an allusion to Mary's 'douz saim' [sweet breast] (I Ch 8: 19) and the concrete image of a pregnant woman carrying a child (I Ch 8: 19). Like many theologians of his day, Gautier revels in paradoxes such as the creator contained in the created, all while painting a simpler and more concrete portrait of Mary as mother.[10] It is then not surprising that one of Gautier's favourite images of motherhood is a mother nursing her baby, an image that paints a humble portrait of the woman Mary. Whereas medieval noblewomen had the choice between breastfeeding their own children and hiring wet nurses, women of humble origins had no choice whatsoever. The image of Mary nursing Jesus, a favourite subject for painters through the ages, especially in the later Middle Ages, also fuelled theological speculation: the idea of divinity dependent upon humanity for its sustenance fascinated medieval theologians.[11] The themes of the Incarnation and Mary as mother represent two sides of a coin, one mysterious and one tangible; yet, both demonstrate how Mary functions as a point of contact between humanity and divinity.

A third theme, marriage to the Virgin, economically illustrates Mary's role as the harmonizing agent between heaven and earth. In evoking this theme, Gautier exploits the acoustic and semantic resonances between the words 'Marie' and 'marier':

> Marions nous a la virge Marie.
> Nus ne se puet en li mesmarïer.
> Sachiez de voir, a li qui se marie
> Plus hautement ne se puet marïer.   (I Ch 4: 28–31)

> [Let us marry the Virgin Mary.
> No one can make a bad marriage with her.
> Know this for certain:
> the one who marries her can marry no higher.]

Marriage to Mary may be taken figuratively to mean devotion or literally as holy vows: Gautier talks of taking holy orders in the same terms in the moralistic *queue* of I Mir 21.[12] But Gautier's insistence on the idea of making a bad marriage moves in two directions: one learned, that is, religious fervour and vocations; and the other popular, for the *chanson de la malmariée* was a prominent thirteenth-century lyric genre.[13]

Like many secular trouvères, Gautier thematizes the act of singing, employs the springtime opening, sets *fine* (sometimes *bone*) *amor* against *fole amor*, and proclaims feudal-like service to the *domna*. Gautier's incipits resemble those of the most secular trouvère: 'Amours, qui bien set enchanter' (I Ch 3/RS 851), or 'Talens m'est pris orendroit' (I Ch 6/RS 1845) or 'Quant ces floretes florir voi' (I Ch 8/RS 1677). Gautier appropriates various socio-cultural understandings of service into his religious conception of service; the verb 'servir' is ubiquitous. Like the vassal who does service to his lord or the trouvère who does service to his Lady, Gautier pledges to serve Mary:

Paradys bien porprent
Et bien i fait son lit
Qui Nostre Dame emprent
A servir par delit.   (II Ch 4: 12–15)

[Indeed does that one reside and
make his bed in paradise,
that one who undertakes
to serve Our Lady gladly.]

However, whereas in trouvère love song, the poet finds himself in a state of perpetual service and ever-delayed rewards, Gautier assures us that all who serve Mary faithfully receive their reward of paradisiac joy. Gautier appropriates the courtly concept of service to the Lady, but infuses the term with new meaning (see my discussion below of II Ch 5/RS 1212, 'D'une amour quoie et serie').

Together with secular motifs, Gautier borrows and converts many musico-poetic elements from other repertoires to his own end.[14] In fact, he organizes his song cycles in *Miracles* through melody. The first song cycle represents a show of melodic diversity as Gautier includes songs in various styles: through-composed (I Ch 3), the *forme chanson* (AAB) (I Ch 4), a *lai* with recurring stanzaic melody (I Ch 5), the *forme chanson* with refrain (I Ch 7), variations on the *forme chanson* (I Ch 6) including variations on the *virelai* (I Ch 9), and even some completely original forms (I Ch 8). In regard to the second song cycle, Kathryn A. Duys illustrates how Gautier borrows various elements from other songs, both secular and religious, thereby turning the cycle into a dazzling display of lyric citation.[15] The songs' melodic sources are easily identifiable and Gautier shows particular poetic prowess when he borrows refrains.[16] In II Ch 5 (examined closely below), Gautier attaches a refrain to a song whose source originally had no refrain. In II Ch 6, he uses a long refrain that alters the words of the Latin motet from which it is taken. 'Ja pour yver, pour noif ne pour gelee' (II Ch 7/RS 520) is a *chanson avec des refrains* in which Gautier combines the stanzaic melody of a song by Blondel de Nesles that originally had no refrain and attaches five different refrains, all with different melodies. Gautier likes to play with secular genres as disparate as the *chanson d'amour* (*canso, grand chant courtois*), the *chanson de femme*, and the racy *pastourelle*. For example, he borrows the incipit of a famous song by Blondel de Nesles: 'Amors dont sui espris.'[17] He borrows equally from musical masterpieces of the Notre Dame school (for example, the *Beata viscera* conductus), and well-known paraliturgical material like the *Laetabundus* sequence.[18]

Gautier's citations help us recall the traditions he is attempting to complement, in the case of Latin devotional works, or supplant, in the case of secular song, all of which points to the important role memory plays in Gautier's literary devotional project. Duys considers the role of memory in the large-scale arrangement of the different pieces of the *Miracles'* manuscripts. As both Frances Yates and Mary Carruthers point out, medieval mnemonics organized materials to be memorized through systems of association, such as complex architectural or manu-script designs. The quintessential element of this system was one's mastery of the mnemonic scheme.[19] If the scheme were not perfectly mastered, one could not thoroughly internalize the new information.[20] By borrowing melodies, melodic schemes, and poetic elements from the most well-known songs of his day, Gautier can easily superimpose Marian material upon compositions that his audience has already learned. Furthermore, Gautier runs little risk of unwittingly promoting secular songs because he relegates them to the background role of mnemonic scheme: it is the new information or new words that occupy the foreground. The interplay of foreground and background illustrates once again a desire to harmonize the human and the divine, which is, unfortunately, lost on the average modern-day listener and now discussed in only the most specialized of scholarly circles.

Finally, highly rhetorical in both senses of its persuasiveness and its reliance upon rhetorical tropes, Gautier's work abounds in word figures such as anaphora and especially *annominatio* and thought figures like apostrophe and metaphor.[21] In his monumental survey of medieval religious lyric, Patrick S. Diehl demonstrates how apostrophe and metaphor bring together disparate elements across time and space. Apostrophe or direct address occupies a privileged position in religious texts, especially highly emotive ones, whether they be poems, songs, or prayers. Similarly, metaphor provides a 'rhetorical means for reducing the distance between the subject matter of religious lyric and the life of the user,' and represents 'the most powerful means of bringing the remote into proximity' (Diehl 198). For medieval poets, theologians, and philosophers, metaphor was not only the most prestigious of tropes, it offered a glimpse into the mind of the Creator, into the mysteries of the God of Genesis who created with a word and of Jesus, the Word Incarnate.[22] In Marian lyrics, metaphor helps the lay listener grasp the most difficult theological points. Many describe her beauty, especially highlighting flowers like the rose; others cast Mary as the source of salvation, likening her to a spring or a well; still others compare her with some agent of mediation such as a bridge, door, or window, illustrating Mary's important role as *mediatrix* between humanity and divinity. We will consider other implications of metaphor in the final section of this chapter in order to show to what extent metaphor governs Gautier's entire lyric enterprise.

As space will not permit close analysis of how Gautier brings together these elements of theme, melody, and trope in individual songs, I offer readings of three particular songs for particular reasons. The first song, 'Amours, qui bien set enchanter' (I Ch 3/RS 851), is the first song of the first seven-song cycle. Its integration into the wider project of the *Miracles* through *annominatio* and its thematization of secular versus religious song make it central to an understanding of Gautier's lyrics. It also shares the reliance on *annominatio* with the song that opens the second cycle, 'Pour la pucele en chantant me deport' (II Ch 2/ RS 1930, 1600), and its melody, in many manuscripts, with two of the Leocadia songs: I Ch 45, 'Las! las! las! las! par grant delit' (RS 1644) and I Ch 46, 'Sour ceste rivage, a ceste crois' (RS 1831). The second song also comes from the first cycle: 'Roÿne celestre (RS 956, 1903).' This song, a *lai*, exemplifies the power of apostrophe and Gautier's musico-poetic prowess while illustrating his attitude towards the relationship between music and words: he always ensures that his religious songs are more than just intricate musical undertakings. As he intimates in I Pr 2, they exist to teach more than to please. Finally, I read 'D'une amour quoie et serie' (RS 1212), a polemical contrafactum of Gilles de Vieux Maisons's 'Je chans mais c'est mauvais signes' to illustrate the generative approach to contrafacture described in my introduction. As in numerous other polemical contrafacta such as 'Quant ces floretes florir voi' (I Ch 8/RS 1677), an imitation of Vielart de Corbie's 'De chanter me semont amours' (RS 2030) or 'Amors dont sui espris' (II Ch 4/RS 1546), which imitates a song by Blondel de Nesles with the same incipit (RS 1545), model and contrafactum are engaged in a dialectical relationship whose synthesis allows Gautier to set the poetry he composes against that which he combats. At the same time, the reading demonstrates the power of metaphor in Gautier's Marian lyrics. I shall read these songs not only against the abstract background of the individual motifs and figures studied above, but also with an eye to the hermeneutical consequences for understanding the first important corpus of Old French Marian songs.

'Amours, qui bien set enchanter' (I Ch 3/RS 851)

'Amours, qui bien set enchanter' opens the first seven-song cycle and illustrates a dexterous use of the thematic, poetic, musical, and rhetorical devices examined above. Rhetorically, the song relies extensively upon *annominatio* to accomplish its twofold aim: the denigration of secular song in favour of religious song and the portrayal of Mary as most worthy of devotion. The journey the believer takes through this song begins with an eschewal of the world, continues with turning towards – a 'conversion,' in the etymological sense of the word – the Virgin Mary, and ends with the reward of eternal joy in the company of God. As such, it may be read as exemplary of Marian songs that perform the communicative act of surrendering one's will to the divine.

Although *annominatio* occurs widely in Gautier's work, as well as in Latin and vernacular didactic writings, it is exceptional in devotional lyric poetry.[23] Moreover, Gautier's use of *annominatio* in 'Amours, qui bien set' is particularly innovative: first of all, the root of the first figure, 'chant,' is the same figure on which the preceding prologue ends. If Gautier manages in the Leocadia sequence to bridge narrative and lyric through an identification of the narrative protagonist with the lyric subject, here he closes the space left between text and paratext through this important rhetorical figure, as its reprise suggests that the song should follow the second prologue. Second, Gautier achieves the formal effect of *coblas doblas* not through rhyme but through *annominatio*. Strictly speaking, the song is written in *coblas singulars* since rhyme sounds change from stanza to stanza. However, the root word used for *annominatio* changes every two stanzas. The first two stanzas elaborate on 'chant'; the next two, on 'cointe'; the fifth and sixth stanzas, on 'pris'; the next two, on 'confors'; the ninth and tenth, on 'servir'; and the last pair employs 'fin.' So *annominatio* secures stability both in the song cycle and in the song itself: stanzas I and II belong together, as do stanzas III and IV, V and VI, etc. However, *annominatio* not only affects the song's transmission but also its performance: the choice to change the *annominatio* every two stanzas, while using new rhymes in every stanza, creates a complex formal patterning that represents a poetic *tour de force*.[24]

The root words resonate distinctively within Marian lyric, and Gautier manipulates them adroitly, weaving together the central argument of

Marian devotion: if we break from the world and turn towards Mary, we will have comfort in this life and in the next one.[25] The first figure on 'chant' allows him to speak of secular song versus love song, while, in the same breath, discussing how love songs cause disenchantment ('desenchanter' 3).[26] Songs to Mary, on the other hand, enchant ('enchanter,' in the sense of 'to cast a spell over') the Devil and his cohorts, which leads us to the figure of the third and fourth stanzas: 'acointes' (21). To join the company ('acointement' 13) of Mary who is noble ('cointe' 15), we must dissociate ourselves ('desacointier' 17, 20, 22) from those acquainted ('acointier' 16, 19) with the Devil. There is no nobler sentiment, according to the singer: he who values ('prisier' 25) Mary's worth ('pris' 29), for she is the worthy flower where precious, holy flesh took hold ('a prise' 30), and takes himself ('se prent' 34) into her service surprises (in the sense of 'ambush' – 'souspenre' 35) the Devil. Gautier then weaves in apostrophe: Lady, he sings, Lady whose comfort ('confort' 37) comforts ('conforter' 42) all, my sins trouble me ('me desconforter' 38); please comfort me ('conforte moi' 46), as you comforted Mary of Egypt. Those who serve you ('servir' 51, 52, 56, 58) deserve ('deservir' 53, 55, 59) eternal joy. Lady, you are like fine gold ('or fin' 64), and I will serve you for all eternity ('sanz finement' 61), for, at the end of time ('la fin' 65), the faithful will feel joy that will never end ('n'iert finee' 66). Pray to the one who died ('finer' 68) on the cross, the one who is the beginning and the end ('fins' 70), that, at the end, we may experience joy ('joie fine' 72). Using these individual figures as strands, Gautier spins a complex semantic web that constitutes, nevertheless, a cogent argument whose persuasiveness derives in large part from its playful appeal to both ear and mind.

Gautier also turns melody to his rhetorical advantage. The song's melody is through-composed, which often suggests a song whose structure is somewhat elusive, difficult to remember:

1.A - mours, qui bien set en - chan - ter,

2.As plu - seurs fait tel chant chan - ter

3.Dont les a - mes des - chan - tent.

4.Je ne vueil mes chan - ter tel chant,

5.Mes por ce - lui no - viau chant chant

6.De cui li an - gre chan - tent.

Although the melody lacks the internal repetition of the *forme chanson* (AAB), its short, six-verse stanzas, the bipartite and symmetrical poetic structure of those stanzas, and the high degree of repetition throughout its twelve stanzas promote accurate oral transmission of melody. But 'Amours, qui bien set' also benefits from a carefully designed internal melodic structure whose distinguishing feature is an elegant symmetry: the melody rises through the first three verses (or 'lines' in the modern edited text), reaches its climax in the fourth verse, descends slowly, and finishes with a melisma whose finalis is the same tone on which the song begins, namely, c.[27]

The same melody is, of course, repeated for each stanza, and the fourth verse where the melody reaches its apex, that is, c′, is often of vital textual importance. For example, in stanza VIII, after reminding Mary that she has comforted many souls, the melody helps accentuate the fourth verse's plea for personal intercession: 'Conforte moi. Grant confort as' (46). In the tenth stanza, Gautier combines a number of textual, rhetorical, and melodic strategies – an *annominatio* on 'servir' and thus the feudal metaphor of service, the semantically loaded adjective 'las,' an apostrophe to Mary, and a sly use of the fourth verse's melodic pinnacle – to compose a stanza that summarizes the essential message of Gautier's Marian lyric:

> Las, ainz nul bien ne deservi,
> Quar si petit ai Dieu servi
> M'ame a mort deservie.
> Dame, or m'apren si a servir
> La joie puisse deservir
> Ou d'angres ies servie.   (I Ch 3: 55–60)

As I have pointed out, Gautier seeks to teach us that the first step towards salvation lies in the recognition of our utter dependence upon and subsequent surrender to the divine. In the first verse of this stanza, the singer realizes that, given his sinful past during which he served God little, he deserves not salvation but damnation. The signifying potential of the fourth verse's melody becomes combined with the rhetorical power of apostrophe as the singer cries out and asks that Mary teach him how to serve her so that he might be saved. The second syllable – the one sung over the highest pitch of the song – comes over 'or,' that is, 'now,' as if to emphasize the present moment of repentant surrender. Then, in line with the narrative structure of consolation after surrender, the fifth verse speaks to the reward of serving Mary – joy in heaven – and the final verse once again exploits the final melisma by recalling the angels of heaven who wait upon Mary.

The last stanzas focus our attention on what is to be gained through service to Mary: eternal joy in the heavenly company of God. The *annominatio* on 'fin' not only signals the end of the song, i.e., the cessation of singing – but also the song's end, i.e., the acquisition of divine favour and personal salvation. In the last verses, the I/we asks that Mary pray to God

> Qui commencemenz est et finz,
> Touz nous face a la fin si fins
> Qu'aions la joie fine. Amen.   (I Ch 3: 70–2)

'Amours, qui bien set' therefore structurally mimics both Mary's role as *mediatrix* and the Marian song's function as a religious utterance. In this respect, 'Amours, qui bien set' is representative of all of the Gautier's religious songs. Neither Mary nor the Marian songs are ends in and of themselves – they both constitute conduits that lead us ultimately to God.

'Roÿne celestre' (I Ch 5/RS 956, 1903)

The third song of the first cycle is a three-stanza *lai* whose stanzaic and melodic structure is extremely complex. Amongs *lais*, it stands as an exception: most use a different melody for each section but 'Roÿne celestre' imitates the *forme chanson* because it uses the same melody for each of its three sections.[28] Contrary to 'Amours, qui bien set,' 'Roÿne celestre' abounds in Marian metaphors. Its short verses and repetitive melody produce an incantatory effect that Gautier underscores when he introduces an *annominatio* on 'corde' at the end of the third section. Far from a mere aesthetic ornament, *annominatio* serves the song's didactic end: Gautier tells us how Mary brings humanity and divinity into concordance, mirroring the intricate interweaving of words and music in this highly complex musico-poetic work.

Each of the song's thirty-six-verse sections is set in an intricate pattern, which the table below breaks down into a four-part structure based on melodic repetitions. Each subsection is repeated once, thus subsections 'a' and 'b,' within which melodic repetitions and, equally important, variations occur (see the appendix for the song's entire melody). Roman numerals represent the subsection; arabic numerals, the number of syllables in the verse(s); small letters, the rhyme (apostrophes indicate feminine rhymes); and capital letters, the melody where variations are represented by apostophes.

Ia.   5a′ 5b′ 5a′ 5b′
        A   B   A   B′

Ib.   5a′ 5b′ 5a′ 5b′
       A   B   A   B′
IIa.   5c′ 6d′ 5c′ 6d′
       C   D   C   D′
IIb.   5c′ 6d′ 5c′ 6d′
       C   D   C   D″
IIIa. 8e′ 6d′
       E   F
IIIb. 8e′ 6d′
       E   F
IVa.   5d′ 6d′ 8fh 8h 6d′ 4g 4g 6d′
       G   H   I   J   F   E′ F
IVb.   5d′ 6d′ 8h 8h 6d′ 4h 4h 6d′
       G   H   I   J   F   E′ F

Repetition within and across sections is prominent. For example, in the first two sections, Gautier uses only five- and six-syllable verses with four different feminine rhymes; yet, he repeats melodic units A and C while varying units B and D. In the third section, melody and text are perfectly synchronized: two different rhymes and two different melodic units are sung. Section IV represents the most complex intermingling of text and melody. On the purely textual level, a greater metrical heterogeneity sets in just as masculine rhymes are introduced. Moreover, this fourth section employs both new rhymes and melodic units while simultaneously reusing others from the preceding section. For example, in section III, E is sung over an octosyllable ending on a feminine rhyme but, in section IV, E is sung over two tetrasyllables – which add up to an octosyllable – that end in masculine rhymes. What Gautier fails to repeat is just as important as what he does. In the case of 'Roÿne celestre,' melodic units H, I, J, and K are not repeated. By selectively repeating, varying, and combining different melodic and textual elements, Gautier creates a complex musico-poetic structure.

Gautier combines apostrophe with various Marian metaphors, making his *lai* highly lyrical in texture. He begins each section by using a different metaphor to call upon the Virgin. Section one calls Mary the 'Roÿne celestre'; section two, the 'Fontaine de grace'; and section three, the 'Rose fresche et clere.' Gautier uses other metaphors, such as queen, door, window, and fountain, as well. They often appear clustered together as in the opening stanza with its juxtaposition of the metaphors of queenship, door, and window (1–4). The metaphors of queenship as well as those for the Incarnation and Mary's maternity run through the entire song, endowing it with some thematic unity, but Gautier never develops any of them extensively. Instead, he uses now one, now another. He combines and separates, switches back and forth, etc. The song's highly complex but repetitive melodies produce an almost hypnotic incantation.

Before we can let ourselves be lulled by this incantatory piece, however, Gautier changes the rules, for he is not content to produce a song that merely soothes – he sings to teach. As the singer intones the third section, the audience's horizon of expectation regarding the song's complex musico-poetic form is set. At that point, Gautier reorients the song's subject matter and then introduces an *annominatio*. In this third and final section, the song's function becomes less laudatory and more supplicatory. As the second melodic section is intoned, the focus remains on Mary, but as the melody is repeated, attention shifts to the person of the singer:

> Dame, qui tant sainte
> Et qui tant fus eslite
> Que grosse et enceinte
> Fus du Saint Esperite,
> Oies ma complainte
> Et envers moi t'apite.
> Ma lampe est estainte,
> M'ame en enfer escripte.   (81–8)

The same form is employed but instead of praising Mary *sui generis*, the singer implores that she use her power for his sake. But the final subsection of this third section marks not only a sharp shift in tone and focus, but also an introduction of new formal and rhetorical elements. In the reprise of section IV's melody, Gautier, while obeying the rhyme scheme, adds an *annominatio* on 'corde':

> Mere de concorde,
> Fai ma pais et m'acorde.
> Pechiez m'a tout taint et nerci.
> Doiz de douceur, merci! merci!
> A ton doz fil m'acorde.
> Mainte descordé
> As recordé,
> Fons de misericorde.   (101–8)

Ending the song with an *annominatio* reminds us of the overtly moralistic endings of Gautier's narratives that he calls *queues*, signalling that this section is set apart from the preceding material in its moralistic content. In fact, he uses the figure on 'corde' at the end of his Theophilus miracle, a medieval crowd-pleaser; more than perhaps any other *annominatio*, 'corde' accentuates Mary's power as reconciler of heaven and earth. She brings both realms into concordance.[29] When Gautier explicitly draws out his lesson at the end of his miracles, he implicitly reminds us that the miracle story's primary aim is to teach a lesson. Gautier here draws on a favourite didactic device to remind us of the essential function of Marian lyric, that is, the surrender of subjectivity and harmonization or concordance of the human and divine in a piece that weaves or accords music and text to such a high degree. By far the most musically complex of songs in the first song cycle, this piece is indicative of Gautier's compositional prowess. He first lets his audience get accustomed to the intricate patterns at work in the piece before bringing the song's incantatory effect to new heights. Thus, even if 'Roÿne celestre' represents the pinnacle of Gautier's lyric talents, it reminds us that Gautier, as he states in his prologue, means to both please and teach.

'D'une amour quoie et serie' (II Ch 5/RS 1212)

'D'une amour quoie et serie' gains its rhetorical thrust by converting elements of secular song to religious ends. *Conversio*, as Diehl notes, meant both conversion and metaphor in the Middle Ages and religious language depends upon metaphor for intelligibility: preachers, theologians, and religious poets need metaphor to make the divine knowable and known to their respective audiences. While individual metaphors are genuinely important, I would argue that metaphor governs Gautier's poetry on a much broader level. 'D'une amour quoie et serie' illustrates best the reign or rule of metaphor in Gautier's lyrics as the trope is understood in Paul Ricoeur's interaction theory of metaphor: the trope's power lies in a bipolar tension that forces us to see one element as another. From that tension, that instance of 'seeing as,' a new meaning emerges.[30] Saying X is Y, for example, 'Mary is a rose,' puts forth in a very economical way how X, Mary, and Y, rose, are simultaneously alike and not alike without drawing our attention explicitly to the idea of likeness, as in the case of simile when we say 'X is *like* Y.' As Ricoeur puts it in 'Word, Polysemy, Metaphor': 'A novel metaphor does not merely actualize a potential connotation, it creates it. It is a semantic

innovation, an emergent meaning' (79).[31] Gautier's polemical contrafacta are poetic events – acts of predication, to use Ricoeur's terms –
that inscribe the familiar into strange contexts, thereby creating new
connotations. In Gautier's 'D'une amour quoie et serie,' a contrafactum
of Gilles de Vieux Maisons's 'Je chans, mais c'est mauvais signes,' just
such transformations occur. Gautier accomplishes this process of metaphorization by relying on his audience's familiarity with Gilles's scornful
lover's complaint or *mala canso* – a type of song for which Gilles was well
known.

To the melody of 'D'une amour quoie,' Gautier also appends a
refrain, one that circulated widely: 'Vilainnes gens, vous ne sentez mie,/
les dous maus que je sent.'[32] The edition of his songs, Jacques Chailley,
points out that Gautier's choice of refrain makes sense musically. The
most distinctive feature of Gilles's melody is its opening gesture. Beginning on d', the melody drops to g before immediately jumping back to
d'. The refrain's melody starts similarly, beginning d'-d'-g-d'. Nevertheless, the two gestures share the melodic trait that Chailley calls a 'saut de
quinte caractéristique' (54):

Incipit of 'D'une amour quoie'

Beginning of refrain 'Vilainne genz, etc.'

However, Gautier's choice of refrain provides more than a mere
melodic echo. First, it provides a new stanzaic cadence, because now
each stanza ends with the refrain. Instead of a slow descent from d' to g,
a melodic sequence that conveys a sense of despair when Gilles's singer
intones it over the last words of the initial stanza, 'devant sa mort,' the
singer of Gautier's song refers to the refrain that follows, ensuring that
both singer and audience are already looking past this slow descent, the

narcissistic climax of Gilles's stanza, and towards the refrain. Moreover, at the end of the refrain, instead of descending slowly from d' to g, the melody ascends more quickly from g to d', thereby reversing the direction of Gilles's cadence and substituting a sense of optimism for Gilles's despair.

Second, and more important, the d'-g-d' sequence constantly reinforces the importance of *vilannie* in the song, as it is sung over 'gart vilains,' 'vilainement,' and 'vilainnes gens' each time the refrain is sung. 'Vilains' is a cultural term that functions on at least two levels: it describes a code of conduct and a social class. Two moments of Chrétien de Troyes's *Yvain* illustrate best the term's polyvalence. In the opening lines of that romance, Guenièvre calls Keu, King Arthur's seneschal, who travels among aristocratic circles, *vilains* when he insults Arthur's knights and speaks in a noncourtly fashion: 'Enuieus estes et *vilains*/ De ramporner vos compagnons' (90–1, my emphasis).[33] Later in the narrative, the second meaning of the term is applied when Calogrenant tells of his meeting a herder of wild bulls, whom he describes as 'Uns *vilains* qui resembloit mor,/ Grans et hideus a desmesure' (286–7, my emphasis). Not only does he not belong to humanity due to his physical stature, but he also does not belong to the high social class of Calogrenant and Arthur's court, a detail revealed a few lines later: his weapon is not the noble sword, but the base 'machue' or bludgeon. Whether 'vilains' is used in the first or second sense, it is primarily employed by the courtly Self to identify the noncourtly Other. As with all cultural epithets, the word says less about the noncourtly Other than about the courtly Self. It exposes the values espoused by courtly culture and reveals how the courtly Self orders the universe. 'Vilains' is a liminal term; it marks a boundary, namely, the boundary between the community of initiates known as the 'cortois,' the courtly, and those excluded, here the 'vilains' or noncourtly. Not only does 'vilains' possess pejorative connotations, but it is also defined negatively, that is, by absence rather than presence. One is called 'vilains' because he does not adhere to the courtly code of conduct or belong to the aristocracy. When Gautier adopts the term 'vilains,' he transforms the meaning to suit his particular ends.

In order to be admitted into Gautier's community of initiates, the Marian faithful, one has to adhere to the code of conduct that 'D'une amour quoie' spells out: one must abandon worldly love and then love the Virgin Mary. The outright injunction to love Mary – 'amons' – appears in verses 17, 34, and 45 (these last two uses occupy the privileged position of first word in a stanza). Elsewhere Gautier uses more impersonal formulae such as 'nus ne l'aimme' or 'qui ne l'aimme' for the Marian faithful or for the *vilains* and draws out the consequences of adherence or a lack thereof to Marian devotion. For example, in verses 7–8 the singer exclaims that the one who loves *vilainement* may not sing this song, not even the refrain, and in verses 17–22 of stanza II we hear:

> Et se l'amons doucement.
> Qui sa douceur a sentie
> Dire puet bien vraiement:
> *Vilaine genz,*
> *Vous ne les sentez mie*
> *Les douz maus que je sent.*

In loving the Virgin Mary, one joins the community of the Marian faithful, winning in the process the right previously denied to the *vilains*, namely, the right to sing the refrain. This particularly apt use of text to weave stanza into refrain melodically represents an important discursive moment. The right to sing the refrain, this granting of voice, symbolizes a border crossing: the imaginary line that separates stanza from refrain emblematizes the line that separates the community of initiates from the community of *vilains*. Singing the refrain separates 'us' from 'them,' because some have the right to sing it while others do not. In turn, what the refrain says perpetuates that separation: '*Vilaine* people, you do not feel at all the sweet pains that I feel.' In singing the refrain, one comes to possess the voice of the Self and may stand on the good guys' side of the dividing line, look across that line at the Other, and say, 'You, *vilains*.'

When Gautier looks across that line and says, 'You, *vilains*,' he looks squarely at Gilles, for the lyric subject of Gilles's song exemplifies the *vilains* in Gautier's song. Gilles is that worldly lover who does not sing the refrain because the refrain is, in fact, absent from Gilles's song. Perhaps ironically, Gilles is *vilains* before Gautier sings his song: an absence of courtly conduct already marks his *mala canso*, so his singing subject is *vilains*. In effect, Gilles rejects courtly love, and it was this trouvère's notorious anticourtliness that sparked a major literary *querelle* between him and many of his illustrious Champenois contemporaries, such as Gace Brulé, Blondel de Nesles, and the Chastelain de Couci.[34] Since Gilles's singer has yet to direct his love towards the Virgin Mary, in Gautier's poem, Gilles is *vilains*. He is literally *vilains* in his poem but metaphorically *vilains* in Gautier's poem. Gautier retains the term's essential sense of liminality before erecting a new hierarchy of values founded upon a redrawing of the boundary that *vilains* demarcates. Instead of separating the courtly Self from the noncourtly Other, Gautier separates his own Christian Self from the non-Christian Other.

The importance of the preceding analysis of the metaphorization of *vilannie* is augmented once we realize that the literal courtly meaning and Gautier's figurative meaning are necessarily incompatible. 'Perception of incompatibility,' Ricoeur writes, 'is essential to the interpretation of the message in the case of metaphor' (*The Rule of Metaphor* 186).[35] The fact that one needs at least two elements to compare and declare incompatible reveals the fundamental paradox behind Gautier's strategy of conversion through contrafacture. Although incompatible with the figurative meaning of *vilains*, the literal definition of *vilains* is no less necessary: without a familiarity with the literal *vilains*, the process of metaphorization could not occur. No matter how desperately Gautier wishes to convert him, the *vilains* is necessary to Gautier just as metaphor is necessary to religious discourse as a means of overcoming the limitations of language. Gautier needs the *vilains* to define himself and metaphor to express himself; without them, Gautier's hierarchy of values would be baseless.

In the final analysis, the similarities and differences in melody and theme suggest that the process of metaphorization that occurs on the level of the word also occurs on the level of the song. The word 'vilains' is literally out of place in Gautier's world view, but metaphorically the term fits. On the level of the song, the attached refrain, although strictly a stranger to Gilles's poem, is nevertheless familiar because of the melodic arrangement of its incipit. In light of the bipolar tension which asserts itself on this broader level of the song, we can recast the conclusion reached regarding the word 'vilains'; despite Gautier's efforts to supplant the secular tradition with his own religious tradition and despite the incompatibilities between the two world views, both are necessary to Gautier's articulation of Marian devotion. Through his use of familiar elements in a new context, Gautier imparts a combined sense of strangeness and familiarity and anchors the performance and reception of his contrafactures upon an oxymoronic feeling of familiar strangeness.

Familiar strangeness as a mode of both performance and reception seems entirely appropriate to Marian lyric: Mary constitutes a liminal figure, like and unlike other women, out of place and at home on both earth and in heaven. Moreover, the dialectic between familiarity and strangeness is the interpretive site of all cultural artifacts. As Gadamer puts it:

> Hermeneutic work is based on a polarity of familiarity and strangeness; but this polarity is not to be regarded psychologically, with Schleiermacher, as the range that covers the mystery of individuality, but truly hermeneutically – i.e., in regard to what has been said: the language in which the text addresses us, the story that it tells us. Here too there is a tension. It is in the play between the traditionary text's strangeness and familiarity to us, between being a historically intended, distanciated object and belonging to a tradition. *The true locus of hermeneutics is this in-between.* (*TM* 295 original emphasis)[36]

Gautier's poetry represents then an intervention, which may be called innovative on some level, into more than one tradition. Individual types, figures, and melodic forms, traditional through and through, come to Gautier through centuries of Marian tradition as well as through contemporary poetic repertoires. If his message is conventional, it is announced in an unconventional way, that is, through vernacular lyric song, and Gautier infuses new life into an old message. The subsequent analyses and discussions in this study will focus on poets who followed Gautier's lead and composed songs both familiar and strange when compared to Gautier's lyrics. Gautier sets himself up as an example for subsequent poets to follow, vary, refute, or even ignore altogether. Subsequent poets, as we shall see, do all four.

chapter two

Thibaut de Champagne, Genre, and the Medieval Taste for Hybrids

Gautier's lyrics belong to a religious poetics of conversion and citation, but Thibaut de Champagne (1201–53) composed a more aesthetically playful religious poetry. This playfulness manifests itself especially at the level of genre, for genre has guided, and sometimes befuddled, the king of Navarre's medieval compilers and modern editors alike. Axel Wallensköld's early twentieth-century edition and Kathleen Brahney's more recent edition both arrange Thibaut's songs in a nearly identical order according to their perceived genre: first his love songs, then his debate songs, and then other genres – *chansons de croisade, pastourelles*, etc. – and finally his devotional songs and *lai religieux*. The approach readily demonstrates the wide range of the trouvère's abilities: Thibaut composed songs sublime and erotic, profane and sacred. When we review the manuscripts that transmit Thibaut's work, we also find 'anthologies'; however, they do not follow the order proscribed by modern editors. They do demonstrate, nevertheless, an awareness of the king's skill when composing in different genres. Considering devotional songs within the context of these anthologies leads us to observe how Thibaut, still active nearly two decades after Gautier's death, created highly pluralistic, hybridized songs to Mary.

Eight of the no fewer than twenty-four manuscripts that transmit Thibaut's songs preserve his lyrics in large numbers. The manuscript family *MtVKX* (the central, interpolated part of ms. *M*, Paris, BnF fr. 844; Paris, BnF fr. 24406; Paris, Arsenal 5198; and Paris, BnF fr. 1050, respectively) all transmit Thibaut's pieces in an order similiar to one another (but far different from modern editions), while ms. *N* (Paris, BnF fr. 845) and *Tt* (a section in ms. *T*, Paris, BnF fr. 12615) preserve fewer songs and reorder them differently. Ms. *O*, the Cangé manuscript (Paris,

BnF fr. 846), is organized alphabetically by incipit, and therefore, preserves a different order altogether.[1] Ms. *S* (Paris, BnF fr. 12581) inserts a number of Thibaut's lyrics among prose works such as the *roman du graal*, examples of erudition like Brunetto Latini's *Thesaurus*, and short texts such as prayers, *fabliaux*, and *contes*. I propose using the order preserved in *Mt*, the *Chansonnier du roi*, as a baseline for analysing the choices of scribes and compilers in ordering Thibaut's work before turning to slight variations found in some manuscripts and more signficant differences in others to suggest the major role that genre played in the early reception of Thibaut's lyrics.[2] The context provides us with valuable insight into the generic status of Thibaut's devotional corpus and the next generation of Marian song after Gautier.

Ms. *Mt*, an interpolation of two gatherings in trouvère ms. *M* (BnF fr. 844), highlights generic diversity in Thibaut's corpus by opening with a love song, a crusade song, a pastourelle, another love song, and a *débat*, respectively. At this point, the compiler takes a different approach by offering series of love songs, among which we find the hybrid love/crusade song, 'Dame ensi est qu'il me convient aler.' With this series ended, we arrive at the midpoint of the anthology where we encounter, a different kind of love song, one that proclaims love for the Virgin: the *lai*, 'Commencerai a fere un lai.' We will examine this piece in great detail at the end of this chapter as it encapsulates the generic playfulness at the heart of Thibaut's work. Suffice it to say for now that since the scribe had to provide music for the entire *lai*, its extreme lyrical character is readily apparent on the page, making this display of pure lyricism at the near centrepoint of the collection a statement about the highly lyrical nature of Thibaut's work. After the compilation's midpoint, we find another mélange of love songs, *pastourelles*, Marian songs, *débats*, and Thibaut's religious *sirventois*, 'Dex est ensi conme li pellicans.' A few *débats* are included among the heterogeneous – and heterogeneric – series described above, but after the second of such series, the compiler offers another series of songs closely related in genre: eleven *débats* and *jeux-partis*. This more homogeneous series provides counterpoint to the earlier series of love songs by playing the dialogic nature of the former off the monologic character of the latter. In the final section, we find, in this order, three love songs (one of which some might consider a Marian song), a crusade song, another love song, a Marian song, and, finally three more love songs. *Mt*'s preservation of series of generic diversity alternating with series dedicated to one genre emphasizes in two different but powerful ways the wide spectrum of genres represented in Thibaut's work.

Other manuscripts either preserve a variation on *Mt* or take a more radically different approach to ordering Thibaut's work. Mss. *KVX* present only slight variations of the order found in *Mt*. For example, *K* shores up the series of dialogic pieces by taking one of the *débats* found in the 'miscellaneous' sections of *Mt* into its long series of debate songs. Mss. *N* and *Tt*, however, make larger, significant alterations to their compilations of Thibaut's work. The former preserves only roughly half of Thibaut's works, and the choices made are of particular importance in understanding the role of genre in reading Thibaut. After an initial display of generic diversity in the first five songs, eleven love songs are preserved, and then the series of debate poems follows, followed in turn by nine more love songs. The compiler of *N* therefore cuts out the 'miscellaneous' parts to concentrate on the two major genres in which Thibaut composed. Similarly, the compiler of *Tt* would seem to want to emphasize Thibaut's love songs by displacing the initial flourish of generic diversity and opening with four love songs. After these, we find a number of songs belonging to different genres and then the long series of love songs. The series of debate poems, however, is cut in two: half comes after the central sequence of generic diversity, and half completes the compilation.

In these compilations, Thibaut's love songs earn pride of place, thereby justifying to some extent the choices of modern editors and critics; just as important, however, is the fact that these compilations emphasize the generic breadth of Thibaut's lyric abilities. As to the question of his devotional works in the context, we must recognize, first and foremost, that they are not grouped together in any codex. These songs form, rather, part of the series highlighting generic diversity, which is by no means a denigration of their status; on the contrary, their context invites us to consider generic hybridity, as we pointed out in the introduction, for Thibaut's devotional lyrics represent cases of extreme generic hybridity. For example, Thibaut's bitter satire, 'Dex est ensi comne li pellicans,' is indeed in the vein of the *sirventois*.[3] However, if the lyric does indeed treat, as scholars think, the dispute between Pope Gregory IX and Emperor Frederick II over the destination of knights for the sixth crusade, could we not call the song a crusade song? In a nod to the work's incorporation of devotional motifs, Wallensköld even offers the hybridized generic term, 'serventois religieux.' Another example is 'Tant ai amors servie longuement,' which comes amid the final songs of ms. *Mt* and that both Wallensköld and Brahney classify as a love song. When beginning his nuanced reading of the song, Pierre-

Marie Joris apparently questions the song's generic status by referring to it, in conjunction with Wallensköld's edition, as 'sa chanson IX, *dite d'amour*' (99, my emphasis). Brahney also questions the generic category of this song but prefers to leave the question open rather than advance a hypothesis (xxx).

It is certainly not the case that Thibaut rejected Gautier's brand of Marian song altogether. On the contrary, Thibaut composed songs very much akin to Gautier's corpus, and I propose reading them first and foremost to demonstrate continuity between the first and second important composers of known Marian lyricists. From there, I will move on to those songs that highlight overlapping generic boundaries to illustrate how many of Thibaut's songs may be read as examples of Marian song or other genres, depending upon the perspective one adopts. We will finish this chapter with a musico-poetic reading of Thibaut's *lai religieux*, which recalls several formal considerations of our reading of Gautier's 'Roÿne celestre.' However, although Gautier's *lai* represents a significant deviation in the history of the *lai* in its use of the same melody for each section, Thibaut's *lai* apparently questions the very idea of the *lai* as a genre.

Thibaut in the Line of Gautier

Two of Thibaut's Marian songs, 'De chanter ne me puis tenir' and 'Dou tres douz non a la virge Marie,' resemble Gautier's production insofar as their primary aim is the expression of unwavering devotion to the Virgin. Like many of Gautier's songs, Thibaut takes his melody from a love song: Thibaut de Blason's 'Amors, que porra devenir' (RS 1402) the melody of which is also used in a love song ascribed to Gautier d'Espinal, 'Se par force de merci' (RS 1059). The resonance between secular love song and Marian lyric come through therefore to listeners familiar with one or both of these songs. The incipit of 'De chanter ne me puis tenir' thematizes singing, and the metaphors of service, queenship (12), the morning star (16), and flowers (29–30) remind us of Gautier's preferred figures. Thibaut also employs anaphora (2–6), and refers repeatedly to the Incarnation (6, 19, 38). He makes use of biblical reference: King David spoke with the voice of the Holy Spirit when he foretold that Mary would be born of his lineage. In stanza V, Thibaut heaps praise upon Mary and ends with a plea for mercy: 'Dame, aiez de nouz pitié!' (40). The envoi elaborates upon this plea for mercy, specifying his hatred of sin and fear of damnation. In short, the entire song resembles

Gautier's lyrics in form and function: by emphasizing Mary's role as *mediatrix*, the harmonizing agent between heaven and earth, the singer acknowledges his utter dependence upon Mary for salvation.

There are nonetheless moments in 'De chanter' where Thibaut reshapes traditional figures. Gautier may combine traditional figures in innovative ways, but he rarely alters the figure itself. In 'De chanter,' however, the singer refers to God in each of the song's five stanzas. God's heightened role might have something to do with Thibaut's social status – perhaps the king of Navarre could relate better to the King of Glory than could the humble prior of Vic-sur-Aisne. The increased significance accorded to God the Father even affects the most traditional of Marian metaphors: the flower. In the fourth stanza, the singer exclaims:

Vos [Mary] n'iestes mie a florir,
Ainz avez flor si puissant:
C'est Deus qui onques ne ment
Et par tot fet son plaisir.   (29–32)

Thibaut first applies the metaphor to Mary, as is traditional. But then, he refers to Jesus as a flower. Perhaps we should understand God as a flower and Mary as a plant that gives birth, in a way, to the flower. Jacques de Cambrai will adopt the same figure in his 'Retrowenge novelle,' but then again, Jacques relies heavily on Thibaut's poetry for his own lyric production. A similar slippage exists in the biblical reference to David: 'David le sot premierement/ Que de li devïez issir' (25–6). To the best of my knowledge, no psalm is regularly interpreted as foretelling the virgin birth. Perhaps Thibaut is obliquely alluding to the genealogy in Matt. 1 that puts Jesus in David's house. But how did David know *first* that Jesus would come? Why first? The genealogy in Matt. 1 goes back, in fact, to Abraham. Why then should Thibaut stop at David?

These discrepancies with tradition should not be read as mistakes on Thibaut's part or as disregard for tradition. As Marie-Noëlle Lefay-Toury points out in her work on animal, mythical, and, to a lesser extent, religious symbolism in Thibaut's poetry, Thibaut often adopts popular symbols only to modify them to suit the particular thematic and poetic ends of a song ('Les masques du *je* amoureux chez Thibaut de Champagne'). These moments of slippage from Mary to God and from Abraham to David function to surprise the audience and shore up, in a subtle way, the audience's understanding of traditional symbolism. The meaning of the refigured symbol might be less important than the refiguration itself: it points to a playfulness on the part of Thibaut. Gautier, of course, abhors such poetic flourishes because words are supposed to refer to something beyond themselves. In Thibaut's song, however, the Marian figure points to Mary while drawing our attention to itself in its reconfigured state.

Thibaut's 'Dou tres douz non a la virge Marie' also calls our attention to the process of signification but more directly. The song constitutes a pseudo-scholastic explanation of the individual letters M-A-R-I-A, and from the very first verses, Thibaut calls our attention to the process of signification:

> Dou tres douz non a la virge Marie
> Vos espondrai .v. letres plainement:
> La premiere est *m*, qui *senefie*
> Que les a*m*es en sont fors de torment.   (1–4, my emphasis)

Thibaut's song not only conveys its message but also calls attention to itself as an act of signification: in other words, the message is the meaning. Such is the nature of all poetic language, but Thibaut's text stands out in its medieval context as an early example of a vernacular text that relies on the written word, i.e., the word 'Maria' as it would be written down.[4] Moreover, while medieval poets often used vivid visual imagery in poetic compositions, Thibaut fuses traditional visual imagery with the visual nature of written language.

As Thibaut meditates on each letter, he includes many points pertaining to Catholic dogma and Mary's cosmological role. Alluding to the alphabet in the second stanza, Thibaut comments on Mary's highly significant role in salvation history as he broods upon the first 'a' of Mary's name. He makes reference to the first position of 'a' in the alphabet – '*A* vient aprés; droiz est que je vos die/ Qu'en l'abecé est tot premierement' (9–10) – before saying that we should pray 'le salu' or 'Hail Mary' to the one who bore Jesus. Thibaut's reference to the Incarnation plays on the paradox of the creator contained: Mary had to be on earth already in order to give birth to Jesus. Yet, God precedes all things. Who came first, Mary or Jesus? The stanza also links this first letter with the first man whose name also began with 'a': 'Premiers fu *a* et premiers devint hom,/ Que nostre lois fust fete n'establie' (15–16). All these interlinked types are anchored in the knowledge of the alphabet and written language.

Perhaps the most clever play on written language comes in the fourth stanza's explanation of 'i.' The entire stanza is worth citing:

> *I* est toz droiz, genz et de bele taille.
> Teus fu le cors, ou il n'ot qu'enseignier,
> De la dame qui por nos se travaille:
> Biaux, droiz et gens, sanz tache et sanz pechier.
> Por son douz cuer et por enfer brisier
> Vint Deus en li, quant ele l'enfanta.
> Biaus fu et bel, et bien s'en delivra;
> Bien fist semblant Deus que de nos li chaille.   (25–32)

Starting with a consideration of the form of the grapheme 'i,' the singer offers a vision of an upright and beautiful body. From her exterior beauty – 'biaux, droiz et gens, sanz tache' – we are led seamlessly to her inner beauty, a result of her being born without original sin: 'sanz pechier.' A final movement from the inside to the outside occurs as the singer alludes to the Incarnation, a central salutary act – indeed, an emblematic act – in which Mary participated as mediator between God and the human race.

The song ends with an envoi that exhorts us to beg mercy of Mary through the greeting that begins 'Ave Maria.' Thus, in that last communicative act between the singer and the community of believers, the entire song is summarized by citing the incipit of the most famous Marian prayer. 'Ave' recalls the primary discursive function of 'Dou tres douz non' – to praise – and 'Maria,' the means by which that act is accomplished – a meditation on Mary's name. 'Dou tres douz non' then, with 'De chanter,' show a formal and thematic continuity from Gautier's to Thibaut's lyric production; second, they provide a backdrop against which we can read Thibaut's hybridized Marian songs. As such, they make the differences among Thibaut's Marian lyric production more readily perceptible.

Thibaut's Hybridized Marian Songs

Thibaut's other Marian songs share many formal and semantic motifs of the songs above; however, they differ in that Mary plays a secondary, though still important, role. At first, in fact, her role in determining a song's genre might not even be apparent. However, when those moments where Mary appears are more closely studied, the rest of the song reorganizes itself around her, rendering it possible to read the song as an expression of Marian devotion. I will employ a pluralistic reading strategy in reading four songs: two belong to the more general devotional song, and the other two are crusade songs. This multicentred, pluralistic reading strategy illustrates the high degree of playfulness at work in Thibaut's lyrics; this playfulness, in turn, will provide a useful means of reading Thibaut's highly lyrical *lai religieux*, which, as we have already seen, occupies a central position in some of Thibaut's most important manuscripts.

One devotional song that endows Mary with a secondary role is 'Mauvez arbres ne puet florir,' a song that uses the same melody as Thibaut's *jeu-parti* with Raoul de Soissons, and a listener familiar with the debate song might, in hearing 'Mauvez arbres,' remember the playful and even bawdy tone of the debate: Raoul asks Thibaut if it is better to see and never touch or touch and never see one's beloved, and Thibaut defends this second, fleshier choice. The headier, rarified allegory of the religious song begins by paraphrasing a teaching found in the gospels: 'By their fruits you will know them' (Matt. 7:17–20; 2:33–7; Luke 6:43–5).[5] Throughout the rest of the song, Thibaut collects a number of meanings pertaining to tree, fruit, and, to a lesser extent, flower symbolism. The reuse of a melody from an off-colour debate song might act as almost a corrective of that debate much as in Gautier's contrafacta. Then again, a listener familiar with the religious song hearing the debate song for the first time might find the latter more humorous for the parodic and almost sacrilegious overtones that the contrast would produce.

Mary's explicit presence is fleeting in 'Mauvez arbres,' yet symbols with Marian resonances abound in the text and, with each example, Thibaut plays with our understanding of the symbol. In the first stanza, vague associations are made with the Incarnation and with the Ave Maria when the singer intones: 'Fleur ne fruit de cointe semblant/ Porte cil en qui naist amors' (5–6). In the second stanza, Thibaut obliquely alludes to Mary as the second Eve:

Par le fruit fu li premiers plors,
Quant Eve fist Adan pechier;
Mes qui dou bon fruit veut mengier,
Dieu aint et sa mere et son non,
Cil quiaudra le fruit de saison.   (18–22)

The opposition between the fruit eaten by Adam and Eve and the good fruit that comes with loving God and Mary reminds us of the Marian type of the 'second Eve.' Yet, Thibaut never draws out the type explicitly, and so our understanding of the symbolism is either assumed or suspended.

A second kind of play on our horizon of expectation occurs over the next three stanzas. The singer begins to use the characteristic subject of religious discourse, the I/we, but the characteristic religious attitude of abandonment to the divine emerges only slowly. The singer wishes rather reluctantly to abandon a sinful past. After comparing the 'fruit meür' that God's people gather to the green fruit 'Qui ja en moi ne meürra: / C'est li fruiz en qu'Adans pecha' (28–9), the singer continues:

> De ce fruit est plains mes vergiers;
> Des que ma dame vi premiers,
> Oi de s'amor plain de cuer et cors
> Ne ja nul jor n'en istra fors.   (30–3)

The singer's regret may stem from a lack of success in past erotic adventures – the 'vergiers' is, after all, the highly eroticized *locus amoenus* of secular song – or from the realization that carnal love is sinful. Thibaut prolongs the ambiguity, and rejects carnal love in favour of a purer, 'Marian' love, only in the last stanza:

> Par vostre [God's] douz conmandement
> Me donez amer la meillor;
> Ce est la preciëuse flor
> Par qui vos venistes ça jus,
> Dont li Deablez est confus.   (51–5)

The singer now communicates an attitude proper to Marian lyric and the figure of the flower, employed earlier to evoke Mary only indirectly, becomes explicitly associated with Mary.

Moreover, Mary takes on her familiar role as the agent of harmony between the human and the divine in the song's envois. However, we should note that the envois do not survive in every manuscript; therefore, in the absence of these texts, as in, for example, ms. *K*, the song becomes much less Marian. In the first envoi, the singer rejects his past, and the last piece of the puzzle has fallen into place:

> Mere Dieu, par vostre douçor,
> Dou bon fruit me donez savor,

Que de l'autre ai je senti plus
C'onques, ce croi, ne senti nus.   (56–9)

The I/we sings of his past folly in the past tense instead of in the present tense, which is proper to the I/we of Marian lyric. Even variants in the manuscripts can reorient our understanding of the song's genre. For example, in *Mt* only this envoi survives, but it begins not 'Mere Dieu' but 'Pere Dieu,' meaning that God the Father is the final figure in view. In ms. *S* where the envoi begins 'Mere Dieu,' a second envoi survives. In this second envoi, the subject calls upon someone called Phelipe to emulate this act of conversion and leave aside love songs in favour of religious songs, citing the incipit, Te Deum Laudamus. The primary aim of 'Mauvez arbres' is confirmed as it was in 'De chanter': in the latter, Thibaut cites the incipit of the Ave Maria in his envoi, but in 'Mauvez arbres,' in one version Mary is not addressed at the end and in another version, the second envoi brings us back to God. Thibaut's song in each version functions primarily as one of praise to God, not to Mary, but Mary becomes a means to that end, depending upon the version heard. The symbolic networks of tree, flower, fruit, and the casual reference to Mary in stanza II only suggest her presence. What constitutes an even craftier manipulation is the I/we's slow abandonment of himself to the divine, the seminal communicative act of Marian lyric.

Like 'Mauvez arbres,' 'De grant travail' exploits a number of poetic, parabolic, and allegorical figures, creating a textual fabric that is singular in intent but varied in approach. Mary's presence is relatively subdued in the song. Its overall tone is moralistic: the I/we entreats us to forsake the world, which the Devil manipulates, in favour of obedience to God's commandments which lead us to salvation. When read from that perspective, that is, as a general devotional song, we find ourselves wedged in between God and the Devil, a spatial relationship evoked in the singer's characterization of our situation in the world:

Ainz avons si le deable troussé
Qu'a li servir chascuns pense et essaie.
Et Deus, qui ot pour nos la cruël plaie,
Avons mes tuit arriere dos bouté.   (5–8)

Having turned our backs on God, we find ourselves between God and the Devil. In the next stanza, the singer lays out the consequences of serving the Devil as he warns that God would have thrown one out of every two of us into Hell had Mary not intervened.

Mary's intervention constitutes a study in contrasts, for she is represented as the tender queen seated next to the wrathful king:

Dex, qui tout set et tout puet et tout voit,
Nos avroit tost un entre .ii. geté
Se la Dame, plaine de grant bonté,
Qui est lez lui, pour nous ne li proit.
Si tres douz moz plesanz et savoré
Le grant coroz du haut Seigneur rapaie.   (10–15)

Two things are striking about this passage: first, Mary is next to God, 'lez lui'; she is not at the centre of attention but rather on the side. Second, the singer draws particular attention to the words the Virgin uses, her 'tres douz moz pleasanz et savoré.' By emphasizing Mary's rhetorical prowess, the poet directly comments on Mary's power and the efficacy of religious speech.

In the next three stanzas, the poet adapts material from medieval bestiaries, employs allegorical figures, and adopts a metaphor drawn from the economic sphere. In stanza III, the poet draws a contrast between us who seek only hell and the mouse that diligently prepares for the long winter, intimating that we should imitate the mouse. The fourth stanza employs allegorical figures and casts the Devil as a fisherman – perhaps ironically as Jesus called his apostles fishers of men in Luke 1:17 – intent on catching us with four allegorical hooks: covetousness, arrogance, lust, and wickedness. The stanza ends enigmatically, alluding to the Devil's shore 'Dont Dex nos gart par son conmandement,/ En qui sainz fonz nous feïsmes honmage' (35–6). The meaning of the verses and especially of the sacred fount, the 'sainz fonz,' to which we pay homage is, as yet, obscure, although it may represent the baptismal font: baptism represents a covenant with God as the rite of vassalage constitutes an act of homage whereby one enters into a covenant with a lord.

Again, Mary takes a prominent role in the envoi, and her function invites us to reorient our interpretation of the entire song. The envoi is an indirect address to Mary through the song:

A la Dame qui touz les biens avance
T'en va, chanson! S'el te veut escouter,
Onques ne fu nus de meilleur cheance.   (46–8)

The feudal metaphor of the Lady, the thematization of the communicative nature of the poetic act, and the appeal to the sense of hearing all

work to reorient our reading of 'De grant travail.' If we do homage to
Mary as a Lady, perhaps the fourth stanza's sacred fount to which we do
service is indeed Mary. After all, similar figures such as the spring or the
fountain occur in Gautier's works. If so, then service to Mary is what
saves us from the Devil's allegorical hooks; Mary interposes herself
between us and the Devil, and just as the song's discursive centre
becomes displaced when read from this second perspective, Mary moves
from the margins of the text and centres herself. The last time Mary
interposed herself occurred in stanza two where she put herself between
us and God. In that stanza, her sweet words save us from God's wrath. If
her words are powerful enough to move God to mercy, we hope that
Mary will listen to our words. Mary's words are essential to our salvation,
thus the love mentioned in the last verses of stanza II could be read as
love for Mary as well as for God. After all, the outcome of the struggle
between the Devil and God would be all but inevitable if it were not for
Mary. Homage to Mary, God's sacred fount, keeps us from the Devil's
grasp as it keeps us in God's good graces.

   The first sentence of the second stanza of 'De grant travail' offers, in
retrospect, a kind of grammatical analogy for the relationship between
the primary and secondary generic categories of the song. Although we
deserve death, we are granted pardon: 'Dex [...] / Nos avroit tost un
entre .ii. geté / Se la Dame [...] / [...] pour nous ne li prioit' (10–13).
Mary acts in the dependent clause and God in the independent clause.
The independent clause stands alone as the primary statement made in
the sentence; however, the dependent clause conditions the meaning of
that clause: we pray to Mary that she interpose herself and save us from
ourselves, the Devil, and God's anger. Somehow the locution 'God would
have thrown us into hell' implies that an explanation follows – the listener awaits the reason for God's change of heart. In the same way that
the dependent clause plays an important, if not vital role without being
grammatically essential to the meaning of the independent clause, Mary
here plays a vital role in the term's etymological sense: she shows us the
path to life.

   We also find Mary playing a important, although secondary, role not
only in more general devotional songs, but also in two crusade songs.
These songs ascribe to her a role to play in one of the most important
movements in medieval history. Mary's inclusion among the crusade
songs has literary historical significance: of the twenty-five crusade songs
edited by Bédier (texts) and Beck (melodies), Mary figures in only
Thibaut's pieces. Moreover, she appears in the two types of crusade

songs that Bédier identifies: the exhortation to crusade ('Seignor, sachiés') and the crusader's sorrowful departure from his beloved ('Dame, einsi') (ix–xi). In the latter, Mary comes to replace the earthly lady that the crusader must leave behind. The former takes a more strident tone, making it a curious constrast with the more tender divine love songs that poets like Gautier and Thibaut sing to her. In so doing, Thibaut illustrates his range of abilities and mastery of the poetic game.[6]

'Seignor, sachiés qui or ne s'en ira' is a song designed to move men to action. Its passionate tone is worthy of a Bernard de Clairvaux or Robert d'Arbrissel: Thibaut glorifies those who take up the cross, vilifies those who do not, and coerces those who waver. The singer urges his aristocratic listeners, the 'seigneurs,' to go on to the Holy Land and, by extension, to heaven:

> Or s'en iront cil vaillant bacheler
> Qui aiment Dieu et l'eneur de cest mont,
> Si sagement vuelent a Dieu aler. (15–17)

To those who will go on crusade, the singer juxtaposes those who stay, casting them in a most unfavourable light: 'Et li morveux, li cendreux demorront' (18). Those men who stay have fallen from grace and into folly. The action verb 'aler' occurs frequently (1, 4, 15, 17, 25), as does its opposite 'demorer' (8, 18, 29), and thus the song moves dialectically between going and staying.

The main theme of the song is duty: one's duty to God and the state. Whereas in songs like 'Dex est ensi' and in Gautier's lyrics, God's values are at odds with those of the secular world, the powerful rhetorical thrust of 'Seignor, sachiés' lies in its reconciliation of the two world views. The crusader honours both value codes, but the ones who stay behind 'por si pou pert la gloire du mont' (21). The so little for which they sacrifice worldly glory is specified in the second stanza with a particularly dramatic flourish, as Thibaut mimics the speech of these cowards before passing judgment on them:

> Et chascuns dit: 'Ma fame, que fera?
> Je ne lairoie a nul fuer mes amis.'
> Cil sont cheoit en trop fole atendance. (10–12)

The speech of the hesitant crusader cited above provides a counterpoint instance of direct discourse in the fourth stanza's imitation of Christ's speech. The stanza describes an apocalyptic Judgment Day scene:

'Vos qui ma crois m'aidastes a porter,
Vos en irez la ou mi angle sont;
La me verrez et ma mere Marie.
Et vos par cui je n'oi onques aïe
Descendrez tuit en enfer le parfont'   (24–8)

With this imitation of Christ's speech, Mary makes her first appearance.
Once again, Mary is seen alongside God and, although her presence is
fleeting, the rhyme 'Marie/aïe' is significant. The association between
Mary and help belongs generally to the Marian tradition and specifically
to this song. The rhyme summarizes a central point of Mariology and it
offers us a glimpse of what is to come in the song's envoi.

In the fifth stanza, the singer dispels what he sees to be the myth that
it is safer to stay in France than to go on crusade: 'Chascuns cuide
demorer tout haitiez/ Et que jamés ne doie mal avoir' (29–30). The
singer points out that the danger to the body might be avoided, but
great danger to the soul remains. When knights shirk their duty, both
the Devil and sin lay hold of their souls until, as the I/we says, 'il n'ont
sen, hardement ne pooir' (32). The stanza finishes with a plea to God
that such thoughts might be expelled from the minds of the cowards:

Biaus sire Diex, ostés leur tel pensee
Et nos metez en la vostre contree
Si saintement que vos puisons veoir!   (33–5)

The envoi, which immediately follows, contains a similar plea for intercession, this time to Mary:

Douce Dame, roïne coronee,
Proiez pour nos, virge bone aüree!
Et puis aprés ne nos puet mescheoir.   (36–8)

This second juxtaposition of God and Mary augments Mary's significance in the song: whereas the singer merely mentions Mary together
with God in verse 25, here she fulfils a more significant function,
namely, that of intercessor between God and us. Although the plea to
God appears to apply only to the demonstration in stanza V of how staying in France poses danger to one's soul, the plea to Mary is more subtle
but equally applicable. We might read the request that Mary pray for us
so that no evil befall us – 'ne nos puet mescheoir' – as a general plea for

protection. Then again, we could posit that the evil about which the singer speaks is that of staying in France. After all, the use of 'mescheoir' echoes an important pronouncement made by the singer in the second stanza. After mimicking the cowards' speech, the singer judges the cowards: 'Cil sont *cheoit* en trop fole atendance' (12, my emphasis). With the last word of the envoi, we are brought back to a critical moment of the singer's argument, and we understand how Mary plays a role that is crucial both in the sense of important and in the word's etymological sense: taking up the cross has become a gesture of Marian devotion.

By contrast to 'Seignor, sachiés,' with its impassioned and inflammatory incitement to religious fervour, Thibaut's 'Dame, einsi est qu'il m'en couvient aler' adopts a more personal tone. The song is sung from the perspective of a crusader who must leave behind his *amie*, and so for the first half of the song, the audience wonders if the lyric is a love song or a crusade song. Yet, with the switch of tone and perspective from 'Seignor, sachiés' to 'Dame, einsi' we hear a familiar voice in the latter, a voice that spoke in the former. The I/we in this latter song ridicules the one who asks such selfish questions as 'What will become of my wife, of my friends,' but in 'Dame, einsi,' Thibaut's speaker asks the same personal questions of himself. By taking up different concerns in these two crusade songs, Thibaut shows how well he defends contrasting positions.[7] In fact, there is even a contrast of positions with the song: the crusader laments the impending loss of human love and his earthly lady in stanzas I–III before he replaces these parts of his life with divine love and Mary in stanzas IV–V and the envoi.

The first three stanzas are marked by the I/we's reluctance to leave his lady. In this, the song resembles 'Mauvez arbres' in which the singer acknowledges his sinful past but only belatedly abandons himself to the divine. In 'Seignor, sachiés,' staying in France leads to hell, but in 'Dame, einsi,' France is cast as the 'douce contree/ Ou tant ai maus sosfrez et endurez' (2–3). In keeping with the shift in values between the two crusade songs, the Holy Land does not represent the gateway to eternal life, but rather a hostile entity that tears lovers apart. In a moment, the I/we of 'Dame, einsi' questions God desperately: 'Deus, por quoi fu la terre d'Outremer,/ qui tant amanz avra fet dessevrer' (5–6). In the second stanza, the singer looks back longingly at his sentimental education while looking ahead towards a desolate future without love's comfort:

Trop ai apris durement a amer;
Pour ce ne voi comment puisse durer

Sanz joie avoir de la plus desirree
C'onques nus hom osast merci crïer   (13–16)

The sorrow felt at departing becomes acute in the third stanza where
the singer cries out and repeats his prediction for a miserable future:

Trop par en sui dolens et esbahiz.
Par maintes foiz m'en serai repentiz,
Quant onques vols aler en ceste voie
Et je recort vos debonaires dis.   (21–4)

Critics have pointed out how much memory in Thibaut's songs consoles
the singer or causes him pain, but memory in this poem serves to bolster
the singer's reluctance.[8] The memory of the lady's gracious words functions as an obstacle to the willing commitment to his duty.

In the last two stanzas, several substitutions take place and the singer's
attitude changes abruptly as he concerns himself now with serving God
instead of his own pleasure. In the first two verses of the fourth stanza,
the singer turns to God, forsaking everything else. As the singer intones
the rest of stanzas IV and V, a number of semantic elements that
describe the lover's situation earlier in the song resurface to describe
now the pious person's situation. As the singer praises God for being a
worthy lord, the word 'esbahiz' used in stanza III's exclamation, 'Trop
par en sui dolens et esbahiz,' recurs, but all the sting has gone out of the
word: 'Si bon seignor avoir je ne porroie:/ Cil qui vos sert ne puet estre
traïz' (31–2). If the lady in stanza II is called 'la plus desirree,' in stanza
V the word is now used to describe religious devotion as opposed to
other more worldly affairs:

Bien doit mes cuers estre liez et dolenz:
Dolens de ce que je part de ma dame,
Et liez de ce que je sui desirrans
De servir Dieu, cui est mes cors et m'ame.   (33–6)

Verses 33–4 represent one final return to worldly regret as expressed in
the first three stanzas, but from that moment on, the crusader looks
back no more. No longer desirous of his lady, the singer now desires to
serve God; and whereas in the fourth stanza the singer complains of
leaving 'mon cuer et ma joie' for God, in the fifth stanza, God is now
'mes cors et m'ame.' Love for Mary replaces love for the earthly lady of

trouvère love song, and from the fourth stanza on, Mary's presence is felt more and more: 'Li guerredons en doit estre *floris*,/ Quant por vos [God] per et mon cuer et ma joie' (27–8, my emphasis) would seem to make Mary the flowery reward for the crusader who leaves his earthly lady to do his duty.[9] At the end of the fifth stanza, the traditional Marian metaphors of the ruby, emerald, and gem, describe the divine love the singer now embraces.

Mary often appears most explicitly in Thibaut's envois, and 'Dame, einsi' is no exception:

Dame des cieus, grant reïne puissant
Au grant besoing me soiez secoranz!
De vos amer puisse avoir droite flamme!
Quant dame par, dame me soit aidanz! (41–4)

The envoi's first verse constitutes another semantic echo, reinforcing the metonymy established in the previous stanza: there, 'iceste amors' is 'puissanz,' but here Mary is a 'reïne puissant.' As in so many love songs, Mary supplants the earthly dame, a substitution that transforms the very nature of love. 'Dame, einsi' is a crusade song first and foremost, but it is also an expression of Marian devotion.

In these crusade songs, Thibaut demonstrates yet again how well he can manipulate the universe of his poetry. Mary plays a role that serves both sides equally well in the polemics that surround the crusades, as Thibaut depicts them in these songs. In 'Seignor, sachiés,' she serves the valiant preacher/crusader's inflated rhetoric of God and country by shoring up the coward's courage while being part of the crusader's heavenly reward. In 'Dame, einsi,' she fills a vacuum left in the life of the knight who aches at the thought of leaving his lady. Thibaut puts Mary to a similar use in these very different songs: although she plays a role on both sides, she always turns us to our duty. Moreover, the hermeneutical subjectivity that characterized the reading process of 'De grant travail' and 'Mauvez arbres' functions in these two crusade songs: the reader (or listener) may read the songs from at least two different perspectives and arrive at complementary but not contradictory readings.

'Commencerai a fere un lai': Genre and Aesthetic Play

Like Gautier, Thibaut composed a *lai* employing some of the most traditional Marian motifs. And if, as pointed out above, Gautier modifies the formal properties of the *lai* by reusing the same melody for each of its three sections, Thibaut stretches the genre to its very limits. As such, 'Conmencerai' represents a final example of how Thibaut plays with our horizon of expectation on the level of genre. Indeed, the witnesses that transmit 'Commencerai' preserve a piece with a highly irregular structure, leaving scholars to struggle when editing or reading the text for over a century.[10] Not surprisingly, therefore, debate over the *lai* as a genre has raged on throughout the twentieth and into the twenty-first century.[11] The debate seems often directly related to the decision to include Thibaut's song among other *lais*. For example, Pierre Aubry contends that *lais* are arranged melodically either through repetition or in a more freely developed style, using a through-composed melody without any apparent, fixed rules (Bedier and Aubry xxi). Such remarks are tantamount to saying that anything could be a *lai*, and it is only upon closer scrutiny of Aubry's corpus that one realizes that only Thibaut's *lai* exhibits no evident division into sections and no consistent pattern of repeated musical phrases. We can only assume that this is the reason why Hans Spanke, in his attempt to form *lai* families, places Thibaut's in a group all by itself.

Thematically and rhetorically 'Conmencerai' resembles Gautier's 'Roÿne celestre' in its pervasive use of apostrophe, but differs strikingly from it in regards to metaphor and doctrinal content. 'Roÿne celestre' employs an extraordinary number of metaphors ('porte,' 'fenestre,' 'rose,' 'fontaine,' 'doiz,' and 'fons' among others) while stressing the doctrinal tenets of the Incarnation and Mary's maternity. As in Thibaut's other religious lyrics, Mary and God both have their own parts to play. Mary plays the very familiar role of *mediatrix* between God and us and, in fact, the movement back and forth from Mary to God is what orders this *lai*'s discursivity. Mary and God are the focus of a nearly equal number of verses – Mary is the focus in verses 1–18 and 37–44 and God in verses 19–36 and 45–6. Mary always leads us to God, and so the song ends with a final plea to God:

> Ci laisserai;
> Et Diex nos doint sans delai
> Avoir son secors veray!   (44–6)

Thibaut's *lai*, although fluid, displays a certain logical coherence: when feeling anguish, we pray to Mary to gain access to God. This movement from Mary to God in the fabric of the text is highly reminiscent of

Gautier's 'Amours, qui bien set enchanter': beginning with an acknowl-
edgment and rejection of a sinful past, the I/we calls upon Mary and is
led ultimately to God. One major difference between the two songs,
however, lies in the use of melody. Gautier's song employs a rising and
falling melody to help emphasize key points in his song, but the corre-
spondences between music and text in Thibaut's *lai* prove more elusive.
Thibaut's *lai*, therefore, displays a certain discursive coherence by textually inscribing Mary in her role as *mediatrix*: twice, the singing subject
prays to Mary and is led to God.

However orderly the piece progresses discursively, 'Conmencerai' displays extreme musico-poetic irregularities. Because no scribal clues –
punctuation, indentation, spacing – indicate where Thibaut's song
might break down into sections, we have to rely on internal textual
evidence alone. Syntax and prosody do not align in any evident way: different rhymes and different metrical combinations appear in each
syntagm, making the desire to discern a pattern among them overwhelming.[12] It is, however, in vain: once a pattern begins to emerge, it
quickly dissipates, leaving us with a perhaps pleasurable, perhaps unset-
tling, sense of poetic free-fall, which is the same in the music: over the
first six verses, we hear a regular melody – ABC ABC – but it soon gives
way to a far looser style of composition. Attempts to discern melodic patterns recreate the to-and-fro movement between possibility and reality
as seen in the song's syntax and metrics. Hans Spanke speculates that an
instrument might have repeated melodic phrases in performance, even
if, as Dominique Billy points out, no concrete, supporting evidence
exists. Spanke even suggests that perhaps Thibaut, in using the technical term 'lai,' might be toying with us. Refusing to give up, Tischler characterizes the *lai*'s melody as through-composed, appends it to his first
layer of pre-Machaut *lais*, defined as 'the works and work families contained in JBA [Jeanroy, Brandin, and Aubry]' (*Trouvère Lyrics* vol. 15:5),
and contends that melodic cohesion occurs through the interrelation of
musical phrases through motifs. However, one has to ask: at what point
does a musical phrase incorporate too many variants to be called a repetition? For example, would the audience recognize the four following
phrases as Tischler sees them, in other words, as variations on a single
phrase?

21.Ou   se - ra   mer - ci   tro - ve - e,

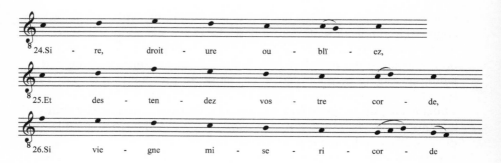

Is this repetition? Sophisticated members of Thibaut's audience like Tischler might believe so, but less initiated listeners might hear not repeated phrases, but rather a bewildering concatenation of differing musical phrases among a few obvious repetitions.

After Spanke, I contend that an audience experiences 'Conmencerai' in performance as a to-and-fro movement between affirmation – 'I am listening to a *lai*' – and negation – 'I am not listening to a *lai*.' The song's first six verses' regular ABCABC melodic structure and generic self-characterization leads the audience members to believe that they are listening to a *lai*. With verse 7's syntactic link to, but melodic departure from verses 4–6, Thibaut begins to play with our horizon of expectation. Verse 8 apostrophizes the Virgin for the first time and the melody of this verse is repeated four verses later, in verse 12, where Thibaut evokes the principal enemy of Mary, the Devil. Many verses are then sung before another obvious melodic repetition occurs. Some members of the audience may suspect that the piece is not a *lai* after all. However, more sophisticated audience members may detect repeated motifs in the first verses of this part and conclude that they are hearing a particularly clever *lai*. But then no motifs are repeated for some time, so that even the most sophisticated members of the audience might waver in their understanding. Later, repeated motifs, some more obvious than others, might be again detected, leading the sophisticated back to their original affirmation and helping lesser initiates, who might be desperate for a point of reference. However, at the end of the piece, repetitions of neither phrase nor motif occur and members of the audience are just left hanging, wondering what they have just heard. Could the near-final expression '*sans* de*lai*' be some wink to the audience and their confusion: a *lai* without being wholly a *lai*?

Instead of trying to fit Thibaut's piece into some preconceived generic notion, we might consider Thibaut's play as play, in the way that Hans-Georg Gadamer relates the concept to aesthetic consciousness. To experience a work of art is to give oneself over completely to a kind of game. This is not to suggest that we stop taking Thibaut's work seriously, for Gadamer carefully points out that seriousness in playing is what makes play legitimately play (*TM* 102). Anyone who pretends to play is, in fact, not playing. A playful to-and-fro movement occurs in the performance of 'Commencerai' on the rhetorical level – in the apostrophizing of Mary, then God, then Mary again, and then God again – and on the musico-poetic level through the repetition or nonrepetition of musical phrase, leading individual audience members to puzzle over whether or not they are indeed hearing a *lai*. Does the audience ever decide if the song is a *lai* or not? Some may decide yes, others no, and still others may refrain from deciding. In any case, it matters little. To measure the success of the game by a satisfactory answer to the question is to miss the point of playing. The object of play is not any end result; rather, the object of play is play, that is, the renewal of play in constant repetition (*TM* 103). Most importantly, although we are the players, we do not master the game. The subject of the game is not the player, but the game itself, and the game takes primacy over human subjectivity (*TM* 106). One's goal should not be to resolve the question, but to ask it willingly.

'Commencerai' constitutes then the apex of Thibaut's playful, hybridized Marian poetry. Whereas his stanzaic songs invite us to choose from among different interpretive centres, 'Commencerai,' by contrast, invites us to participate in a kind of play that prevents us from arriving at a final interpretation and understanding of genre. In turn, we are forced to abandon any teleological hermeneutic. Time and time again, Thibaut transforms Marian motifs and figures as he transforms genres through the hybrid songs that he composes. We feel suspended in mid-air, helpless to see which way he is heading. If Gautier never strays from the path he clearly maps out from the very first verses of the *Miracles*, Thibaut lets us wander, feel our way around, and make our own judgments. Gautier strips the reader of hermeneutical subjectivity when he ties his poetry to dogmatism, but Thibaut restores to us our interpretive freedom. We cannot see behind Thibaut's lyric masks – and that is the point! Thibaut invites us to join his masked lyrical ball and experience Marian song for ourselves.

chapter three

Voicing Marian Devotion in Women's Devotional Song

The Marian songs of Gautier and Thibaut are cast in voices that purport to speak for all humanity, but there are devotional songs, a number of which are Marian, sung in a specifically female voice. How do such songs differ from male-voiced songs? What might such differences entail? One similarity, as the editors of the recent *Songs of the Women Trouvères* (hereafter *SWT*) point out, is that 'the nonliturgical devotional songs of the trouvères are closely modeled on the secular repertoire, sharing its vocabulary, metaphors, and motifs, as well as its forms' (Doss-Quinby et al. 164). On one level, this is undeniable, but we must keep ourselves from seeing in the 'modelling' a one-way or derivative relationship: we should focus on the editors' comment that the two repertoires *share* elements and, as my readings of Gautier's 'D'amors coie et serie' and study of Thibaut's hybridized Marian songs demonstrate, out of the process of adoption and adaptation, a new message is created. One difference concerning this relationship is that women's songs tend to share elements not with the *chanson d'amour*, but with the *chanson d'ami*. As the editors of *SWT* provide an overview of past work on Old French women's songs, it only bears mentioning that little work has been done on Old French women's *devotional* songs. The one exception has been Blanche de Castille's male-voiced Marian song, 'Amours, u trop tart me sui pris,' which scholars have mainly studied for the question of attribution. To the best of my knowledge, no one has undertaken a reading of women's devotional song *comme telle* or against the backdrop of men's devotional song. In this chapter, I propose reading women's devotional songs both on their own terms and in the wider context of male devotional songs within their historical, manuscript, and musical contexts, all of which reveal, as I will argue, substantial dif-

ferences between the two corpuses. Moreover, even if they share characteristics and voice similar concerns, women's voices are distinct not only
from men's voices but also among themselves.

Reading these songs on their own terms and especially in their manuscript context suggests an approach grounded in the concept of voice.
Doing so provides us with three distinctive groups: three songs in the
voice of Everywoman, two songs in the voice of religious women, and
one song in the voice of the Virgin Mary herself. Two of the three Every-
man songs are published as *Recueil* no. 86, 'Chanter m'estuet de la virge
puchele' (RS 611a) and *Recueil* no. 132, '*Du dous Jhesu souvent devons
chanter et lire*' (RS 1195); the other is published as *SWT* no. 40: '*Li solaus
qui en moy luist est mes deduis*' (RS 1936a, 2076). One of the songs in the
voice of women religious is *SWT* no. 39, '*Li debonnaires Dieus m'a mis en sa
prison*' (RS 1646); the other is *Recueil* no. 131 '*Ave Maria, j'aim tant.*' The
last song is a *planctus Mariae*, most likely from the thirteenth century,
'*Lasse, que devendrai gié*' (RS 1093).[1]

As the editors of *SWT* include only songs authored by women or that
are cast in a grammatically determined female voice, the three songs
from the *Recueil* are rightly excluded from their anthology, since these
three songs are cast in voices that are grammatically determined as neither masculine nor feminine (except in the special case of '*Ave Maria*' in
which a female voice is cited and which Bec publishes in volume 2 of his
Lyrique Française among women's songs). However, if nothing in these
texts casts them definitively in the female voice, nothing assures us that
they belong to the male voice.[2] Some might object that only songs
explicitly marked in women's voices should be considered women's
songs, to which I must respond: why is the default voice male? Moreover, there is compelling textual evidence to justify reading them as
women's songs. For one, they share formal properties common, but
not exclusive, to women's songs: they are all refrain songs and employ
dancelike musical forms. If songs in the male voice also use these forms,
one should note that out of the twenty-seven monologic *chansons* anthol-
ogized in *SWT*, twenty-two incorporate refrains, are composed in dancelike forms, or both, whereas far fewer male-voiced songs display such
formal properties. For another, the themes of pain and longing, so prevalent in the *chanson d'ami, ballettes*, dawn songs, and devotional songs
gathered in *SWT* are present in these three songs. To put it succinctly:
while nothing prevents us from reading these songs as women's songs,
formal and thematic elements invite us to do so.

The six songs come down to us in two different contexts, one of which is already familiar to us: 'Chanter m'estuet,' is transmitted in Paris, Arsenal 3517, one half of a vastly extended compilation of Gautier de Coinci's *Miracles*.[3] The other five songs are preserved in trouvère ms. *i*, Paris, BnF fr. 12483, a work commonly known as the *Rosarius* that has held the attention of philologists since Jubinal in the mid-nineteenth century. This work is a voluminous collection of devotional songs, *contes*, and miracles, compiled in honour of the Virgin Mary by a Dominican friar from Poissy in the early fourteenth century (Svenqvist argues for a later date), although many of the narratives and songs most likely date from the thirteenth century. The dedicatory function of the work heightens Mary's importance throughout this work, which the compiler has ordered in a very specific fashion: the compilation is divided into two books, which are further divided into chapters, which are each, in turn, dedicated to a different 'chose': typically an animal, plant, or stone. The item is then described and its attributes are applied to the Virgin Mary. These descriptions are derived from bestiaries and works of natural history, especially those of Pliny and Isidore, but the comparisons to Mary are regarded by modern scholars as original compositions.[4] A devotional tale, either a miracle or *conte*, ensues, followed by a *dit* or song.[5] Variations exist – sometimes more than one devotional tale or song is included, sometimes the application of the thing's qualities to the Virgin Mary is continued after the song or *dit*, etc. – but the basic chapter structure remains evident.

The *Rosarius* context proves especially important for a reading of these female-voiced songs, for their particular voicings of Marian devotion echo or provide counterpoint to other voices heard within their context. In fact, even the identification of the voices speaking is sometimes problematic. For example, in chapter 47 of book 2 and in the midst of comparing the falcon to Mary, the speaker abruptly switches from indirect to direct discourse and from a didactic to an endearing tone, addressing the reader as 'chier filz' (47–51).[6] This parent then incites the son to turn away from this world in order to love God and Mary by singing '*Amis, amis,/ Trop me laissi[ez en] estrange pais*,' the opening refrain of a (grammatically determined) woman's song (*SWT* no. 35; RS 747). As the song is in the female voice, perhaps we should also read the parent's voice as feminine, i.e., a mother's? Does that mean that the speaker of the whole chapter is feminine? The parent encourages the son to sing a woman's song, thus adopting a female voice. What does it mean that the parent wants the son to assume a female voice? In short, this chapter, among others, presents us with a number of disruptive moments we might call 'cross-voicings,' which evoke many questions concerning the work's public and reception, but which lie outside of this study's scope. We might conclude with Susan Boynton that, as medieval literary voices were fluid, either women or men could sing both women's and men's songs.[7] On the other hand, Boyton risks assimilating the female voice to a default, male voice, a problem that Matilda Bruckner considers in trobairitz (women trouba- dour) song and E. Jane Burns in the *chanson de toile*. Both of these crit- ics argue that reading women's voices in a poetic system largely determined by men is problematic.[8] Similarly, we need a way of listen- ing to the distinctively female voices expressing Marian devotion in a conventional poetic system while not muting their differences. As in Gautier and Thibaut's lyrics, the womens' voices of these songs stake a claim to transcendence. And yet, these songs introduce different motifs and themes, some of which apply differently to women than to men. As a result, we encounter a new multicentred reading strategy that is analogous to the one at work in Thibaut's songs, based not on generic function, but on voice: whose voice, what it says, and what we take away from that difference.

Songs in the Voice of Everywoman

Three songs, two of which others might call gender-neutral, make room for both universal application to all humanity and particular application to women. The first, 'Chanter m'estuet de la virge puchele,' contains a grammatically neutral voice, but in this refrain song the singer high- lights the themes of longing and pain, central to woman's song, and alludes to the miracle of the pregnant Jewess in the final stanza, all of which makes reading the song in the female voice compelling. The sec- ond is '*Du dous Jhesu souvent devons chanter et lire*,' another song in a grammatically indetermined voice, and may be read as a female-voiced song for the same reasons as 'Chanter m'estuet' as well as for the charac- ter of its refrain: the use of 'dous' to qualify Jesus is strongly reminiscent of the *chanson d'ami*. Finally, there is '*Li solaus qui en moy luist est mes deduis*,' composed in a grammatically determined female voice. When we read all these songs as women's songs, we come to realize that they speak for no particular woman, but for women in general, that is, Every- woman. Their voices resonate with the universal male voices of Gautier and Thibaut's work in some ways; however, in contrast to the male voice, they give us insight into not only devotional attitudes towards Mary and God, but also attitudes towards life on earth.

Preserved in Arsenal ms. 3517, 'Chanter m'estuet' is the last poem in the first lyric cycle of the compilation that includes both monophonic and polyphonic compositions in either Latin or French. Although Mary is addressed in 'Chanter m'estuet,' the singer longs for Jesus, and so the Virgin assumes her familiar role as *mediatrix*. This augments her importance even as it seems to diminish it: she may not be the desired end, but she is the efficacious means to that end. The song intertwines two particular themes: calling on Mary and the Incarnation. It is only through calling on Mary that the believer finds aid, and the Incarnation, as we saw in Gautier's lyric production, represents perfect communion between humanity and divinity, a kind of unity now sought by the singer. The two themes are inextricably tied together in every stanza: as God made his way to humanity through Mary, so can humanity make its way to God through her.

The final stanza, however, treats the concomitance of childbirth and the calling to Mary differently, prompting questions of performance, reception, and public:

Cheste miracle est aperte provee:
Ja Juïse n'iert de son fruit delivree
Se la mere Dieu n'est avant reclamee;
Por ce l'aimme je et la voel tous jours amer.
Priés vostre fil ...   (25–9)

The singer here makes reference to the miracle of a Jewish woman delivered from a painful and potential deadly childbirth. The miracle survives not in Gautier's work, but in various collections of medieval miracles, sermon exempla, and devotional songs such as the *Speculum Historiale* by Vincent de Beauvais, Johannes Herolt's *Sermones discipuli de tempore et de sanctis cum promptuario exemplorum et de beata Virgine*, Johannes Gobius's *Scala Coeli*, and the *Cantigas de Santa Maria* of Alfonso X. Some descriptions of the woman's agony are explicit, as in Alfonso's cantiga 89:

Ela assi jazendo,
   que era mais morta ca viva,
braadand'e gemendo
   e chamando-sse mui cativa,
con tan gran door esquiva,
   que desanparada

foi; e desasperada
A Madre de Deus onrrada. $(22-9)^9$

[Lying there thus,
more dead than alive,
agonizing and shuddering,
and wailing over her very wretched state,
experiencing such pain,
she felt abandoned
and desperate.
To the honoured Mother of God.]

The woman has no choice but to call on Mary, who immediately saves her and her child. However, the attendant Jewesses become enraged at her act of betrayal and call her 'ereja' (58), 'renegada' (59), and 'crishāna tornada' (60): 'heretic,' 'traitor,' and 'Christian turncoat.' They ready themselves to attack, but the newly converted Jewess immediately flees to a church where she is baptized along with her children.

The allusion to the miracle creates an effect of *mise en abyme*: a call within a call. It also creates a link between lyric and narrative discourse, as the song survives in a collection of miracles. In regard to performance and reception, though, the allusion might cast a dark shadow for women singing or hearing the song and remind them (men too, but especially women) of the many dangers women faced in medieval society. Childbirth represented a happy event then as now, when it did not go awry, which happened far more frequently than today. Moreover, the miracle reminds listeners of the dangers faced by women, whether Jewish, Christian, or Muslim, who disobeyed the tenets of their community: witness the harsher penalties for women committing adultery. Maternal protection is also thematized in the miracle and thus insinuated in the song: the mother flees not alone, but with her children. Of course, men and women alike may understand the song, but the inclusion of motifs and allusions that apply differently to the historical situation of women leaves space for a distinctively feminine reading. Its implicit focus on women's issues, while not completely foreign to men, could make it differently understood by women. Although men certainly sympathize, they could not as easily empathize when song and miracle are applied to women's historical conditions.

The second and third songs in the voice of Everywoman, '*Du douz Jhesu souvent devons chanter et lire*' and '*Li solaus qui en moy luist est mes deduis/ Et Diex est mes conduis*' do not focus on the dangers of this world, but their theme of the desire to flee from it is suggestive of an attitude similar to that found in 'Chanter m'estuet.' '*Du douz Jhesu*' comes in chapter 42 of the second book of the *Rosarius*, 'Rossignol,' in which both Mary and Jesus are compared to the nightingale.[10] '*Li solaus*' comes in chapter 46 on the camel.[11] After describing the beasts' longevity, ability to survive with little sustenance, and their endurance, the compiler moves to another figure, one that serves as a transition to our song: the sun. Jesus is first and foremost the sun, but Mary is never far from him or our minds. With the next verse begins '*Li solaus*,' a song clearly cast in the feminine voice as the fourth stanza begins: 'Hé mi, lasse, que feray?' (21). Thus this chapter and this song serve as further examples of cross-voicing.

'*Du douz Jhesu*' thematizes the desire to flee from this present world and find a new, more comforting world, one that Mary represents and to which she gives us access. Jesus is the little nightingale in the song and the singer's interlocutor: 'Rossignolet, Jhesu de piteus estre,/ Assié nous tous delez toy a ta destre' (39–40).[12] Jesus-nightingale plays, in fact, two roles in the song: he urges worldly lovers to flee the world, and he becomes the sacralized lover with whom the singer wishes to flee:

> Menez m'ou bois o vous en la gaudie.
> La serons en deduit
> Et le jour et la nuit,
> Et si l'orons, celui
> Qu'amours firent ocirre.   (19–23)

There is an almost wistful quality about the stanza: the speaker desires so ardently what she does not have presently that she speaks of it as something that *will* happen. It is, in fact, her *will* that comes through in these verses, that is, her desire to be elsewhere.

In the last stanza of the nightingale song, Mary is strongly associated with that desired future far from this world of pain:

> La verront cil Marie
> Qui l'averont servie
> De cuer et en purté;
> La seront a seurté
> En pardurable vie;

Bele est la compaignie.
Jhesus nous doint que nous n'i faillons mie.   (47–53)

Mary is already in the place that the singer desires to be, alluded to time
and time again throughout the song as 'ça jus' (6), the 'bois' (19), 'paradis' (41), or simply 'la' (20, 43, 47, 50). Mary looms large in that desired
place, and she is indeed the conduit by which one gains access, since the
key to finding paradise is service to her. Moreover, the preponderance
of verbs in the future accentuate the singer's desire to move into this
future 'seurté,' intimating that the present is one of less security.

'*Li solaus*' also thematizes the desire to flee this world and find a place
of respite. The song is highly emotional in tone, and its musical properties highlight this tone. The stanza's melody is highly structured, and con-
strasts with the more free-flowing refrain. Nevertheless, the refrain ends
and the stanza begins on the same note; this makes for a seamless transition from stanza to refrain to subsequent stanza. The melody over the
first three verses of the stanza contains wide leaps but stays in the upper
register; however, the whole octave is explored in the fourth verse and
refrain. These musical characteristics enhance the text on the semantic
level. For example, the oscillation between joy and despair is accentuated
in turn by the melody's wide leaps over the first verse of stanza I:

Moreover, the fourth phrase's melismatic qualities enhance the description of Jesus as sweet. Likewise, in stanza IV, the melody functions in the
same way when sung over its lyrics:

Hé mi, lasse! que feray? N'i puis aler.
Esperance et fine amour, quar m'i portez,
Qu'aprez ceste mortel vie i puisse aler:
Ce sont tous mes deduis.   (21–4)

The juxtaposition of these melodically enhanced passages brings out a significant thematic nexus: like 'Chanter m'estuet' above, the song focuses on the desire to flee and a promising future; however, we should note that it dwells just as much on the pain of living in 'ceste mortel vie,' this 'temporary' and 'deadly' life. She describes herself as weary ('lasse') and searches for 'esperance,' the hope for a future beyond this deadly life.

The way to escape this world is, of course, to appeal to Mary, and this is accomplished in the song's final stanza:

Dame Marie, priez a vostre fil
Qe tant com vivons en ce mortel essil,
Sa grace nouz doint, par quoy soions si fil,
Et en son livre escrit.   (27–30)

Life as a mortal exile is a depiction that echoes the previous stanza's use of the expression, 'mortel vie.' If the song is characterized melodically by wide leaps, it is also the case thematically: the singer wishes to make the wide leap from this life to the next. Her attitude towards this life focuses on its temporary state, tinged not with regret or terror, but with hope: this world is profoundly marked by death, which brings us back to the first verses of the song in which the woman asks Jesus if it is her death that he wants. With the final appeal to Mary, we come full circle, and it is precisely this circle from which the singer wishes to break free.

The three songs in the voice of Everywoman focus on reunion with God, as with men's songs, but we also clearly hear a desire to flee from this world, which is less apparent in the men's songs. At work in these songs is a temporal and spatial opposition between now and the future, a 'here' and a 'there,' and one perceives that where one is now – and in a song like 'Chanter m'estuet' through its allusion to the pregnant Jewish woman, the here and now is extremely painful – is not the place where one ultimately wants to be. This sense of uneasiness or of out-of-placeness is far more developed in these songs than in the male-voiced songs. Gautier and Thibaut both express a desire to find paradise, but the same urgency is largely absent from their songs. In the Everywoman songs, an ardent desire to leave the 'here' and to reach the 'there' lies at their heart: it remains to be seen if the same holds true for the songs in the voices of particular women.

Religious Women Voicing Marian Devotion

Two songs are cast in the voices of religious women: '*Li debonnaires Dieus m'a mis en sa prison*' is in the voice of a Dominican nun and '*Ave Maria, j'aim tant*' in that of a beguine. These songs bring fresh perspectives to the conclusions reached above; however, whereas in songs like 'Chanter m'estuet' that include motifs particular to women's experience in the secular world, i.e., childbirth, these two songs include or suggest motifs related to women's religious institutions. Both the Dominican nuns, or *jacobines*, and the beguines constituted newer religious movements that failed to fit earlier models of ecclesiastical life. Moreover, if both cloistered orders and urban, parochial clergy scorned the Dominicans (and other mendicant orders like the Franciscans), the *jacobines* were held in contempt and feared by their male counterparts in the Dominican order.[13] In fact, extraordinary efforts were taken to regulate the behaviour of Dominican nuns, even to the point of contradicting the very mission of the order. As Jo Ann Kay McNamara notes, Dominican nuns were supposed to remain not only cloistered but also silent: 'Dominic urged the women to fast, maintain cloister, and obey, stressing the importance of silence, an ironic commandment for even the most marginal members of a preaching order' (313). On the other hand, diocesan clergy as well as cloistered and mendicant orders were wary of the beguines, who occupied a middle ground between the religious and secular worlds (Grundmann 140). Nevertheless, it is worth noting that Mary holds a prominent role in the history of this movement, the members of which took Mary, a poor and virginal woman living in the wider world, as the founder of their state in society. In light of these historical considerations, it is paramount to remember that a Dominican friar compiled the *Rosarius*, for his world view surely affects the representation of both women.

'*Li debonnaires Dieus*' is integrated into the chapter on the dove, a bird noted in the text for its various colours, mournful song, and meditative but generous nature.[14] We are also told in this chapter that Mary serves as an example of one who never sings foolish songs, but sincere and often contrite ones (248–63). This detail links her to both the dove and the singer of '*Li debonnaires Dieus,*' and although a singer in the Middle Ages would have sung the song in a personally comfortable range, it is compelling to analyse the song on levels of both music and text as it is written. The through-composed and conjunct melody is quite low, often staying close to c, especially in the refrain, and although it rises as high as c′, the melody dwells mostly in the lower register between d and a. Given this, it is interesting to juxtapose both words and melody in the refrain:

Li   de - bon - nai - res   Dieus   m'a   mis   en   sa   pri - son.

Refrain of '*Li debonnaires*' (Ed. E. Aubrey, *Songs of the Women Trouvères*)

I would suggest that the melodic properties lend a sorrowful tone to the words. In light of this observation, the first stanza could be read as a lament or even an accusation:

> *Li debonnaires Dieus m'a mis en sa prison.*
> Vous ne savez que me fist
> Jhesuscrist, li miens amis,
> Qu[ant] jacobine me fist
> Par grant amours.
> *Li debonnaires [Dieus m'a mis en sa prison.]*

Is this merely the metaphorical prison of love converted from secular songs like those of Thibaut, or is there some hint at the convent in these lines? The rising melody over the stanza's third verse draws our attention to the action that was 'done to' the *jacobine*, most likely when she pronounced her vows. If the nun is regretting her taking of vows, then 'li miens amis' and 'par grant amours' may be, in fact, ironic; furthermore, other motifs, such as the Ovidian arrow of love that inflicts pain in stanzas II and III may hint at an existential, even physical pain rather than emotional or spirtual rapture. This reading becomes even more credible when we hear the longing for paradise in stanzas III and IV and the mention of tears, sighs, and the nun's melting heart. McNamara is careful to point out that strict claustration was not always observed among *jacobines* and that cloistering was more a state of mind than a physical condition: 'If women were averse to cloistering, the sources have silenced them' (290). I would posit that this song may very well be a source of discontent, albeit a subtle one that suggests rather than explicates the nun's ill feelings.

Mary was the model of humility and submission that nuns were supposed to emulate. However, when the *jacobine* mentions Mary in the final two stanzas, she expresses not admiration but 'jalousie':

Quant je pense a Marie,
Qui fu [de] nete vie,
J'ai une jalousie
Que [...] bon.
Li debonnaires ... (27–31)

The word should not be understood in its contemporary English context, but rather more in its contemporary French one: 'jalousie' means less 'envy' than it does a kind of 'possessiveness.' The *jacobine*'s wish to guard Mary jealously may be read two ways: for one, it may be that she embraces her religious life; then again, it may be all she has left, a final refuge, for underlying any feeling of possessiveness is fear: the one who is 'jaloux' lives constantly in the fear that what is loved will suddenly be lost. Of course, since the stanza is fragmented, we cannot read it with any more certainty.[15]

Like many songs, '*Li debonnaires Dieus*' ends with an appeal to Mary, after which the nun expresses hope in one day joining Mary in paradise:

Prions [a] la pucele,
Qui fu saint[e et] honneste,
Qu'en paradis nous [mete]:
C'est mout biau don.
Li debonnaires ... (32–6)

Once again, Mary is qualified as exemplary, a model of saintly conduct, and the song ends with the desire to enter paradise. One cannot, however, ignore what leads up to that final request: overshadowing that request for heavenly reunion is a lament concerning an implicit desire to escape the prison in which the *jacobine* now lives, but perhaps paradoxically also a fear of losing that very prison as it might constitute the nun's only earthly refuge.

Reading the song as one in which the *jacobine* celebrates her divine prison of love is certainly possible, but alongside the possibility of reading the song as a celebration of the religious life, I would suggest, it is possible to see a projection of male desire to cloister women strictly either physically, mentally, or both. In this reading, the song speaks less of the *jacobine*'s fear than that of the *jacobin* who compiled the work. At some level, whether or not Dominican nuns actually kept cloister is less important if they mentally did so: their prison becomes portable. At the same time, in the same male fantasy, the friar would like to imagine that the women enjoy their claustration: thus the use of an almost violent love vocabulary to describe the feelings about what Jesus 'did to me.' From among these readings, it is possible to support one over the other depending upon one's perspective, and thus friars and nuns could very well have understood the song differently: friars might have felt their fears assuaged upon hearing about how much this nun enjoys her imprisonment, how much she clings to the model of humility that Mary provides, and how the *jacobine* longs for reunion with Mary and God in heaven. Then again, if nuns were constantly reminded of their duty to stay indoors and silent, perhaps the song resonated differently with them. Perhaps they understood that the *jacobine*'s desire to leave this life and join the next one is double-edged.

By contast to the cloistered *jacobine* in '*Li debonnaires Dieus,*' in '*Ave Maria, j'aim tant,*' we encounter an errant beguine. The song is found in chapter 41 of the *Rosarius* on the sky, which also includes a celestial vision that Saint Dominic had of Mary and a *dit* of Renart. In the first, Dominic visits heaven and is saddened to see only adherents to other orders present. However, when Mary pushes back her hood, she reveals numerous Dominican friars underneath. Dominic returns and exhorts all to renounce *papelardie*, a kind of false religious fervour of which the beguines were often accused – in fact, they were often referred to as *papelardes*. Similarly, in the Renart poem, the poet laments the *renardie* or hypocrisy in his day, and he spares no one from his satiric barbs, especially the religious orders. In one stanza, we find a resonance with not only our song but also Dominic's vision:

> Prestres, moingnes, jacobins,
> Cordeliers et li béguins
> Qui font bien le papelart,
> Sous leur chapes ont Regnart.   (53–6)

> [Priests, monks, friars,
> Franciscans and Beguines
> Who play the hypocrite,
> They keep Renart under
> their hoods.]

If the passage takes the beguines to task through its explicit association of beguines with 'le papelart,' we should also not fail to notice that the Dominicans too are the subject of ridicule here.

Between these two passages we find our song, in which each stanza is punctuated with a refrain expressing Marian devotion: '*Ave Maria, j'aim tant.*' The song employs a through-composed melody and the fluid compositional nature of the song highlights the beguine's emotional state as she makes her way into a church to contemplate the wounds of Christ.[16] The scene is not at all far-fetched: private meditative practices were the norm for women religious since they could not administer the sacraments. However, we not only observe this beguine's actions and perceive her feelings, we also hear her speak as she exclaims how she fears the day of judgment, for it will be terrible for her and all humanity. Beguines and other women religious were often mystics who reported having visions, especially of purgatory and hell, which gave them spiritual currency and often helped curb priestly abuses of power.[17] In the final stanza, in fact, the beguine names priests as well as a host of people arranged hierarchically in descending order who will have to account for their conduct on judgment day:

Prestre, clerc et chevalier,
Damoiseles, escuier,
Bourgois et gent de mestier
I seront tuit en present.   (27–30)

The beguine's foreboding vision contrasts sharply with Dominic's peaceful, celestial scene. We should also note that only male religious and secular women are listed; in other words, women religious are spared. Thus, much to the contrary of Dominic's assertion that 'Ne papelart ne glorieus/ Ja ne monteront es sains ciels' and the Renart poet's scorn for the beguines, it would seem that they are among the few to be saved. The ideological dispute among these three texts ends with a zero sum.

The two songs in voices of religious women develop the theme of the desire to flee, so prevalent in the songs in the voices of Everywoman. The women speakers in these songs express their loneliness and isolation in two different situations, both of which belong to the sphere of religious life. The *jacobine*'s imprisonment, perhaps physical, but assuredly mental, due to her condition as a Dominican nun, comes through both text and melody in her dovelike, mournful song. The beguine's isolation, on the other hand, takes place in the wider world, and like the *jacobine*, she feels an overwhelming sense of isolation from all sectors of society, be they ecclesiastical or secular. This isolation among the masses is intimated even in the very format of the chapter: the beguine's voice is heard within a song that finds itself surrounded by hostile ecclesiastical and secular voices alike. Mary's role in both cases is subdued, but significant in its own right: she may be all that the *jacobine* has left, and the beguine invokes the mother of Jesus to witness her pain and suffering.

Mary's Voice: 'Lasse, que devendrai gié'

If any woman stands alone among other women, it is the Virgin Mary herself, as the title of Marina Warner's book intimates: *All Alone of Her Sex*. Mary herself speaks in 'Lasse, que devendrai gié,' a thirteenth-century *lai* and *planctus Mariae*, a genre that flourished in Latin and the vernaculars from the twelfth through the sixteenth centuries. The genre is intimately connected with the Passion play, as it comprised the moment in which Mary sings of her suffering at witnessing the death of Jesus.[18] A song sung in the voice of Mary herself stands both apart from and at the very centre of women's songs. Mary was, as the same time, familiar in her roles as wife and mother, and strange: she stood apart from women through her unique role as Theotókos, the Mother of God. Despite this paradox, Mary served as a model for medieval women: as such, she sets a worthy, but unattainable, goal in terms of virtue, humility, and status. It only stands to reason, then, that an examination of Mary's voice in lyric should hold a prominent place in this discussion: to what extent does Mary's voice exemplify the women's voices heard thus far and to what degree does she voice concerns unique to her station?

Although the history of the *planctus* and the Passion play lies beyond the scope of this study, it is noteworthy that the first *planctus*, found in the twelfth-century Latin Passion of Montecassino, is in a vernacular: Italian.[19] The effect of the linguistic switch, best articulated by Robert Edwards, is to join the witness of ordinary speech to that of biblical language (55). There occurs in this moment a real identification between Mary and the public. We should be mindful of this link when reading 'Lasse' and when drawing conclusions about the significance of these Marian poems in the voices of women. We should also note that for most of the Middle Ages, Western theologians depicted Mary at the cross as stoic, steeled by the knowledge that Jesus' death had higher meaning. As the Middle Ages progressed, however, Mary was depicted as more human, but her human qualities would usually be tempered by a kind of premonition of the impending redemption.[20] As we shall see, no such balance is struck in 'Lasse.'

'Lasse' is a piece of high musico-poetic complexity that comes down in the *Rosarius* chapter on balm that treats one of the most complex of questions ever pondered: death. The work is heterometric and a new melody is introduced with each of its ten sections. Each section is bipartite in nature whereby the same melody is used for the first and second part of the section, although section nine doubles the structure to produce a bipartite stucture wherein each subsection is, in turn, bipartite. Slight variation usually characterizes the melody's repetition, and the melody of the entire *lai* may be schematized as follows: AA BB′ CC′ DD′ EE′ FF GG HH′ II′JJ′ KK′. The length of these sections runs between four and eight phrases, endowing the piece with a metrical complexity that belies the seeming orderliness of the proposed melodic scheme. Yet, despite these differences, the entire piece shows unity on the level of octave species: the entire piece uses the a octave species transposed to d with a reciting tone of a, which divides the octave into the fifth d-a and the fourth a-d′. These divisions are explored systematically over the entire song: the melody of sections I, II, and III remains in the lower half of the octave, exploring the fifth in an extremely conjunct fashion. This melodic restraint serves to build tension, for with section IV, a much different approach is employed: section III ends on d, but section IV begins a whole octave higher on d′. With that gesture, the entire octave is explored sometimes conjunctly, but just as often through jumps of a fifth – especially between d and a and vice versa – and jumps of an octave. The final tone of phrases within sections is often a, the reciting tone, but just as often it is e, a tone higher than the finalis of each section, d, which repeatedly creates tension.

Syntax often plays along with or against these melodic tendencies and divisions. For roughly the first half of the *lai*, that is, sections I through V, syntax and melody work together: where the melody is completed, one finds a hard stop. Thus a new clause is begun where the melodic repetition begins. However, these neat patterns become interrupted in the second half of the *lai*, especially towards the end. For example, in sections VII and section IX, at the middle of each section, the syntactical arrangement of the sentence is such that the whole idea is not expressed within the subsection. Below is section VII:

Onques ne senti doulour,
Biau filz, quant vous fustes nez,

Ne ne muay la coulour:
Ne pouoit estre esgenez
Li cors qui de tel seignour
avoit esté [estrenez.]
Or ai duel; nus n'ot greignor
Dont vous estes si menes.

The melody starts over with 'li cors' but that expression is the complement of the verb at the end of the preceding line that marks the end of
the first occurence of the melody. As such, syntax spills over into the
next melodic unit, and these misalignments will become important as
we interpret the words of the Virgin.

In 'Lasse,' the Virgin pours out her heart to her audience upon seeing
the horrific sight of the public humiliation and death of her son. The
present moment of performance is always in view, accented by the high
emotional tone of the song; yet, the present and the future are also of
prime importance to the Virgin's complaint. Three pasts are highlighted:
the recent past of Jesus' death, the happy childhood past shared by Mary
and Jesus, and the prophetic past, by which I mean the Virgin's several
allusions to prophecies of Jesus' death and her grief, especially that of
Simeon, the priest who said at Jesus' presentation in the temple that
Mary's soul would one day be pierced by a sword. Throughout the first
three sections, all three pasts are mingled, gathering together moments
of joy and pain, as is admirably demonstrated in the third section:

Toute riens fu esbaudie
Quant mes ventres t'ensfanta.
Nis la bele compaingnie
Des celz en rist et chanta.
Quant la mort vint soz ta vie,
Li cielz s'en espouenta;
Mult deüst estre garie
Dame qui tel enfant a.   (27–34)

The joy experienced in heaven and earth at the birth of Jesus is treated
in the first half of the section; the second half, in which the same melody is repeated, both subject and tone have changed: now the focus is
on death and sorrow. The relationship between melody and semantics
is clearly complex: the same melody accompanies verses of opposite
meaning and tone, creating a startling contrast.

Shifts in melody come at times of high emotion. Throughout the first three sections where the melody is confined to the fifth, the Virgin paints the picture of a painful and uncertain future. But with section IV, uncertainty gives way to outright despair, and the melodic range is suddenly doubled and higher in register. At that very moment, the tone of the song changes, pivoting on the contrastive conjunction 'mes':

The realization of the future's uncertainty comes with a realization of how radically the present differs from the past: she has been stripped of her motherhood. The second half of the section repeats not only the melody but also a similar syntactical pattern, this time with the contrastive conjunction 'or':

> Or si l'a mis en sa prison,
> La mort dure et amere.
> Li prophete que nous lison
> Y prirent leur matere.   (39–42)

The figure of the prison resurfaces, but there is no ambiguity here as in the *jacobine*'s song. Death is a hard and bitter prison.

The intensity of the pain that she feels is sometimes enhanced in the remaining sections where we observe discontinuities between melody and syntax. For example, in the last verses of section VII, after just such a discontinuity, we hear, 'Or ai duel; nus n'ot greignor,' an exclamation that sets Mary apart from other women not through her perpetual virginity or immaculate conception, but through her extreme pain. The disconnect between melody and syntax that occurs in these final sections works in tandem with the creation of tension when each internal phrase ends a second higher than the final. Both accomplish an important semantic and thematic function in the *lai*: the creation of tension paired with discontinuities between syntax and melody are suggestive of the anxiety and the emotional tearing felt by a woman witnessing the public execution of her son. The song's failure to end with a permanent release of this anxiety and pain suggests, I would argue, that the cycle is thought to never end.

When discussing her role as co-redemptrix of humanity, medieval theologians gave Mary an essential part to play in the Passion: her suffering held a redemptive value.[21] However, this *lai* omits exactly that: redemption. There is only pain, presently felt and sure to continue into the future. As the Virgin's voice falters, there is no indication of impending change, except in the minds of the listeners who already know how the story will turn out. Nevertheless, to the Virgin of 'Lasse,' the future is bleak, and if theologians since Justinian have seen Mary as the antithesis of Eve, we find here common ground between the two: for one, they both share in the grief of losing a son in a violent episode; for another, they share the experience of exile, for among Mary's last words, we hear, 'or m'en irai en essil.' As these female archetypes share pain and exile, they partake of the feelings that we have seen time and time again in these women's devotional songs: isolation, pain, suffering, and longing. When considered in this literary context, Mary is, indeed, exemplary.

Devotional songs, whether voiced by men or women, enact the same speech act – the surrender of will to the divine – but women's songs make this call through varied voices. From the voice of Everywoman to those of religious women to that of Mary herself, these voices relate devotion indirectly but no less poignantly to women's affairs in this life, characterized as an 'estrange païs,' a 'prison,' a 'mortel vie,' and 'mortel essil.' I am not suggesting that these songs are autobiographical in nature; they do, nevertheless, make an important contribution to a medieval discourse on women. Male-voiced songs treat pain and suffering more abstractly, usually filtering them through the concept of sin; this is present in women's songs too, but far less so than in men's songs. Uniquely female experiences are entwined in these songs in their references to childbirth, to the taking of holy orders perhaps unwillingly, and to persecution from various sectors of society for failing to conform to models of behaviour exacted by either ecclesiastical or secular authorities. After all, are not the figures of Jesus and Mary themselves nonconformist: one, a radical preacher and the other, a virginal mother? The contributions of these songs to a social discourse are both representational and prescriptive: they affect a realistic vision of women's suffering on earth while intimating that the situation could be far worse if they were to try to break free from the norms prescribed. As such, these songs leave room for a uniquely female reception by carving out a small but significant space for voicing the spiritual needs felt by women. Mary herself illustrates best in 'Lasse' that at the centre of women's devotional song lies a desire less for reward than for deliverance. There may be a fine distinction, but it makes all the difference between male-voiced and female-voiced Marian devotion.

chapter four

Jacques de Cambrai, Distinctive Traditionalism, and Kaleidoscopic Contrafacta

Jacques de Cambrai, a little-read poet about whom we know nothing outside his seven devotional songs, four *chansons d'amour*, and one *pastourelle* was active most likely in the third quarter of the thirteenth century at a time and in a place where the Marian lyric tradition was in full bloom.[1] Although hardly innovative in the current sense of the word, Jacques exploited the tradition to its fullest. I should point out that traditional does not necessarily mean staid or static; on the contrary, as we shall see, Jacques made choices of form, theme, and model that render his lyric production distinctive. By noting a poet's choices first and then seeking to understand how those choices articulate a particular message, we see that traditionalism becomes a dynamic process of gathering types from the available stock to produce new songs that become, in turn, incorporated into the tradition for others to employ, exploit, and plunder. As did Gautier, Jacques composed many polemical contrafacta, but his particular formal and semantic choices place his works in a highly allusive lyric discourse that transcends the boundaries of genre, register, and even language, endowing them with a kaleidoscopic character in performance.

Jacques's religious songs survive mostly as *unica* in trouvère ms. *C* (Bern, Stadtbibliothek 389).[2] The manuscript orders songs alphabetically by incipit, creating a more 'neutral' context in regard to author, genre, and interpretive frame: within each grouping, secular and religious songs survive juxtaposed to each other with no paratextual material to guide our reading as in the *Miracles* or *Rosarius*. Some attributions are given, but although staves were drawn for each song, no melodies survive. Rubrics paraphrase the incipit of the song whose melody was meant to accompany Jacques's religious songs, with the notable exception of one, as we shall see. It is unclear when and why the rubrics were provided: perhaps they were added later when the melodies were discovered missing; perhaps they were there to help the later work of a musical scribe. Nevertheless, the rubrics stand as evidence of how well established the practice of contrafacture had become by the later thirteenth century. Scholars like Bec might read the manuscript context as evidence of the parasitical nature of the songs. However, just as reading Thibaut's devotional songs in the context of the 'miscellaneous' sections of his manuscripts leads us to a critical observation regarding the Marian song's hybridity, a similar positive conclusion may be drawn concerning the Bern codex: we see that religious songs, placed side by side with other songs, have become full participants in the wider lyric tradition. They are freed of the constraints placed upon them by the exigencies of a Gautier de Coinci or a compiler gathering and ordering the songs of a particular author, i.e., the king of Navarre, or a Dominican friar with a particular ideological bent. Marian song has, in one sense, matured. In fact, the genre at this moment in history is on the verge of going its separate way from secular song, as we shall see in our conclusion.

Choices of Motif, Theme, and Model: The Case for Distinctive Traditionalism

As I noted above, a poet's choices from among available types marks his or her poetry as distinctive, even if those types are traditional. Thematically, Jacques's songs both resemble and differ from the other lyrics studied thus far. Like the previously studied poets, Jacques relies heavily upon the Incarnation to illustrate Mary's role as *mediatrix*. However, Jacques's songs differ from the other two poets' works in his repeated juxtaposition of the Incarnation and the Passion. Apart from the insistent pairing of the two themes in 'Lasse,' the other works studied here treat them separately. In Gautier's elaboration on the Incarnation, the accent is always on Mary's maternity. Thibaut's poetry pairs the Incarnation with the Passion in 'De chanter ne me puis tenir,' but the reference is fleeting and peripheral; in 'Seignor, sachiés,' Jesus briefly refers to the crusaders as those who helped him carry his cross.[3] Moreover, although obviously the Virgin's role is crucial – one must be born to die – Jacques's thematic juxtaposition highlights Jesus' self-sacrifice, not the Virgin Mary's, as the ultimate redemptive event. Of Jacques's seven Marian songs, only 'Grant talent ai k'a chanteir me retraie' contains no mention of Jesus' Passion. Every other song, to one degree or another, relies on the topos to accomplish its spiritual and didactic aims.

Related to Jacques's pairing of the Incarnation and the Passion is his accentuation of Jesus' humanity, implied already in the doctrine of the Incarnation drawn out more explicitly in Jacques's songs.[4] In two songs, he introduces the theme subtly: in 'Haute dame, com rose et lis,' he refers to Jesus as 'li *hon*/ Ki nos metroit hors de prixon' (44–5, my emphasis) and in 'Retrowange novelle' Jacques mentions Jesus' 'chair belle' (5). However, in two other lyrics the topos is treated more extensively. In 'Kant je plus pens a commencier chanson,' the third stanza begins with an elegant parallelism: 'Sires, ki es et vrais Deus et vrais hons.' Even more explicit are the first lines of 'Meire, douce creature':

> Meire, douce creature,
> Ou li fils Deu volt venir
> Et prendre humainne nature
> Por sa deïteit couvrir
> Et morir.   (1–5)

These explicit treatments of Jesus' fully human and divine natures might appear innocuous, if it were not for a specific verse from 'Haute dame, com rose et lis.' After treating Jesus' Passion, the singer draws out the consequences for nonbelievers in this seminal event of salvation history in an ominous, contemporary historical reference: 'En enfer o les Abejois/ Alaist chascuns sens nul retor' (24–5) The Albigensians denied Jesus' humanity, and although historians would certainly debate the reasons of it, the crusade led against them in the thirteenth century caused them great pain and suffering.[5]

Jacques's formal choices – stanza length, metre, and often rhyme scheme – are dictated by his choice of lyric models.[6] Like Gautier, Jacques used melodies from well-known love songs. Table 3.1 lists Jacques's songs by incipit and Raynaud-Spanke number, the song's model, and any other contrafacta using the same model. Jacques's choice of models from well-known songs allows his audience to grasp his new texts more easily, as we saw in the case of Gautier. Even Colart's love song, although imitated by no one else (to the best of our knowledge), enjoyed relatively wide circulation: according to Tischler, his 'Loaus amors et desiriés de joie' survives in seven different manuscripts. Only one song has no model that has been positively identified, 'Retrowange novelle,' for the rubricator fails to give any indication of the model – the

Table 3.1 Jacques's choices of model[7]

Song by Jacques (RS no.)	Model (RS no.)	Other contrafacta based on same model (RS no.)
'Grant talent ai k'a chanteir me retraie' (RS 114)	'Loaus amors et desiriés de joie' by Colart le Boutellier (RS 1730)	Unknown
'Haute dame, com rose et lis' (RS 1563)	'Ausi conme unicorne sui' by Thibaut de Champagne (RS 2075)	'De fin cuer et d'aigre talent' attributed to Pierre de Gand (RS 734)
'Kant je plus pens a commencier chanson' (RS 1856)	'Tuit mi desir et tuit mi grief torment' by Thibaut de Champagne (RS 741, 991)	'Je ne cuit pas qu'en Amours traïson' by Jehan de Maisons (RS 1902); 'Quant fine yvers, que cil arbre sont nu' anonymous (RS 2057)
'Loeir m'estuet la roïne Marie' (RS 1178)	'De bone amor et de loial amie (me vient)' by Gace Brulé (RS 1102)	'Souvent me vient au cuer la remembrance' anonymous (RS 247); 'De bone amor et de loial amie (saurai chanter)' anonymous (RS 1102a); 'Chanter m'estuet de la Virge Marie' anonymous (RS 1181a); 'Minne gebiutet mir, daz ich nu singe' (RS –) by Rudolf von Fenis
'Meire, douce creature' (RS 2091)	'Quant voi la glaie meüre' by Raoul de Soissons (RS 2107)	'Dieus, je n'os nommer amie' anonymous (RS –); 'Aussi com l'eschaufeüre' by Philippe de Remi (RS 2096); 'Virge des ciels, clere et pure,' by Perrin d'Agincourt (RS 2112); 'O constantie dignitas' (RS –) by Adam de la Bassée
'O Dame, ke Deu portais' (RS 380, 197a)	'Aïmans fins et verais' by Gauthier d'Espinal (RS 199)	'Aïmans fins et verais (debonaires)' by Lambert Ferri (RS 158)
'Retrowange novelle' (RS 602)	Unknown [perhaps a *pastourelle* or a *ballette*], if any	Unknown, possibly 'Quant voi la flor nouvele/ paroir en la praele' (RS 599)

rubric reads simply 'Jaikes de Cambrai – De Notre Dame.' Perhaps there is no model and that is what Jacques means when he calls the song 'novelle,' a question to which we will turn later in the chapter.

If the musical practice of contrafacture marks the lyric production of both Gautier and Jacques, music also provides an important difference between their devotional works. As I demonstrated in chapter 1, Gautier chose not only popular models but also those that furnished him with a wide variety of melodic styles. Among Jacques's models, we find two that are through-composed: Thibaut's 'Ausi conme unicorne sui' and Gauthier d'Espinal's 'Aïmans fins et verais.' Both were apparently very popular since the same melodies appear in other contrafacta – a point to which we will return below – and they survive in several manuscripts.[8] Three of Jacques's models – Gace's 'De bone amour,' Thibaut's 'Tuit mi desir,' and Colart's 'Loaus amors' – conform to the common AAB structure of trouvère love songs, and Raoul's 'Quant voi la glaie' is arranged in a slightly irregular, but no less repetitive melodic structure: AA'BB. Jacques's predilection for more regular and repetitive melodies, the two popular through-composed melodies notwithstanding, might in part be explained in light of the time separating Gautier from Jacques: the former lived during the earlier stages of trouvère composition when experimentation was more common. On the other hand, Jacques might have found repetitive melodies appealing as models because they were easily memorized, a crucial aspect of polemical contrafactures.

Like Gautier, Jacques produced contrafactures that polemically engage their models. Gautier does so on the levels of both form and discourse by adding refrains and transforming key elements of his model. Jacques does so not by adding refrains, but rather through the seemingly deliberate complication of his model's formal patterns in a process we might call formal one-upmanship. For example, in 'Kant je plus pens a commencier chanson,' Jacques employs *coblas unisonnans*, a more difficult formal convention than Thibaut's *coblas doblas*. In his 'Haute dame, com rose et lis,' a contrafactum of Thibaut's famous 'Ausi conme unicorne sui,' Jacques uses different rhyme sounds but complicates the rhyme scheme by employing the convention of *coblas retrogradadas:* Thibaut's rhyme scheme is *abbaccbdd* throughout, but Jacques uses that scheme for only odd-numbered stanzas. For his even-numbered stanzas, Jacques reverses the *a* with the *b* rhyme and the *c* with the *d* rhyme to produce the scheme *baabddacc*. One contrafactum, however, Jacques's 'Loeir m'estuet la roïne Marie,' pales in formal comparison to its model, 'De bone amor et de loial amie (me vient),' in which Gace Brulé demonstrates his mastery of such difficult formal conventions as *coblas capcaudadas, capfinidas, retrogradadas,* and *retronchadas* (Rosenberg, Danon, and van de Werf 331). Nevertheless, the exception proves the rule and the case for formal one-upmanship is clear: since a great part of the trouvère art form is formal, what better way to show up a competitor than through the adoption and deliberate complication of his formal patterns?

Poets, both medieval and modern, make choices when they compose lyrics. Even if those choices were made before by other poets, a poet's particular choices from among the endless possibilities available make his or her lyric production distinctive. In the case of Jacques, we can go one step further: *because* he makes choices that others have made before him, especially in regard to melodic model, his religious poetics, like Gautier's before him, is one that is readily understandable to an initiated audience. However, unlike Gautier, Jacques was composing later in the thirteenth century, and the practice of contrafacture in Old French song had become established, as the work of ms. *C*'s rubricator suggests. In this period, more and more contrafacta were being composed, often using the same melody. It is therefore now time to think more multidimensionally about this dynamic, which is both general to medieval poetics and particular to Jacques, for medieval composers like Jacques take their material from many sources. In turn, those from whom a composer takes source material also appropriate types and figures from other poets and traditions; the end result, as we shall see, is dazzling.

Towards a Generative Model of Kaleidoscopic Contrafacture

The issues of reception and understanding at work in the generative model of contrafacture that we employed when reading Gautier's 'D'une amour quoie et serie' also hold true for Jacques's polemical contrafacta. However, whereas Gautier was the first to engage in this kind of devotional poetic activity, Jacques is one of many. Moreover, Jacques was often not the only composer to use a given melody, meaning that the complex associative webs created in the minds of listeners were potentially far more extensive than in the case of Gautier's early thirteenth-century audience. A fully initiated listener of the late thirteenth century might have experienced Jacques's songs in a dizzying, almost kaleidoscopic way, depending upon how familiar he or she was with the songs and traditions involved. A brief look at three examples and a longer treatment of a fourth illustrate the density of the Marian lyric tradition at this time in French literary history.

Jacques's 'Loeir m'estuet la roïne Marie' uses a number of secular motifs from love songs to articulate its message of praise and adoration for the Virgin. For example, in the second stanza, Mary is addressed and described as follows:

Dame, tous biens et toute courtoisie
Est dedans vos et maint a remenance,
Nuls n'en diroit la centisme partie.   (9–11)

In addition to its reliance on secular love motifs, the song shares its
melody with two Old French love songs, one by Gace and the other by
Thibaut, as well as another anonymous devotional song. Interestingly,
the anonymous devotional song, 'De bone amor et de loial amie,' takes
its incipit and rhyme sounds from Gace's song, making it a particularly
close contrafactum that recalls Gautier's inversion of incipits by poets
such as Blondel de Nesle. Undoubtedly due to the fame of the original
composer and its subsequent adaptors, the melody apparently spread
far and wide, for it also survives in a *minnelied* by Rudolf von Fenis. Only
one stanza is extant:

Minne begiutet mir, daz ich nu singe,
Unde wil niht, daz mich iemer verdrieze;
Han ich von ir weder trost noch gedinge,
Daz ich mins sanges iht gen ir genieze.
Si wil, daz ich iemer dien an solh statt,
Da noch vil kleine min dienest ie wac
Und(e) al min staete gehelfen niht mac.
Nu waer min reht, möch ich, daz ich ez lieze.[9]

[I sing now of how Love appeases me
and doesn't want me always to be vexed.
I have from her neither solace nor hope
that I may give her any pleasure through my song.
She wishes that I should always serve in such a state
that my service should always weigh little [on me],
and all my constancy I cannot help.
Now I wish that my moral code would give in.][10]

Rudolf's love vocabulary, like Gace's and Thibaut's, not to mention
Jacques's adaptation of this vocabulary, is entirely conventional. However, the situation of a melody used by composers of both secular and
devotional works in both Old French and Middle High German endows
the melodic nexus with a depth that one might call, for all of its contemporary connotations, multicultural: Romance and Germanic as well as
secular and religious cultures come together around similar themes –

love, service, reward – announced in different languages – Old French and Middle High German – to different ends: earthly love or divine favour.

Jacques's 'Meire, douce creature,' a piece that survives in three different versions in three different manuscripts, belongs to a nexus of five songs: four in Old French and one in Latin.[11] Three of the vernacular pieces are secular love songs: Raoul's 'Quant voi la glaie meüre,' the apparent model; the anonymous 'Dieus, je n'os nommer amie'; and 'Aussi com l'eschaufeüre' by Philippe de Remi. As was the case with 'Loeir m'estuet,' the intersection of secular and religious is keenly felt, especially as the last secular work is Marian: 'Virge des ceils, clere et pure' by possibly Perrin d'Agincourt. Listeners to Jacques's 'Meire, douce creature' or Raoul's song might then already associate the melody with devotional song. It is, however, the Latin intertext, a conductus, 'O constantie dignitas,' by Adam de la Bassée, that provides an especially interesting point of contrast:

O constantie dignitas,
Fundamentum gracie,
Te illuminat claritas
Divine iusticie,
Glorie
Pacis et letiticie;
Sic illos Dei largitas
Premiat, quos feritas
Non vicit requicie.
Sed de belli acie
Fervens retulit caritas
Tropheum victorie
Dignum celi requie.[12]

[O honour of constancy,
foundation of grace,
the brightness of
divine justice,
of glory,
peace and happiness illuminates you.
Thus the generosity of God
rewards those, whom the savagery
of wickedness has not overcome,

but from the battleline of war
fiery charity has brought back
the trophy of victory
worthy of heavenly rest.][13]

Adam's conductus also belongs to the secular sphere, but its praise of heroic virtue in war and a chivalric ethos add a new dimension to the listener's experience. Of course, a famous rapprochement between chivalry and Christian devotion comes in the previous century in Bernard de Clarivaux' *De laude novae militiae*. Now similar intersections occur when concepts such as dignity, grace, and justice announced by Adam resonate in the Marian tradition in which supplicants describe Mary as full of grace and beg her to intercede for them before divine justice.

Our third example of kaleidoscopic contrafacture, Jacques's 'Kant je plus pens a commencier chanson,' shares its melody with two love songs 'Tuit mi desir et tuit mi grief tourment' by Thibaut and the anonymous 'Quant fine yvers, que cil arbre sont nu.' It also shares its melody with Jehan de Maisons's more satiric love song, 'Je ne cuit pas qu'en Amours traïson,' a song that recalls Gilles's *mala canso*. Its initial stanza reads:

Je ne cuit pas qu'en Amours traïson
Poïst norrir, que qu'avenu m'en soit.
Ainz sai et di et moustre par raison
Qu'au dieu d'amors asfiert bien q'il essait
Les fins amanz, si en fet ce q'il doit.
Bon fet sousfrir le mal et la prison,
Dont a la fin vient l'en a guerison.[14]

[I do not think that in Love I can nourish
treachery, whatever may befall me.
Rather I know and say and demonstrate through reason
it is fitting that the god of love test
true lovers, thus he does what he must.
One does well to suffer pain and prison,
At the end of which one becomes cured.]

Compare these thoughts to the last verses of Jacques's initial stanza:

Ki s'amor [the Virgin's] ait en honor et en pris,
Serait sauveis el grant jor del juïs,

Et qui ne l'ait, Deus! si mar ains fut neis
Ke sens mercit serait mors et dampneis.

(4–7)

This cluster of songs focuses on the relationship between love and torment but in the nuanced dynamic among the traditional secular love
songs, devotional 'love songs,' and satiric love songs: all three speak of
the relationship between love and torment. For Thibaut and Jehan, torment and desire are inextricable from the experience of worldly love,
for better or for worse, but Jacques wishes to avoid the pain of an after-
life of torment by loving the Virgin Mary. Similar concepts and terms
may be used, but the paradigm of love and suffering is turned on its
head.

All of these examples are noteworthy, but Jacques's 'Haute dame,
com rose et lis' takes this associative web to a new level through its intersections with not only lyric but also other literary traditions, namely,
bestiaries. Medieval bestiaries gather and interpret, in Latin or in the
vernacular, both natural and supernatural beasts as ciphers of God's
transcendence in the natural world. But familiarity with bestiary material did not mean that one had access to a bestiary or even a written
source. On the contrary, as Debra Hassig points out in her introduction
to an anthology of essays dedicated to bestiaries, and despite the reserva-
tions of scholars like Ron Baxter who rightly point out that not all animal symbolism is derived from bestiaries, bestiary figures were available
not only through textual and visual sources, but also by word of mouth.
In the case of Jacques's 'Haute dame, com rose et lis,' we would have to
add to 'word of mouth,' something like 'songs' for constantly reinter-
preted bestiary figures tie together model and multiple contrafacta.

'Haute dame' uses the melody from Thibaut de Champagne's 'Ausi
conme unicorne sui,' in which the unicorn becomes desacralized and
eroticized; Marcel Faure has called this poem a pure expression of
erotic desire. The song was apparently very popular; it survives, as noted
above, in no fewer than fifteen sources, eight with musical accompaniment. The second contrafactum is Pierre de Gand's 'servantois' or song
in service to the Virgin, 'De fin cuer et d'aigre talent.' This work survives
only in ms. *C* where Jacques's song is preserved and in trouvère ms. *V*
(Paris, BnF fr. 24406, the *Chansonnier de la Vallière*) with music. Formal
one-upmanship is in evidence in this lyric exchange: Thibaut employs
coblas doblas, the convention where rhyme sounds change every two stanzas, but Jacques utilizes different rhyme sounds in his *coblas retrogradadas*, or stanzas where the rhyme scheme is inverted from stanza to

stanza. So, like Thibaut, Jacques employs the scheme *abbaccbdd* for his first stanza, but the *a* and *b* rhymes as well as the *c* and *d* rhymes switch position in the second stanza to produce the scheme *baabddacc*. The third stanza reverts to the first stanza's scheme. New rhymes are introduced in the fourth stanza and they change position in a similar fashion in the fifth. Pierre de Gand takes an intermediate path by inverting only the *a* and *b* rhymes, but leaving the position of the *c* and *d* rhymes unaltered. It is against the backdrop of the repeated stanzaic melody and manipulated rhyme schemes that figural borrowings create the highly allusive texture that we are now ready to examine. (Full texts for all three songs are given in the appendix.)

In the first stanza of 'Ausi conme unicorne sui,' Thibaut compares himself to the unicorn of medieval lore. The unicorn was said to be a fierce beast: if today we depict unicorns as rather effeminate, one should keep in mind the name used in Greek bestiaries: 'rhinoceros.' According to legend, the unicorn could only be captured with the aid of a virgin girl. When the unicorn comes upon the virgin girl, he becomes docile, approaches, and falls asleep in her lap. In bestiaries such as the one Pierre de Beauvais compiled at the same time that Thibaut composed his song, this scene is allegorically interpreted as the Incarnation and Passion. In traditional bestiaries, hunters kill, not capture, the docile unicorn, but in Thibaut's song, both occur: Love and the lady kill him and take his heart prisoner. Thibaut's contribution to the legend of the unicorn is then to desacralize and interpret it to a new, secular end. The song continues in an allegorical vein, but it leaves aside bestiary or other animal symbolism to focus on the lover's heart and the amorous prison, a topos highly favoured by Thibaut, in which he wastes away. The song ends, as so many trouvère love songs do, with the lover suffering, begging for mercy, with no relief in sight.

If Thibaut secularizes bestiary material in his song, similar figures retain religious connotations in the contrafacta: thus, the contrafacta function as religious correctives to Thibaut's secular composition. Neither contrafactum includes the unicorn, but omission can be as significant a gesture as allusion or citation: as the singer of either contrafactum intones the first phrases of the melody, the unicorn is there in the minds of the listener. Pierre does, however, wax eloquent on the salamander, the lizard that reportedly extinguished a fire were it to fall into it; bestiary compilers interpreted it sometimes as the just one who would not burn in hell and sometimes as a sign of miracles performed by saints. Pierre reinterprets the figure to comment on the virgin birth: like the salamander that is unharmed and unaltered in the fire, Mary was left unchanged by the experience of childbirth. We have here then not a desacralization, but rather a different sacred interpretation of the figure. Pierre also mentions other animals, although these figures may not necessarily come from bestiaries. In stanza IV, the singer makes sure to mention that even if all the earth were to praise Mary, she could not be adequately praised. Among the creatures of the world, he mentions not only men, but also birds, beasts, and fish: the list is then highly inclusive as it comprises creatures of the sea, air, and land. In the final stanza, Pierre mentions the lion and the lamb, both of which figure among bestiaries as figures for Jesus. The lion is, in fact, the initial entry in many bestiaries, including the *Physiologus*, the prototype for medieval bestiaries. Again, Pierre subtly alters these figures because he uses them to praise not God, but Mary, by using them in expressions such as 'mother of the lion' or 'mother of the lamb.' Pierre reshapes them to suit his particular religious aim; he plays freely with both bestiary and animal symbolism, choosing particular figures as well as interpretations of those figures while leaving others aside.

Jacques begins his song with a different figure for the Virgin: the rose. Although most bestiaries in the High Middle Ages limit themselves to animals, earlier compilations such as the *Physiologus* and even later, radically refigured compilations such as the *Rosarius* include plants, stones, and other intangible items such as the sky and the sun. The mutual reliance on simile in both Thibaut and Jacques's initial stanzas through the word 'com' casts into relief a grammatical shift from the first person to the third person that economically conveys the thematic shift from narcissism in Thibaut's song to selflessness in Jacques's contrafactum. Jacques's song is, after all, centred on the Incarnation and the Passion as events demanding self-sacrifice, and even if the two songs are at odds here, they do find common thematic ground in betrayal and death: Thibaut's lover is betrayed and killed by Love and the Lady, and Jesus was betrayed by Judas and killed by the Romans. An initiated listener would hear the first strains of Thibaut's melody, recall the desacralized unicorn legend, and thus hear Jacques's new text on the Incarnation and the Passion, which is the usual allegorical interpretation of that legend. The contrafactum serves to restore the traditional link between lore and allegorical interpretation in a subtle but perceptible way.

Like Pierre, Jacques mentions the lion and the lamb in his fourth stanza as symbols of Jesus, and thus establishes perhaps a link between contrafacta. Unlike Pierre, though, Jacques does not reshape these figures to praise Mary: he uses them in their usual sense to connote Jesus. Jacques includes, however, two more figures that must be mentioned here – the pelican and phoenix – as they endow Jacques's contrafactum with a more allusive texture. The pelican, also representative of Jesus, is a bird whose young are either murdered by the pelican himself for their having rebelled or by the owl, interpreted in some bestiaries as the Jews, as Mariko Miyazaki has shown in a recent article on medieval English misericords. The pelican then revives its young three days later by means of its tears or blood. The pelican does not appear in 'Ausi conme unicorne,' but it does in Thibaut's political song, 'Dex est ensi conme li pellicans,' in which he criticizes papal hypocrisy during the sixth crusade. Similarly, in 'Haute Dame,' Jacques utilizes the phoenix, the legendary Arabian bird that lives centuries but that periodically perishes in a plume of flames only to be reborn from the ashes. As Valerie Jones has recently shown, some variability exists in the figure's interpretation, reflecting competing theologies of the resurrection: a Jewish corporeal theology or a Hellenistic, spiritual theology. This bird represented Jesus as well, and it figures among Thibaut's songs, this time in his love lyric, 'Chanter m'estuet, car ne m'en puis tenir.' In this particular lyric, the singer decries how Love and his lady mistreat him, a theme that it shares with many love songs, including 'Ausi conme unicorne sui.' The singer of 'Chanter m'estuet' says that he will surely die of grief, consumed in the fire of his passion as the phoenix. Thibaut leaves out the part about resurrection, though, which either completes the picture of despair that he paints or suggests that he still harbours hopes that his Lady will one day come around.

The associative web goes on and on and we understand that contrafacture is hardly two-dimensional, an affair that pertains only to the new song and the song to which the melody was originally set. Rather, by the end of the thirteenth century, the process constituted a multi-dimensional dynamic in performance. Jacques's Marian songs play off songs that use the same melody: secular love songs, both traditional and satiric; devotional songs in more than one vernacular tongue; secular, heroic song in Latin; and even literary traditions usually considered peripheral to lyric, i.e., bestiaries. An initiated public would have made connections with the wider lyric and literary traditions, and experienced these kaleidoscopic contrafacta differently, creating a highly allusive texture that resonates differently with different members of his audience, depending upon individual experience and knowledge of those traditions.

Traditionalism, Innovation, and 'Retrowange novelle'

Jacques's 'Retrowange novelle' proves unique among his other songs in several respects. First, it is the only song for which no rubric clues us into a lyric model. However, it shares its dancelike metrical structure and streamlined rhyme scheme, *a'a'a'a'a'ba'b*, with two songs: the Marian lyric, 'Quant voi la flour novele' (RS 598); and the *pastourelle*, 'Quant voi la flor nouvele/ paroir en la praele' (RS 599), which Rivière suggests might very well be the model for Jacques and that Jacques 'veut sans doute dire que c'est la rotrouenge qui est nouvelle par rapport à la pastourelle' (*Pastourelles*, 2:138). What also distinguishes 'Retrowange novelle' from Jacques's other songs, however, can be seen on the level of discourse. In the other songs the fluid, *mouvant* quality of lyric composition is in evidence. The most extreme case in Jacques's corpus is 'O Dame, ke Deu portais.' In each of the two extant stanzas of 'O Dame,' very similar syntactical and rhetorical patterns are used: the singer apostrophizes the Virgin and Jesus once in each stanza, repeating rather than innovating on a small number of lexical units and syntactical structures. When addressing Mary, the singer exclaims 'O dame, ke Deu portais' in verse 1 and 'He! dame de paradis' in verse 19. Similarly, the apostrophes to Jesus are repetitive: 'Sires Deus' (9) and 'He! sires Deus' (16). In both stanzas, the singer calls upon Jesus to remove him from the waste of a life that he leads:

> Ma vië est vis et *orde*;
> *Sires Deus*, a vos me plaing
> Ke vos *m'osteis* cest mahaing!   (8–10, my emphasis)

> He! *sires Deus* Jhesuscris,
> Ki por moi la mort souffris,
> *Oste moi* de cette *ordure*'   (16–18, my emphasis)

The repetitive texture of this lyric demonstrates a high potential for *mouvance*, for the song's themes are developed from one stanza to the next using the associative logic of trouvère lyric. One might easily imagine the two stanzas switching position, although the interjection 'O' would seem to make the first stanza a more likely initial stanza. In any case, this potential for interchangeability, that is, the degree of *mouvance*, in most of Jacques's lyrics is very high indeed.

Such is not the case, however, with 'Retrowange novelle': the song's beginning is truly that – a beginning – and the stanza could not come in the second or third position and still be effective. As in many of Jacques's other songs, Mary is not evoked by name but rather through some reference to her role in salvation history:

> Retrowange novelle
> Dirai et bonne et belle
> De la virge pucelle
> Ke meire est et ancelle   (1–4)

Whereas the first four verses concentrate on Mary, the last four focus on the figure of Jesus and the sacrifice made in the Passion. The equal attention paid to each figure is not at all surprising in the context of Jacques's lyrics. What is unusual is the lyric subject's confidence in humanity's salvation:

> Celui ki de sa chair belle
> Nos ait raicheteit,
> Et ki trestout nos apelle
> A sa grant clairteit.   (5–8)

The verses do not constitute a direct plea for salvation. The use of the past indicative – 'ait raicheteit' – conveys a sense of surety in salvation: Jesus' sacrifice bought us back from sin. There is no uncertainty detected in the lyric voice. The subsequent present indicative – 'trestout nos apelle' – imparts the same confidence: Jesus calls each and every one of us towards his light. The next two stanzas continue to share the focus between Mary and Jesus but use scriptural paraphrase to reach their end.

A close relationship in argument exists between stanzas II and III. The second stanza paraphrases two prophecies made in Isaiah: the virgin birth (Isaiah 7) and the newborn's belonging to the house of Jesse (Isaiah 11). The stanza's orderly development brings to mind a preacher giving a sermon to his congregation. He begins by telling us the source of his comments: 'Se nos dist Isaïe/ En une profesie' (9–10). Then he paraphrases the passage:

> D'une verge delgie,
> De Jessé espanie,

Istroit flors, per signorie,
De tres grant biaulteit.   (11–14)

The use of the conditional – 'istroit' – suggests that the prophecy has already come true: if the prophecy had yet to be fulfilled, the poet might have used the future. In any case, the last two verses confirm that the prophecy has come true: 'Or est bien la profesie/ Torneie a verteit' (15–16). On the word 'verteit' the stanza ends and the singer's focus changes from announcement to interpretation.

The last stanza expertly illustrates the function of the subject of religious discourse, the I/we, by calling attention to both the objective meaning of the prophecy – Mary is the staff and Jesus the flower – and its subjective meaning through hermeneutical application. The recurrence of key words and the close sonorous relationships in the syntagm, 'Celle verge delgie/ Est la virge Marie' (17–18), recalls Jacques's streamlined song, 'O Dame, ke Deu portais,' as well as the acoustic play in Gautier's lyrics. An audience easily grasps these verses for two reasons. First, practically all of the words are reused from previous stanzas, which is what locks this stanza in the third position: one cannot begin a stanza 'Celle verge' without having previously mentioned the staff. Second, Jacques creates an acoustic parallelism in 'verge delgie' and 'virge Marie.' The rest of the stanza interprets the flower figure as Jesus and, like the first stanza, puts forth the redeeming quality of his suffering:

La flor nos senefie,
De ceu ne douteis mie,
Jhesucrist ki la haichie
En la croix souffri,
Tout por randre ceaus en vie
Ki ierent peri.   (19–24)

The incitement to cast aside doubt in verse 20 furthers the preacher's tone of the verses. Moreover, the same confidence that we perceived in the first stanza comes back in these last verses. No rhetorical flourishes are needed to bring salvation history to bear upon personal history: the two coincide naturally in this song. Nor is there a plea (at least, no direct plea) for salvation, for the singing subject seems sure that salvation lies ahead of him.

In conclusion, 'Retrowange novelle' is both formally and discursively unique among Jacques's songs; one might even say innovative. Formally, the unusual rhyme scheme distinguishes the song acoustically from the others that belong more to the tradition of the *chanson d'amour*. Stanza II's paraphrase of Isaiah and stanza III's interpretation of that paraphrase do not link these stanzas associatively as in other songs: they are fixed discursively. Finally, the confidence in one's salvation exuded throughout the piece combined with the lack of a direct plea for salvation sets 'Retrowange novelle' apart from most of Jacques's other songs. This confidence runs throughout the piece and provides a link between stanza I and the rest of the song: the reassurance in the final two stanzas that Isaiah's prophecy has come true justifies the confidence in salvation that shines through in the first stanza's proclamation that Jesus has bought back our souls. Because of its formal and discursive properties, 'Retrowange novelle,' invites a purely linear reading. If Jacques's other six Marian songs permit a measure of freedom in performance or hermeneutical subjectivity to performers, 'Retrowange novelle' denies it to the performer. Behind this lyric, one detects the mind of a preacher *à la* Gautier de Coinci. One must begin with stanza I, proceed to stanza II, and finish with stanza III. Neither omissions nor changes in order will be tolerated.

The Future of Old French Marian Song

Once again, the exception proves the rule: the unique status of 'Retrowange novelle' casts into starker relief the extent to which Jacques's songs are traditional. His choice of themes and motifs in the wider Marian tradition reveals nothing unexpected, even if he does incorporate more Christological themes than other composers of Marian lyric. Nevertheless, even these are traditional. Moreover, his choices among lyric models for his creation of polemical contrafactures are hardly unique: other poets choose the same models for their contrafacta in French, Latin, or German. In the final analysis, Jacques was not an innovator; nor was he a mere imitator: Jacques was, in a word, a participant. Each text is a fragment that finds its complete meaning in a wider textual and cultural context that can never be completely known, although on some plane, it does exist. The dialectical relationship between text and tradition finds its hermeneutical correlate in the concept of the hermeneutic circle: each reading provides a part of the tradition where the whole already exists. Each song sets in motion its own distinct understanding or realization of the Marian lyric tradition.

After Jacques de Cambrai, the Marian lyric tradition evolved in the direction of the *serventois* and the *chant royal*, genres marked by fixity in form, close textual citation and manipulation of models, and a less effusive and more didactic tone.[15] The *chant royal* did not come about until much later in the French Middle Ages, but the *serventois* – not to be confused with the *sirventés*, for Gros posits an etymology of the generic label in the 'service' to the Virgin that these texts promise – began to take shape in the later thirteenth century (*Le poème du puy marial: étude sur le servantois et le chant royal du XIVe siècle à la Renaissance* 22). Nevertheless, the technical term, 'serventois,' appears in three surviving Marian songs of the thirteenth century: Järnström's *Recueil* X, XXXIX, and XL. After examining the first, Gros notes a number of characteristics that would mark the *serventois* generically in the subsequent century:

> De plus, outre l'imitation du modèle profane, apparaissent ici quelques linéaments du genre qui ne se fixe qu'au siècle suivant: la séquence de cinq couplets, l'apostrophe à fonction d'envoi, et aussi l'image qui, pour concise qu'elle soit dans une rapide comparaison, n'est pas sans préfigurer la construction allégorique. (*Le Poème du puy marial* 23)

We have seen that Jacques's songs are anything but fixed in their form. But do they have nothing to do with the subsequent tradition studied by Gros?

All three songs – *Recueil* X, XXXIX, and XL – have, in fact, links to Jacques's lyric production. *Recueil* X (RS 734) is Pierre de Gand's 'De fin cuer et l'aigre talent' which shares, as we saw above, the same lyric model as Jacques's 'Haute dame, com rose et lis,' namely, Thibaut de Champagne's 'Ausi conme unicorne sui.' Is it possible then that Jacques's song is also a *serventois* or proto-*serventois*? After all, Jacques's song shares with Pierre's song many characteristics named above: Pierre's and Jacques's songs are each five stanzas long; neither text appends an envoi, but addresses Mary directly in the final stanza; and in light of their numerous bestiary figures, allegory abounds. Moreover, *Recueil* XXXIX is Lambert Ferri's 'Aïmans fins et verais (debonaires)' (RS 198) which models itself after Gauthier d'Espinal's 'Aïmans fins et verais,' as does Jacques's 'O Dame, ke Deu portais.' Ferri also composed the *Recueil* XL, 'J'ai tant d'amours apris et entendu' (RS 2053) and Gros, based on all of this evidence hypothesizes that Ferri belonged to a *puy*.[16] The form and length of Jacques's contrafacture may differ from Ferri's song, and Jacques may not engage in the same kind of close citation that marks Ferri's composition or the fourteenth-century *serventois*, yet the evidence is compelling. Given the fact that so many of Jacques's con-trafacta share models with other contrafacta, many of which use or are linked to songs that use the term *servantois*, is it not possible that Jacques was involved in a *puy* at Cambrai or even those of Arras or Valenciennes? After all, it was during these poetic competitions that poets composed religious songs on an agreed-upon secular model. Were more evidence unearthed and a case made, the benefits to literary history would be sub-stantial.

These questions invite further research, but I have chosen to pursue a different path in this study of Marian lyric. The material of my first four chapters leads up to and announces the forms of the fourteenth and fif-teenth centuries, the world of the *puy* and its highly regularized lyric forms. Marian devotion in thirteenth-century French literature also fol-lows another path, the one I now take, the one that leads to spoken poetry, that of Rutebeuf in particular. Many of the motifs that we have seen as characteristic of Marian lyric as well as the core communicative act of Marian devotion survive in Rutebeuf's poetry, but they are recast in his spoken poetry. Furthermore, Rutebeuf integrates his Marian poetry into his diverse oeuvre that adopts different voices and leans towards the dramatic rather than the lyric.

chapter five

Rutebeuf: Beyond the World of Marian Song

It may strike some readers as strange that I include Rutebeuf in this study of thirteenth-century lyric. In the strictest sense of the word 'lyric,' Rutebeuf did compose within the tradition I am studying. Although none of Rutebeuf's Marian poetry survives with accompanying melodies – indeed most of it was not meant to be sung – to this rule, there is an exception: 'C'est de Notre Dame' adheres to a traditional style of composition and relies heavily on courtly love song and Latin liturgical materials for its formal and thematic properties. Rhetorically, the text relies on *annominatio*, a figure familiar to Marian lyric, which relies on variation, and anaphora, a figure based on repetition. Each of the first four stanzas uses a different *annominatio* that resonates within the Marian tradition, but the fifth stanza relies on anaphora, not *annominatio*, to develop the theme of Mary's perpetual virginity through the metaphor of the light-pierced window and an anaphora on 'vierge.'[1] Placed side by side with Gautier or Thibaut's production, it would be indistinguishable.

In the remainder of Rutebeuf's Marian corpus, melody cedes its prominent place to timbre, the rise and fall of the human voice. Several 'lyrical' pieces, that is, works that are neither narrative nor dramatic, figure among Ruteubeuf's works. They survive in twelve different manuscripts, all meticulously described by the poet's editors, Edmond Faral and Julia Bastin (1:11–31). Three of these codices preserve large collections of Rutebeuf's poetry: ms. *A* (Paris, BnF fr. 837), ms. *B* (Paris, BnF fr. 1593), and ms. *C* (Paris, BnF fr. 1635 [formerly 7633], the second and third of which are ordered, according to Sylvia Huot, rather haphazardly. However, also according to Huot, Marian devotion defines the author's persona (*From Song to Book* 217–18). Indeed, if 'lyric' seems at first out of place in Rutebeuf criticism, the application of 'Marian' to the poet's corpus presents the opposite problem: Mary looms large throughout Rutebeuf's works, even if many poems contain only casual references to her.[2] Leaving aside Marian narrative poems such as 'La Vie de Sainte Marie l'Egyptienne,' 'La Vie de Sainte Elysabel,' and 'Le Sacristain et la femme au chevalier,'[3] as well as 'Les neuf joies Notre Dame' for its surely false attribution, I define Rutebeuf's Marian lyrical corpus as comprised of six works: 'C'est de Notre Dame,' already examined above; 'La Mort Rutebeuf' and 'L'*Ave Maria* Rustebeuf,' two poems that recast the relationship between Marian poetics and polemical poetry; Théophile's repentance and subsequent prayer to the Virgin, which we find excerpted from the whole play in one manuscript; and, finally, 'Un Dist de Nostre Dame,' in which Rutebeuf imagines what the Virgin says when she intercedes on our behalf.[4] As we shall see, in the hands of Rutebeuf, the vernacular Marian tradition proves most malleable and supple. In many ways, in fact, Rutebeuf's poetry represents the culmination of the tradition that I am studying: he takes Gautier's predicatory and polemical tone; he defends contrary positions and stretches generic boundaries like Thibaut; as in the women's songs, he sometimes adopts the universal speaking subject or 'I/we,' sometimes specific voices.[5] Like Jacques, Rutebeuf shows himself to be a full participant in the tradition while taking the tradition a step further, a step beyond the world of lyric song and into the wider vernacular literary tradition.

Rutebeuf's Polemical Marian Poetry

The link between Marian devotion and polemical poetry was there from the start when Gautier used contrafacture to combat values that he found antithetical to his Christian world view. However, in two of Rutebeuf's Marian poems, one entitled alternatively 'La Mort Rutebeuf' or 'La Repentance Rutebeuf,' and the other, 'L'*Ave Maria* Rustebeuf,' Rutebeuf brings polemics and Marian devotion together in new ways. The persona who speaks in these two poems is a polemicist, one who has written satirical, sometimes propagandist poetry over his lifetime, and this persona, both for his self-description and also for the inclusion of the proper name in the rubrics, reminds us of Rutebeuf himself.[6] However, whereas the 'Repentance' puts the vocation of polemicist with Marian devotion in a relationship of opposition, the '*Ave Maria*' reconciles them, demonstrating Rutebeuf's remarkable ability to defend either side of a question in much the same way we saw Thibaut do in his crusade poetry.[7]

For the 'Repentance Rutebeuf,' Rutebeuf uses the *strophe d'Hélinand*, a form used by Hélinand de Froimond for his *Vers de la mort* and by Artesian poets for *congés*, that is, poems in which the poet takes leave of his community. By using this form, Rutebeuf suggests that he is treating either death or a departure. In fact, he does both: aware of his own mortality, the speaking subject turns inward, examines his conscience, and repents before death. Necessary to his repentance is a departure from the viciousness of polemical poetry, and the 'Repentance Rutebeuf' constitutes the inner monologue and the call to Mary as the poet's way out of his sinful situation. At the outset of the piece, the poet expresses his dismay at having engaged in slanderous poetry for so long (2–3). As he has shown no concern in the past for his immortal soul, he decides that now he must do so. To that end, he turns to the Virgin as his sole means of gaining salvation:

> Se por moi n'est au Jugement
> Cele ou Diex prist aombrement,
> Mau marchié pris au paumoier.   (10–12)[8]

Poets typically invoke the Incarnation as an exemplary moment of Mary as *mediatrix*, but the gaming motif in the last verse creates a curious mixture of the sacred and profane. Rutebeuf uses motifs from worldly society to describe the religious problem in which this repentant poet finds himself: it is not his money, but his soul that is at stake. The polemicist realizes that he has wasted his God-given talents and lived on other people's money. He broods upon his past deeds, or rather, misdeeds, his principal fault being slandering some people to please others; this sets this poet apart from the lyric subjects of Gautier's aristocratic poetry.

Poetic corpus and the poet's corporeality become intermingled as the poem progresses. Adopting the traditional dichotomy of body and soul, the repentant poet explains that he sacrificed the latter to indulge the former. In his call upon Mary, he casts the Virgin as a physician beyond compare who can cure his ills (49–55). As in other Marian poems, the poet aims to persuade the Virgin to intercede on behalf of humanity in general and the individual speaker in particular. To help make his case, the speaker employs the exemplum of Mary of Egypt, who together with Mary of Magdala, represented for the medieval public the consummate sinner who found forgiveness and salvation.[9] She fits perfectly in this context for two reasons: first, by including the example of Mary, a repentant prostitute, the poet reinforces his previous insistence on the

body; second, the allusion suggests that the polemicist is a kind of prostitute. Instead of selling his body, however, the polemicist sells his
poetry to whoever will pay good money, so that he may, in turn, indulge
in the pleasures of the flesh: gambling, drinking, and brawling. After all,
in Rutebeuf's version of the legend, Mary of Egypt turns to prostitution
not for money, but for physical pleasure: 'son cors livrer/ Du tout en
tout *a la luxure*' ('La Vie de Sainte Marie l'Egyptienne' 46–7, my emphasis).[10] For these reasons, Mary of Egypt represents a perfect choice for
this polemical poet's confession.

Despite the life of debauchery that the poet has led, he intimates in
the final stanza that his intentions were always good. The speaker begins
the final stanza by admitting that he can do no more and hopes that his
plea does not come too late. While awaiting God's judgment, he reflects
upon his intentions and alludes to another popular literary figure,
Renart, seen previously in our discussion of '*Ave Maria, j'aim tant*' in
chapter 3:

> Je cuidai engingner Renart:
> Or n'i valent engin ne art,
> Qu'asseür est en son palés.   (79–81)

The poet believed that he could make a difference, and his mention of
Renart constitutes one final polemical comment on the world – those in
power are tricksters – but the poet's last words are tinged with regret.
He wanted to expose them, but they remain entrenched in positions of
authority. He thus leaves this world:

> Por cest siecle qui se depart
> M'en covient partir d'autre part:
> Qui que l'envie, je le lés.   (82–4)

One might interpret the verse as leaving this life literally – thus the title
'La Mort Rutebeuf' in ms. *A* – or figuratively as entering into religion.
Or one might interpret the verse as an eschewal of worldly pursuits,
including poetry making.[11] As the voice of the repentant polemicist falls
silent, the final meaning is ambiguous. Then again, as Rutebeuf's
poetry was so closely tied to issues of authorship for both the manuscript
compilers of *A* and modern readers, perhaps, at some level, the cessation of his poetry is equivalent to the death of Rutebeuf: corpus and corporeality amount, in fact, to the same thing.

An analogous inner struggle arises in Rutebeuf's '*Ave Maria*,' a poem composed in Rutebeuf's metrical specialty, the *tercet coué*.[12] The poem begins with a particularly polemical prologue criticizing both ecclesiastical and secular leaders for their bad faith, reminding us of the beguine's diatribe in '*Ave Maria, j'aim tant*':

> Chanoine, clerc et roi et conte
> > Sont trop aver;
> N'ont cure des ames sauver,
> Més les cors baignier et laver
> > Et bien norrir.   (11–15)

The prologue ends with the poet announcing his attention to say a 'salu de la douce Dame' to keep us from harm's way, thus effecting a shift in tone from the polemical to the devotional. His 'salu' is comprised of Latin expressions from the Ave Maria interwoven into a French text at irregular intervals: 'Ave' (34), 'Maria' (43), 'Gracia plena' (73), 'Dominus' (76), 'Tecum' (83), 'Benedicta tu' (88), 'In mulieribus' (110), 'Et benedictus' (133), 'Fructus' (134), 'Ventris tui' (147), 'Amen' (164).[13] Expressions in the two languages are interwoven, not merely juxtaposed. If French predominates on one level by virtue of the fact that there is more French than Latin, we should realize that reading the Latin expressions one after the other results in coherent discourse, i.e., the Ave Maria; however, as Latin expressions are often, for example, the subjects or complements of French verbs, the same does not hold true for the French. The discursive relationship between the two insinuates that the text is first and foremost an expression of Marian devotion. The manuscript context supports this conclusion: nearly every Latin expression comes at the beginning of a verse, marked by a capital. Therefore, a mere glance at the page serves to highlight first and foremost the Latin.

If the poem is primarily devotional, a polemical subtext nevertheless remains, reminding us of the generically pluralistic texts that make up Thibaut's Marian corpus. In addition to expressions from the Ave Maria, Rutebeuf uses traditional Marian motifs: Mary is called, for example, the 'roïne coronee' (34); he alludes to her perpetual virginity (82); and a final appeal for mercy is made at the end of the piece. As in the 'Repentance,' Rutebeuf uses exempla: a short allusion to Mary of Magdala and, more importantly, extensive use of the story of Theophilus. Yet, mixed into these Marian motifs and exempla are moments where the speaker rails against arrogance, faithlessness:

Fols est qui en toi ne se fie.
Tu hez orgueil et felonie
   Seur toute chose.   (112–14)

Fols est cil qui pensse autre part
Et plus est fols qui se depart
   De vostre acorde.   (124–6)

These verses fit perfectly within a devotional context, but retain a polemical tone in light of the prologue that precedes the Ave Maria proper. Those who prove arrogant and faithless are precisely the ones that Rutebeuf criticizes in his opening verses for thinking 'autre part': priests and aristocrats who think less about service and protecting the weak than pampering themselves. The Ave Maria, perhaps the ultimate expression of Marian devotion, becomes also then a polemical rallying cry against secularism and faithlessness.

These two poems constitute expressions of Marian devotion that also thematize the creation of polemical poetry by either putting them into opposition as in the 'Mort/Repentance Rutebeuf' or reconciling them as in 'L'*Ave Maria* Rustebeuf.' Of course, Rutebeuf is not the first to reconcile the worldly and spiritual spheres: Thibaut's 'Seignor, sachiés' does the same. Rutebeuf's two poems are also similar in their use of intertextual allusions. One might wonder whether Rutebeuf composed *Le Miracle de Théophile* before 'L'*Ave Maria* Rustebeuf' or the 'Renart' before the 'Repentance.' However, as my readings demonstrate, that line of inquiry would be pointless, for Theophilus, Renart, and Mary of Egypt all held symbolic value in the Middle Ages. Knowing Mary of Egypt's perverse pleasure in sin helps colour the repentant poet's confession just as a familiarity with the Theophilus story aids in associating the words 'Ave Maria' with that character's plight. Reading the 'Repentance' and the '*Ave*' side by side illustrates how Rutebeuf expresses Marian devotion using similar subjects and common themes but with different goals and from different angles.

Marian Devotion Dramatized

One of Rutebeuf's most famous Marian pieces is dramatic in nature: *Le Miracle de Théophile*. The entire play survives as an *unica* in ms. *A*, but ms. *C* preserves two excerpted passages with titles in the rubrics: the 'Repentance Théophile' and 'Prière Théophile.' These poems embody the moments between Theophilus's bargain with the Devil and the Virgin's intercession on his behalf. To the best of my knowledge, no one has treated the passages that *C* transmits as autonomous works, or rather, how their excerption and entry into the lyric mode of Marian poetry changes our understanding of them. They are most often used for establishing an edition of the 'whole' play. Michel Zink has compared the 'Repentance Théophile' to the 'Repentance Rutebeuf' and notes that these poems, Rutebeuf's saints' lives, and his devotional tales all take their inspiration from a common stock of Marian topoi and motifs ('De la repentance Rutebeuf à la repentance Théophile' 19). Zink suggests that, from a certain perspective, the identity of the speaking subject matters little: whether the speaker is Rutebeuf, Theophilus, Mary the Egyptian, or the anonymous lyrical 'je' of the 'Chanson de Notre Dame,' the sentiments expressed are the same. From one perspective, this might be true; however, as I hope to demonstrate, the hermeneutical consequences of the excerption of the 'Repentance Théophile' and 'Prière Théophile' and their consideration as autonomous pieces are far-reaching: the subject becomes universalized, making an audience's understanding of the Theophilus story more akin to the experience of lyric rather than drama.

The Theophilus poems separate the moments of repentance and calling on the Virgin, which most Marian lyric poems intertwine, and formal features in each poem accentuate the expression of repentance or supplication. The 'Repentance Théophile' is made up of twelve quatrains of alexandrines whose rhymes change with each stanza and never repeat themselves in other stanzas. The quatrain as a stanzaic form is unusual in trouvère poetry; more unusual is the rhyme scheme: *aaaa*. This form accentuates the highly deliberative nature of repentance, which comes with the realization of impending damnation for past evil-doing.[14] In Gautier's poetry, the moment where a narrative character realizes his precarious state precedes a call on the divine: the 'Repentance Théophile' endeavours to amplify that moment of realization. Simply put, the poem performs the speech act 'I repent.' The poem therefore concentrates its energies on the present tense and on the subject 'I' at the expense of a 'you' or 'her' in subtle ways. The first person is the subject of twenty-nine clauses and the third person is the subject of twenty-five clauses. However, the third person subject often refers to the lyric subject 'I' as in such passages as 'Hé! Diex, que feras tu de cest chetif dolant/ De cui l'arme en ira en enfer le buillant' (9–10). The 'chetif dolent' and the soul that constitutes the subject of the verb 'to go' both belong to the third person grammatically, but each refers back to the first-person speaker. The focus on the speaking subject 'I' throughout the entire discourse thus furthers the isolation felt by the speaker, which he has brought upon himself through evil-doing.

Significantly, all time frames – past, present, and future – coincide in the moment of enunciating repentance. The speaker broods upon past sinfulness: 'Or ai Dieu renoié, ne puet estre teü:/ Si ai laissié le baume, pris me sui au seü' (5–6). This deliberation upon the past reaches its climax in the last verse of the eleventh stanza: 'Richesce, mar te vi!' (44). At the same time, repentance often occurs due to fear of future punishment and, significantly, this curse, uttered in the past tense, is followed immediately by a thought of future consequences: 'J'en avrai doleurs maintes' (44). The past and the future are inextricably linked together almost fatalistically: past actions cannot be separated from future consequences. However, the linchpin in the poem's temporal scheme is the present of performance: everything in the past has led up to the present moment of performance and all that ensues will likewise depend upon it. In this respect the 'Repentance Rutebeuf' and 'Repentance Théophile' are identical.[15]

Of course, the medieval audience's familiarity with the Theophilus legend works in favour of granting Mary a pivotal role, but the text itself subtly privileges Mary's place. The key to understanding Mary's role lies in the text's use of *annominatio*. The 'Repentance Théophile' uses the figure sparingly, but a number of uses cluster in the sixth, seventh, eighth, and ninth stanzas. The last verse of the sixth stanza plays on 'char' – 'Ma char charpenteront li felon charpentier' (20) – and in the seventh stanza, the Virgin is mentioned for the first time:

Arme doit hon amer: m'arme n'iert pas amee,
N'oz demandeir la Dame qu'ele ne soit dampnee.
Trop a mal semance en sa maison semee
De cui l'arme sera en enfer seursemee.   (25–8)

The acoustic and semantic play on the words 'ame' and 'amer' gives way to an *annominatio* on 'semer,' a word with important biblical resonance.[16] The eighth stanza employs a brilliant figure on 'baillir' and 'baillier' meaning, respectively, 'to carry, lead, or direct' and 'to govern.' The second verb has distinct feudal connotations, endowing the metaphor with strong political overtones that function to connect Theophilus's sin with this confession: he renounced God so that he might wield worldly political power. Now that he sees the error of his ways, he wishes to redirect his intentions towards the divine and put himself under the authority of the Virgin, 'la douce baillie':

> Ha! laz, con fou bailli et com fole baillie!
> Or sui je mau bailliz et m'arme mau baillie.
> S'or m'ozoie baillier a la douce baillie,
> G'i seroie bailliez et m'arme ja baillie.   (29–32)

This gradual intensification of *annominatio* produces a kind of crescendo: the lyric subject first engages in simple word play before then using a true *annominatio*; a virtuostic figure then ensues, bringing together the central theme of the poem – repentance – and the one persona who has the ability to set him on the right road – Mary. From these dizzying rhetorical heights, the speaker begins to descend slowly: the ninth stanza begins with a shorter figure on 'ordure,' plays briefly on 'durer,' and then finishes with the simple acoustic figure of alliteration:

> Ors sui, et ordeneiz doit aleir en ordure.
> Ordement ai ovrei, ce seit Cil qui or dure
> Et qui toz jours durra, s'en avrai la mort dure.
> Maufeiz, com m'aveiz mort de mauvaise morsure!   (33–6)

Annominatio is often used in expressions of Marian devotion, and the figure in this densely wrought passage focuses our attention first on Mary, 'la douce baillie,' and then on God, 'Cil,' to whom Mary always leads us. In this passage, Mary's role as intercessor is highlighted, suggesting Mary's prominence in the poem, which the last stanza and 'Prière Théophile' bring out in more relief.

The last stanza's mention of the Virgin is perfectly in keeping with other Marian lyrics, especially those of Thibaut de Champagne and the women's songs that mention Mary in the envoi. The last stanza of 'Repentance Théophile' recycles key words and phrases from the earlier display of rhetorical prowess:

> Je n'oz Dieu ne ses saintes ne ses sainz reclameir,
> Ne la tres douce Dame que chacuns doit ameir.
> Mais por ce qu'en li n'a felonie n'ameir,
> Se ge li cri merci nuns ne m'en doit blasmeir.   (45–8)

The speaker's allusion to Mary as 'la tres douce Dame' echoes the eighth stanza's use of the more unusual term 'la douce baillie.' The rhyme 'amer' meaning 'to love' and 'bitter' constitutes a variation of the seventh stanza's play on 'ame' and 'amer.' These acoustic and semantic echoes resemble those used by Thibaut de Champagne to remind us of the Virgin's power in a song's last verses. In the final two verses of the 'Repentance,' focus shifts from the self to the Virgin Mary: 'Mais por ce qu'en li [the Virgin Mary]' (47). The speaker now thinks of how he might possibly escape his future of doom and this possibility becomes thematized in the last verse's use of 'if': 'Se ge li cri merci' (48).

In the 'Prière Théophile,' nine 12-verse stanzas of hexasyllables combine simplicity with complexity through the rhyme scheme borrowed from the *strophe d'Hélinand*: *aabaabbbabba*. Whereas the long alexandrines of the 'Repentance' convey a brooding and deliberateness, the shorter hexasyllables of the 'Prière' produce a more clipped and faster pace, highlighting the poem's tone of urgency. The simple yet complex rhyme scheme creates a more intricate acoustic pattern when compared to the stately rhythm of the 'Repentance.' Rutebeuf makes no other use of the form in the *Miracle*, and thus the 'Prière' stands alone formally in the context of the play; it is the moment where the need to persuade is most felt, and the piece's formal features contribute to the aim of persuasiveness.

The 'Prière' focuses our attention more on the Virgin and less on the speaking subject. Apostrophe predominates the poem's rhetorical level – the poem is, in fact, one long apostrophe – but metaphor is also ubiquitous. The two are sometimes combined through an address to the Virgin using a traditional metaphor. The second-person imperative is employed in every one of the nine stanzas, helping us focus on the Virgin and the principal aim of persuading her. In stanza I, the imperative 'me rapele' constitutes the final, definitive word, as if to punctuate the lyric subject's utmost desire, namely, that the Virgin remind Jesus to be merciful. In similar fashion, the imperative in stanza II combines the command with the first-person object pronoun 'me': 'Car me desenchanteiz' (19). In stanza IV, the subject uses the ill-fated Tantalus as an exemplum and prays that he be spared the same fate:

Gart qu'avec Tentalu
En enfer le jalu
    Ne preigne m'eritei!   (46–8)

In other places in the text, the imperative is followed by certain conjunctions that bring the Virgin's general power as intercessor to bear solely upon the speaking subject's case as occurs, among other places, in stanza III : 'Mon corage varie/ *Ainsi que* il te serve' (26–7, my emphasis). When the speaker combines these cases of direct address through the imperative with various conjunctions, he aims to bridge the gap that his sinfulness created between himself and God. These examples also illustrate how the speaker attempts to channel the Virgin's power to fulfil his need to be reconciled with the divine.

In the 'Repentance' the subject broods over his past, but the 'Prière' highlights the pasts of both the speaking subject and the Virgin. The terms through which the speaking subject's past is evoked recall moments of the 'Repentance':

> En viltei, en ordure,
> En vie trop oscure
> Ai estei lonc termine.   (85–7)

The word 'ordure' echoes the *annominatio* on the same word after the crescendo on 'bailli(e)' in the 'Repentance Théophile.' The speaking subject also evokes events of salvation history, especially the Incarnation as the event par excellence which granted salvation to humanity:

> Si come en la verriere
> Entre et reva arriere
> Li solaux que n'entame,
> Ausi fus virge entiere
> Quant Diex, qui es cielz iere,
> Fit de toi mere et dame.
> Ha! resplendissans jame,
> Tantre et piteuze fame,
> Car entent ma proiere.   (61–9)

The metaphor explains the possibility of the Incarnation and, by extension, the virgin birth. The apostrophe used to address the Virgin after the metaphor is significant: 'resplendissans jame' (67). The lapidary metaphor of the sparkling gem resonates with the previous metaphor's thematization of luminosity. Because this echo is followed by the request that the Virgin hear his prayer, the speaker suggests that divine favour be granted to him as it was to the Virgin.

If two pasts are discussed, so are two futures. The subjunctive mood is used to convey the subject's desired future, one that depends upon the good will of the Virgin. The speaker uses the future indicative for the future that his sinful past has already guaranteed him, a future filled with pain and suffering:

Ci *avra* dure verve
S'ainz que la mors m'enerve
En vous ne se marie
M'arme qui vous enterve.
Soffreiz le cors deserve
Qu'ele ne *soit perie.*   (31–6, my emphasis)

The subject's certain future, one spent forever in hell, is spoken of in the future indicative: 'avra.' However, the subject's desired future, one in which the soul does not perish, is cast in the subjunctive mood: he conveys his desire to ally himself with the Virgin through the metaphor of marriage – 'En vous ne se marie/ M'arme' – and thus save his soul from death – 'Qu'ele ne soit perie.' Because Mary's consent and his soul's salvation are only potential, the subjunctive is used. The grammatical distinction between the two moods is of direct importance to the poem's rhetorical goal, for it is only through the efficacy of the poem as a call upon the divine that the subject's desired future can be realized. Perhaps for this reason, the most potent display of rhetorical prowess is saved for the last stanza.

The last stanza combines the preceding rhetorical strategies with *annominatio* – only this stanza uses the figure – in order to make one last plea for salvation; this reminds us strongly of Gautier's use of the figure in his narrative *queues* and in the last section of his 'Roÿne celestre.' The root word played upon is 'proier,' which means both 'to prey upon' and 'to pray': the demons that prey upon the speaking subject can be fended off only if the 'Prière Théophile' is successful in moving Mary to pray for him:

Li proierres qui proie
M'a ja mis en sa proie:
Pris serai et preeiz,
Trop asprement m'asproie.
Dame, ton chier Filz proie
Que soie despreeiz.   (97–102)

Again, the speaker talks of his sinful past in the same certain terms –
'm'a *ja* mis en sa proie' (98, my emphasis) – as he does for the painful
future that awaits him – 'Pris serai' (99). The imperative of 'pray' is followed by the conjunction 'que' in order to channel the Virgin's power
to his own particular case. Any change in the subject's situation, however, remains only potential and thus uncertain and so a desired outcome is cast in the subjunctive: 'que soie despreeiz' (102). The present
prayer has the power to redirect the subject, to put him on another
path. Thus one final *annominatio* on roots that can mean 'path' as well as
'see,' 'lead,' or 'forbid' ends the 'Prière':

> Dame, car lor veeiz,
> Qui mes meffeiz veeiz,
> Que n'avoie a lor voie.
> Vous qui la sus seeiz,
> M'arme lor deveeiz
> Que nuns d'eulz ne la voie.   (103–8)

The speaker desires to be redirected from his present course and
brought to salvation where the Devil cannot lead or see him but where he
can see both Mary and God. Thus, where the 'Repentance' emphasizes
the act of repentance that precedes the call on the divine, the 'Prière'
focuses on the call itself. These poems concentrate on, rather than isolate
the separate moments: the final verse of 'Repentance' uses 'se' and forces
us to look ahead towards the possibility of salvation that the 'Prière'
emphasizes and works to secure. Likewise, the 'Prière' enters the confes-
sional mode a number of times, recalling the 'Repentance.'

The question of the audience's identification of and with Theophilus
remains. This is really a question of context, for when the two passages
are excerpted from their dramatic context, they change only slightly,
but their context undergoes drastic change. At the same time, though, if
their context changes, so does our understanding of them. The two versions of the *Miracle* survive in the two most complete collections of Rutebeuf's work. The long version survives in ms. *A*, a long and valuable
source of narrative *dits, contes, fabliaux,* and prayers produced in the late
thirteenth century. Rutebeuf's works occupy only a fraction of the
codex – folios 283–332 – and the *Miracle* occupies folios 298v–302v. The
play appears third among Rutebeuf's works after 'La Vie de Saint Elysabel' and 'Le Sacrestain et femme au chevalier.' The last piece in the
anthology is the 'Repentance Rutebeuf,' studied above. Works of a devo-

tional character frame this collection, as Huot notes, but beyond that one observation, we notice a shift in literary subjectivity from third-person exempla at the beginning of the anthology – a saint's life, a devotional tale, and a miracle play – to first-person lyrical pieces at the end of the anthology. Crucial to understanding the impact of the excerption of the 'Repentance' and 'Prière' is the fact the integral 'miracle' here figures among the third-person exempla: reception of the work would then be analogous to Gautier's miracles, that is, through a process of projecting oneself onto the character.

Ms. *C* is similar to ms. *A* in many ways, but the differences between the two assert themselves boldly in the case of the Theophilus excerpts. Thus we are forced to reconsider Huot's assertion that there is no discernable organization to *C*. The first half of the manuscript, with the exception of one folio (an excerpt of the 'Prophecies of Merlin' written in Italian) is dedicated to Rutebeuf's works. An incomplete version of the *Roman d'Alexandre* occupies the second part of the manuscript. The Rutebeuf collection dates from the late thirteenth or perhaps the early fourteenth century. As we have seen, the 'Repentance' and the 'Prière' survive not as one piece, but two, each with its own rubrics: 'Ci encoumence la repentance theophilus' precedes the 'Repentance' and a simple 'explicit' follows; similarly, we find 'C'est la priere theophilus' before the 'Prière' and an 'explicit' after it.[17] Zink remarks that in ms. *C*, the 'Repentance Rutebeuf' and the 'Repentance Théophile' function to frame the anthology *grosso modo*: the 'Repentance Rutebeuf' occupies the third position in the anthology and the 'Repentance Théophile,' the third to last position ('De la repentance' 20). However, if these pieces come third and third-to-last, then the pieces that precede and follow frame the frame. The first two works of the anthology are 'Les Ordres de Paris' and 'La Chanson des Ordres.' The very last work of the anthology is 'Des Béguines.' It is clear that, in contrast to ms. *A*'s devotional frame, satirical and polemical pieces frame the anthology of ms. *C*. Furthermore, as Rutebeuf's editors, Faral and Bastin, comment, eight pieces absent from ms. *A* but present in ms. *C* are related to the crusades, a political controversy par excellence. Both its satirical frame and the sheer number of extant satirical and political texts transmitted in *C* lend to the anthology a highly polemical tone. The cries to God and the Virgin that occur at irregular intervals but significant moments in ms. *C* resound with more urgency, become more acute, when considered in this context.

I posit that through the recontextualization of these pieces as well as the processes of application and appropriation, as outlined in my introduction, the 'Repentance' and 'Prière' move away from constituting a plea made by Theophilus, the deposed bishop of sixth-century Cicilia, and towards becoming a cry in the urban wilderness of thirteenth-century Paris. Every Marian miracle tale is meant to showcase the powers of the Virgin and teach listeners about humanity's utter dependence upon the divine, and the 'Repentance' and 'Prière' constitute Theophilus's call on the divine. I therefore agree with Zink when he calls the two excerpts the 'essentiel' of Rutebeuf's play: the passages function rhetorically as a synecdoche of the whole play, the part that stands in for the whole ('De la repentance' 19). But the hermeneutical consequences of their excerption reach beyond the relationship of the whole to the part: details of Theophilus's life situation, e.g., his confession to to having renounced God, pledged loyalty to the Devil, and spent seven years in the devil's service cross the border separating the dramatic from the lyric mode and metaphorization takes place. These details are no longer understood in the context of Theophilus's story. Announced by the universally applicable lyric subject, these moments fit the life situation of each individual audience member. The renouncement of God that Theophilus literally performed might be understood more figuratively as perhaps a shirking of one's religious duties or a placing of other things before God. The number seven, with its obvious symbolic value, might be understood as simply a significant amount of time, leading a listener to believe he has led a sinful life too long.

One other piece of manuscript evidence supports this reading: the prayer attributed to Gautier de Coinci that survives in ms. *A* on folios 191v–2v. It represents a special case of gap closing between speaker and character. Koenig includes the piece among the final prayers in Gautier's *Miracles de Nostre Dame*, and it survives in no fewer than twenty-six separate manuscripts. Its accompanying rubrics vary widely: 'Oracio domini Galteri prioris de Vi ad piissimam Dei matrem'; 'Une orison devote a la Virgene Marie de lonc temps faite'; 'C'est une oroison a Nostre Dame, etc.' (II Prière 37: notes). In ms. *A*, however, the ending rubric, written in the copyist's hand reads: 'Explicit la priere theophilus.' The rubric above the song, written in a different and later hand, reads, 'La priere theophilus.' An analogous but inverted case of metaphorization has taken place, and we observe a play between the general and the specific. In contrast to those who read the prayer in a more general vein, the scribe and rubricator of ms. *C* read the text in a specific life situation, that of Theophilus. Moreover, and this is directly relevant to the excerption of Rutebeuf's pieces, nothing in Gautier's text has anything specifically to do with the Theophilus legend. Certainly, there are parallels: the speaker admits to having lived a dissolute life, and expresses a fear of hell, of the earth opening and swallowing him whole. These motifs figure in the 'Repentance' and 'Prière,' but they are hardly particular to them. If the excerption of the 'Repentance' and 'Prière' from the *Miracle* present us with the case of the application of the specific to the general through metaphor, the attribution of Gautier's prayer to Theophilus presents the inverted operation: the general to the specific. In some way, the life situation of Theophilus spoke to the copyist, the rubricator, and even a number of nineteenth- and twentieth-century scholars who continued to list the work as 'La Prière Théophile.' They read 'je,' 'I,' but understood 'Theophilus.' As a result of this hermeneutical gesture, the very meaning of the name 'Theophilus' reverts to its etymological meaning, 'lover of God,' to be applied not to one particular literary figure, but potentially to all people, as is the case in the beginning of the gospel of Luke. And we wonder, if Rutebeuf's Theophilus prayers had continued to be copied separately from the whole play, how would subsequent rubricators and copyists have understood the text? Their excerption and separate rubrication already represent an important step towards a more total emancipation from Rutebeuf's play.

In the final analysis, these poems may represent the discursive centre of the *Miracle de Théophile*, but their excerption from their dramatic context has important implications for their interpretation and for our understanding of Marian poetry. When excerpted from the play as a whole, details from the Theophilus story become metaphors for the sins and temptations of the individual audience members. Compelling manuscript evidence confirms this reading as well as the mode of reading religious literature as explained in my introduction. However, one important element that is lost irrevocably when these poems are taken out of their dramatic context is the Virgin's response. And yet, the expressions of Marian devotion that form the object of my study also leave this out. Rutebeuf's 'Un dist de Nostre Dame' fills this lacuna left by previous poets while combining the lyric, dramatic, and narrative modes in a poem that perfectly complements the Theophilus poems.

When Mary Intercedes: 'Un dist de Nostre Dame'

'Un dist de Nostre Dame' is similar to the *planctus Mariae* studied in chapter 3 in that it constitutes a monologue in the voice of the Virgin.

However, the difference here is that the Virgin is not expressing her sorrow at witnessing the death of her son. Rutebeuf's monologue is unique among the works under examination, for it fills a void in the communicative paradigm of Marian devotion whereby we pray to Mary that she, in turn, pray to God. Time and time again we have heard her supplicants, but the subsequent part of the paradigm where Mary speaks has only been implied in these poems. In 'Un dist' Rutebeuf imagines what Mary does say when she intercedes on our behalf. Mary's speech, implicit in every Marian lyric, is, moreover, crucial, for her speech is crucial to humanity's salvation; that it goes unheard in other Marian lyrics is ironic: Mary remains as silent as the courtly trouvère's lady whom Mary supposedly supplants in so many poems. Such passages do occur, however, in Gautier's narrative miracles.[18] One might indeed wonder if the poem's principal influence came through narrative Marian poetry, because Mary's speech takes us into the narrative mode when she recounts seminal events of salvation history from Genesis to Pentecost in chronological order. When Mary speaks, she uses a rhetorical strategy common to Marian poetics: she retells the major events of salvation history, reminding God, in light of all that he has already done to save humanity, that he must not abandon us now.

The first twenty-four verses, spoken in the voice of the lyric subject, praise the Virgin Mary. The passage sounds like an amplified Marian lyric exordium, as the poet combines the inexpressibility topos with the Marian metaphor of the well:

Més l'en porroit avant un puis
Espuisier c'on poïst retrere
Combien la Dame est debonaire.   (4–6)

An initiated public easily recognizes both types; however, the metaphor of the well is usually applied to Mary's inexhaustible goodness, and Rutebeuf applies it to his own speech act. The conflation of the types gives rise to an ambiguity, which was always there in other trouvères' poems using the topos but which Rutebeuf brings out more forcefully: when lamenting the impossibility of describing his lady, is the poet focusing on himself or his lady?[19] Rutebeuf's speaker tells us how difficult it is to choose from among Mary's good qualities. The situation in which the poet finds himself is embarrassing. We should call on the Virgin – 'si la devons requerre' (7) – but where should we begin? Of course, the poem has already begun, which is part of the type's rhetorical effect: secular or religious lyric poets compose in spite of the difficulty. Nevertheless, the abundance of available material remains daunting:

> Besoignex sui par abondance.
> L'abondance de sa loange
> Remue mon corage et change
> Si qu'esprover ne me porroie,
> Tant parlasse que je voudroie.   (12–16)

The repetition of the word 'abondance' in verses 12–13 is structurally significant: since this exordium is 24 verses long, the last word of the twelfth verse and first word of the thirteenth verse constitute the passage's very centre. The central focus of the exordium is the abundance of Mary's virtues, but is the poet's concern for Mary or for his poem? The tension remains to the end and, instead of resolving the ambiguity of these verses, Rutebeuf merely resigns himself altogether: the attempt to write the Virgin's goodness would be in vain even if he were a good writer. Mary's goodness and his poem stand in a relationship of inverse proportionality: Mary is as good as the poem's words are poor. The poet is thus speaking about Mary and his own speech at the same time.

Whereas the lyric 'I' of the exordium talks about both himself and the Virgin, Mary never talks about herself. Rather, she mentions elements of salvation history in order to generate an encomium of Jesus:

> Biax chiers fis, il t'en prist pitiez
> Et tant lor montras d'amistiez
> Que pour aus decendis des ciaus.
> Li dessandres fu bons et biax:
> De ta fille feïs ta mere,
> Tiex fu la volanté dou Pere.
> De la creche te fit on couche.   (41–7)

Mary's use of these events does nonetheless remind us of the rhetorical strategies of other poets: instead of merely recounting the Incarnation, Mary interprets the Incarnation so that her praise of Jesus' goodness is more effective. Marian poets do the same when praising the Virgin, and Mary's use of the strategy to praise Jesus represents a variation on a tried and true rhetorical ploy. Significantly, Mary downplays her own role in the Incarnation, whereas previous poets focused on her role. When

Mary refers to herself, she keeps the focus on Jesus by using third-person pronouns for herself and second-person pronouns and adjectives for Jesus: 'De ta fille feïs ta mere' (45); 'De la creche te fit on couche' (47). These instances of pronoun switching suggest a subtle understanding of the purely mediatory role that the Virgin plays: she has effaced herself entirely to assume a role of pure instrumentality. Furthermore, the length of Mary's speech represents an amplification of previous poets' use of salvation history: whereas they evoked one or two events, Rutebeuf's Mary names many more. As a result, her speech sounds much like a narrative. But the whole point of the retelling is to praise Jesus and to help convince him to have mercy on humanity:

> Biax chiers fiz, por l'umain lignage
> Jeter de honte et de domage
> Feïs tote ceste bonté
> Et plus assez que n'ai conté.   (107–10)

Mary's encomium ultimately benefits humanity, 'l'umain lignage' (107). These verses, the raison d'être of the Virgin's discourse, illustrate how well Rutebeuf conflates the narrative and lyric modes: although narrative in construction, Mary's speech is panegyric in aim.

In the Virgin's last words her one and only use of 'je' occurs. After all that she has said, it is somewhat ironic that 'je' is uttered when speaking of what she did not say: 'plus assez que n'ai conté' (110). We are reminded of the speaker in the prologue who spoke openly and at length in the exordium about what he does not say. A second echo of the prologue occurs in the next verses:

> S'or laissoies si esgaré
> Ce que si chier as comparé
> Ci avroit trop grant mesprison,
> S'or les lessoies en prison
> Entrer, don tu les as osté,
> Car ci avroit trop mal hosté,
> Trop grant duel et trop grant martire,
> Biau filz, biau pere, biau doz sire.   (111–18)

In the exordium, the speaker focused on the Virgin's qualities, which he could not name because they were so numerous; they were, in a way, excessive. In these last words, the Virgin calls Jesus' attention to the

excessive suffering that humanity will endure if he does not save them –
'trop grant mesprison' (113), 'Trop grant duel et trop grant martire'
(117). This suffering would be excessive precisely because Jesus' life and
death occurred so that human suffering would cease; after all, in verses
114–15, the Virgin talks in the past tense of humanity's liberation from
the prison of hell. Mary's rhetoric is keenly honed: while it is true that
sinners of present and future generations may still be damned, Mary
tries to convince Jesus that he can prevent further suffering and thus
make his Incarnation, life, and death ultimately meaningful.

In the last section of the poem, Rutebeuf employs an *annominatio* on
an apt figure, 'corde,' to summarize the Virgin's role as the one who
brings divinity and humanity into concordance:[20]

> Ainsi recorde tote jor
> La doce Dame, sans sejor;
> Ja ne fine de recorder
> Car bien nous voudroit raçorder
> A li, don nos nos descordons
> De sa corde et de ses cordons.   (119–24)

These verses share a focus on Mary and humanity and further suggest
an identification between the poet and Mary in the poem. In the final
analysis, the 'dist' constitutes a poem in which the speaker and Mary
perform the same speech act: the 'je' reminds us of how Mary reminds
Jesus of his infinite mercy. In this way, the dynamic of Marian intercession that previous poets tried to convey – for instance, Gautier in his
'Amours, qui bien set enchanter' (I Ch 3) – is enacted more dramati-
cally. In the very last verses, Rutebeuf exhorts us to join him in calling
upon the divine:

> Or nous acordons a l'acorde
> La Dame de misericorde
> Et li prions que nos acort
> Par sa pitié au dine acort
> Son chier Fil, le dine Cor Dé:
> Lors si serons bien racordé.   (125–30)

In 'Un dist' Rutebeuf continues the work of previous poets, but he reviv-
ifies the Marian poetry of the past by transferring Marian motifs into a
new form that is lyric, narrative, and dramatic. In his first prologue,

Gautier uses the metaphor of resurrection to describe his project of translation, transference, and composition. Rutebeuf's poetry represents an analogous undertaking, whether consciously chosen or not: by reusing traditional material in new ways, Rutebeuf breathes new life into a corpus of texts, inviting us to compare and contrast his Marian poetic compositions with those of his predecessors.

In many ways, my study has come full circle, for Gautier de Coinci cherished *annominatio*, especially on the root 'corde.' Some of the very first poems read in this study, that is, Gautier's Leocadia sequence, play with narrative and lyric modes like Rutebeuf does. Rutebeuf's poetry revisits Gautier's as it recasts questions that Gautier's poetry first posed, such as the relationship between audience and poet and the dynamic interaction of the religious with the secular. Ending this book with Rutebeuf, in fact, brings many elements of my study into concordance. Nevertheless, the same root appears in 'discord': there are many points of discord between Rutebeuf and Gautier, as well as the poets studied in between. Both Gautier de Coinci and Rutebeuf wrote different kinds of noncourtly poetry: although he strove to dissuade us from listening to secular songs, Gautier was greatly indebted to them for his lyric production, and Rutebeuf's urban public cultivated different tastes from the audience at court. Rutebeuf's spoken poetry does not sound like the songs of Thibaut de Champagne, the composers of women's songs, or Jacques de Cambrai. Yet, the Marian songs and poems of all these poets are linked sometimes semantically on the level of motif, sometimes formally through contrafacture, sometimes rhetorically through various tropes. They exist in a relationship of analogy, allowing us to see similarities and differences, concordance and discordance, among them. As expressions of Marian devotion, they all serve the same end – only the means vary.

Conclusion: Contrafacture and Cultural Exchange

I have shown in the preceding pages that Marian devotion in Old French song may very well have drawn on secular and Latin forms and motifs, but vernacular Marian song is anything but staid and static. Quite to the contrary, a dynamic interaction between the religious and secular lies at the very heart of this poetics. The birth of Old French Marian lyric in the devotional and dogmatic context of Gautier's *Miracles* is only a starting point for a genre that would come to know many variations throughout the thirteenth century. Thibaut fully integrates religious song into his wider courtly production in ways that are sometimes surprising, but always playful and enticing. Women's devotional song enacts multiple and various voicings of Marian devotion and blends motifs of women's longing and pain to mark a more troubling, existential crisis when calling on the divine. Jacques de Cambrai's poetry represents the densely allusive tradition that Marian song would become in the later thirteenth century. Finally, like Gautier before him, who revived texts by translating them from the Latin and combining secular and religious components, Rutebeuf lifted motifs typical of Marian lyric and integrated them into a literary project that traverses the boundaries of lyric. Marian devotion in and beyond the world of thirteenth-century lyric is far from derivative, repetitive, and monotonous: it is a vibrant tradition that reinvents itself with each passing generation.

Needless to say, much has yet to be done. The corpus of texts that I have studied represents only a fraction of extant religious lyrics, and the proposed generative model of contrafacture only crudely sketches out the interactive relationships between model and contrafactum. From the painstaking and often time-consuming analyses of individual contrafactures and the outlines of general compositional trends, one might

then move the study of contrafacture beyond the empirical and consider deriving a performative model or theory of contrafacture. The
question is as pertinent today as it was in the Middle Ages: from Monty
Python's 'All Things Dull and Ugly' to Clairol's 'I'm Gonna Wash that
Gray Right out of My Hair,' contrafacta are abundant in film, television,
and radio. Perhaps the anthropological and sociological data derived
from studies of popular culture could give us an insight into the performance and reception of contrafacture in the Middle Ages.

Much work has already been done on the relationship between contrafacture and metaphor, as well as on the nature of religious language
and its reliance on metaphor, allegory, and analogy, but much has yet to
be explored in relation to the corpus of texts I have chosen. Gautier's
opposition between secular and religious speech is only one way, and a
more medieval way, of posing the question. One could situate scholarly
research at an entirely different level, if one were to explore further the
linguistic models of Gadamer and Ricoeur, who draw no distinction
between religious and secular speech per se. Though different on the
level of theme and referent, religious and secular speech and interpretation are the same in the criteria they must adhere to for intelligibility
and understandability. Joel Weinsheimer puts it this way in the preface
to *Hermeneutics, Religion, and Ethics*, a collection of newly translated
essays by Gadamer:

> Gadamer shows, however, that every kind of interpretation, and not just
> that informed by faith, must ineluctably posit the inviolability and self-
> sameness of meaning. Without such a dialectical counterbalance to the
> self-difference of meaning evident in secular interpretation, even nonreli-
> gious interpretation necessarily falls into what Gadamer calls 'hermeneutic
> nihilism' – the premise that every new reading is a new creation – which
> amounts to the denial that interpretation and understanding are possible
> at all. (viii)

Both religious and secular texts must mean the same in the present,
past, and future in order for meaning to be possible at all. The elucida-
tion of the relationship between 'objective' or 'ideal' meaning, existential application, and religious belief or faith would require spending
much time and intellectual energy. I have only scratched the proverbial
surface in this book, planting the seeds for future research into a question that remains vital to the study of religious poetry.

The one conclusion that remains inescapable is that contemporary scholars of Old French should regard medieval vernacular religious poetry in higher esteem. If the present study has not exhausted the many issues relating to the production, reception, and place in medieval culture of these poems, it has posed valid and necessary questions. My attempt at offering at least provisional answers to these questions has come through contextualization and interpretation, which only makes the need for further discussion among students of literature, music, theology, and philosophy more keenly felt. Only through a continuing and evolving dialogue can we hope to come to a better understanding of the secular and the religious in both medieval and modern culture.

Appendix of
Textual and Musical Editions
of Songs and Poems

All text and music is edited and translated by Daniel E. O'Sullivan, unless otherwise indicated.

The appendix is preceded by a table of contents that groups the songs according to their corresponding chapter and provides the following information: incipit, Raynaud-Spanke number (where appropriate), editor and translator, and base manuscript. Although musical and textual editions are available in the standard or recent modern editions, I have reedited a number of texts. Koenig's choice of base manuscript for Gautier was made for reasons of availability and not necessarily quality (see his introduction). I have also reedited several songs by Thibaut de Champagne: Axel Wallensköld's editions do not represent songs as they are found in any one manuscript. Kathleen Brahney's editions are based on trouvère ms. *K* (Paris, Arsenal 5198), which is a fine manuscript for many trouvère works, but in regard to Thibaut's work, trouvère ms. *Mt*, the so-called *Chansonnier du roi* (the central part of trouvère ms. *M*, BnF fr. 844), represents the better choice for both its text and music and its compiler's evident desire to assemble Thibaut's songs. As for the other texts, I rely on Doss-Quinby et al. for some women's songs, Järnström and Långfors for others, Jean-Claude Rivière for Jacques, and Faral and Bastin for Rutebeuf. For each of these, I have checked the editions against the declared base manuscripts and noted errors or new, alternative readings. As for melodies, many in this repertoire are available only through the work of Jacques Chailley and Hans Tischler, who employ a controversial method of mensural notation. I have therefore provided new melodic editions for all songs except those recently edited by Elizabeth Aubrey in *Songs of the Women Trouvères*. Like Aubrey's editions,

mine indicate pitch but not rhythm, and I do not transpose the melodies, even if they seem too high or low for the voice meant to sing : after
all, in the absence of a concept of absolute pitch, medieval performers
sang melodies in a range comfortable to them. In regard to chromatic
inflections, I have tried to remain faithful to the transmitted melody and
only intervened with clear justification. The motivation for appending
these texts stems from the desire to provide the reader with the necessary material for understanding my discussions. The critical apparatus
provides, therefore, rejected readings but not variants: the interested
reader is encouraged to seek such material in the earlier, authoritative
editions. All translations are my own unless otherwise indicated. Finally,
I add the following caveat: given the well-known *mouvant* quality of
medieval literature, editions should be taken only as guides, and translations, literal but readable guides to the original Old French.

Gautier de Coinci

Amours, qui bien set enchanter (RS 851); Paris, BnF nouv. acq. fr. 24541,
    fol. 4v.
Roÿne celestre (RS 956, 1903); Paris, BnF nouv. acq. fr. 24541, fol. 5r–v.
D'une amour quoie et serie (RS 1212); Paris, BnF nouv. acq. fr. 24541, fol. 116v.

Thibaut de Champagne

De chanter ne me puis tenir (RS 1475); Paris, BnF fr. 844, fol. 69v.
Dou tres douz non a la virge Marie (RS 1181); Paris, BnF fr. 844, fol. 67r.
Mauvez arbres ne puet florir (RS 1410); Paris, BnF fr. 844, fol. 75v.
De grant travail et de petit esploit (RS 1843); Paris, Arsenal 5198, fol. 69r–v.
Seignor, sachiés qui or ne s'en ira (RS 6); Paris, BnF fr. 844, fol. 13v.
Dame, einsi est qu'il m'en couvient aler (RS 757); Paris, BnF fr. 844, fol. 64r–v.
Commencerai a fere un lai (RS 84, 73a); Paris, BnF fr. 844, fol. 66r.

Women's Songs (all anonymous)

Chanter m'estuet, de la virge puchele (RS 611a); Paris, Arsenal 3517, fol. 4v.
Du dous Jhesu souvent devons chanter et lire (RS 1195); text ed. Edward Järnström
    and Arthur Långfors; Paris, BnF fr. 12483, fols. 243v–4r.
Li solaus qui en moy luist est mes deduis (RS 1936a, 2076); text ed. and trans. Eglal
    Doss-Quinby et al; music ed. Elizabeth Aubrey, *Music*; Paris, BnF fr. 12483,
    fol. 266v.
Li debonnaires Dieus m'a mis en sa prison (RS 1646); text ed. Samuel N. Rosenberg

and Hans Tischler, cited in Eglal Doss-Quinby et al.; music ed. Elizabeth
Aubrey, *Music*; Paris, BnF fr. 12483, fol. 253r.
Ave Maria, j'aim tant (RS); text ed. Edward Järnström and Arthur Långfors;
Paris, BnF fr. 12483, fol. 240r–v.
Lasse, que devendrai gié' (RS 1093); Paris, BnF fr. 12483, fols 63r–4r.

Jacques de Cambrai

Grant talent ai k'a chanteir me retraie (RS 114); ed. Jean-Claude Rivière; Bern,
Stadtbibliothek 389, fol. 83.
Ausi conme unicorne sui (RS 2075) by Thibaut de Champagne, which served as
the model for Jacques's 'Haute dame, com rose et lis'; text ed. Samuel N.
Rosenberg; Paris, Arsenal 3517, fol. 29r–v.
De fin cuer et d'aigre talent (RS 734) attributed to Pierre de Gand, another con-
trafactum of Thibaut's 'Ausi ...'; text ed. Hans Tischler; Paris, BnF fr. 24406,
fols 150v–1r.
Haute dame, com rose et lis (RS 1563); ed. Jean-Claude Rivière; Bern, Stadt-
bibliothek 389, fol. 90.
Kant je plus pens a commencier chanson' (RS 1856); ed. Jean-Claude Rivière;
Bern, Stadtbibliothek 389, fol. 110.
Loeir m'estuet la roïne Marie' (RS 1178); ed. Jean-Claude Rivière; Bern, Stadt-
bibliothek 389, fol. 121.
'Meire, douce creature' (RS 2091); ed. Jean-Claude Rivière; Bern, Stadtbibliothek 389, fol. 141.
O Dame, ke Deu portais (RS 380, 197a); ed. Jean-Claude Rivière; Bern, Stadt-
bibliothek 389, fol. 167.
Retrowange novelle' (RS 602); ed. Jean-Claude Rivière; Bern, Stadtbibliothek
389, fol. 209.

Rutebeuf

C'est de Notre Dame' (RS 1998); ed. Edmond Faral and Julia Bastin; Paris, BnF
fr. 1635, fol. 82r
La Repentance/Mort Rutebeuf' (RS –); ed. Edmond Faral and Julia Bastin;
Paris, BnF fr. 837, fol. 332r
L'*Ave Maria* Rustebeuf (RS –); ed. Edmond Faral and Julia Bastin (slightly
modified); Paris, BnF fr. 837, fol. 328r
La Repentance Théophile (RS –); Paris, BnF 1635, fols 83r–4r
La Prière Théophile (RS –); Paris, BnF fr. 1635, fols 84r–v
Un dist de Nostre Dame (RS –); ed. Edmond Faral and Julia Bastin (slightly
altered); Paris, BnF fr. 1593, fol. 74r–v

Amours, qui bien set enchanter
Gautier de Coinci

1.A - mours, qui bien set en - chan - ter,

2.As plu - seurs fait tel chant chan - ter

3.Dont les a - mes des - chan - tent.

4.Je ne vueil mes chan - ter tel chant,

5.Mes por ce - lui no - viau chant chant

6.De cui li an - gre chan - tent.

Musical emendations (hereafter ME): 1/6 (verse 1, syllable 6) the neume is written a second too high – 4/3 the consistent flatting of all other b's suggests that the scribe mistakenly omitted the sign here.

Amours, qui bien set enchanter

I.   Amours, qui bien set enchanter,
     As pluseurs fait tel chant chanter
     Dont les ames deschantent.
4 Je ne veuil mes chanter tel chant,
     Mes por celui noviau chant chant
     De cui li angre chantent.

Love, which knows well how to
    enchant,
makes many [people] sing songs
that disenchant the soul.
I no longer want to sing such songs,
but [rather] for her, about whom
    angels sing,
I sing a new song.

II. Chantez de lui, tuit chanteür.
8 S'enchanterez l'enchanteür
     Qui souvent nous enchante.
     Se de la mere Dieu chantez,
     Touz enchantant iert enchantez.
12 Buer fu nez qui en chante.

Sing of her, all singers,
and you will enchant the enchanter
who often enchants us.
If you sing of the mother of God,
every enchanter will be enchanted.
Fortunate is the one who sings of her.

III. Qui veut son cointe acointement
     Acointer s'i doit cointement,
     Quar tant est sage et cointe
16 Que nus ne s'i puet acointier
     Ne li estuit desacointier
     Quanqu'Anemis acointe.

He who wishes to associate himself
    with
her gracious friendship should wisely
    do so,
for she is so gracious and wise
that no one can associate himself
    [with her]
without necessarily dissociating him-
    self
from whatever the Devil teaches.

IV. Ja nus ne s'i acointera
20 Devant qu'il desacointera
     Por li toutes acointes.
     Pour s'amour les desacointiez!
     N'iert acointe Dieu n'acointiez.
24 Nul s'il n'est ses acointes.

No one will ever be associated with
    her
before he dissociates himself
from all other female associates in
    favour of her.
Dissociate yourself for love of her!
No one who is not her associate will be
associated with the right associate.

V. Mere Dieu, tant faiz a prisier.
     Ton pris ne puet langue esprisier,

Mother of God, you do many worthy
    deeds.

Tant en soit bien aprise.
28 Chascuns te prise et je te pris.
La rose ies ou la fleur de pris
Char precieuse a prise.

No tongue can measure your worth,
no matter how skilled [that tongue]
     may be.
Everyone prizes you and I do, too.
You are the rose where the supreme
     flower
took [the form of] precious flesh.

VI. Char precïeuse en tes flans prist,
32 Par quoi le soupernant souprist
Qui touz nos vieut souspenre;
Mais qui a toi servir se prent,
Sa soupresure nel sousprent.
36 A toi se fait bon penre.

In your womb he took precious flesh,
whereby he ambushed the ambusher
who wants to ambush us;
but if someone undertakes to serve
     you,
[the Devil's] ambush does not sur-
     prise him.
[That person] does well to cling to
     you.

VII. Dame en cui sont tout bon con-
          fort,
De mes pechiez me desconfort,
Mais ce me reconforte
40 Que nus n'est tant desconfortez
Par toi ne soit reconfortés.
Tes confors toz conforte.

Lady in whom all comforts lie,
I am distressed by my sins,
but it comforts me [to know]
that no one is so distressed that
he may not be immediately comforted
     by you.
Your comfort comforts all.

VIII. Dame, con grans, dame, con fors
44 Est tes secors et tes confors!
Mainte ame as confortee.
Conforte moi. Grant confort as:
L'Egypcïene confortas,
48 Qui ert desconfortee.

Lady, how great, lady, how strong
is your aid and your comfort!
You have comforted many a soul.
Comfort me. You possess great com-
     fort:
you comforted [Mary] the Egyptian,
who was in distress.

IX. Douce dame, qui bien te sert
L'amour ton douz fil en desert.
Bien est droiz c'om te serve.
52 Touz cil qui bien te serviront
Joie sans fin deserviront.
Diex doint je la deserve!

Sweet lady, he who serves you well,
deserves the love of your sweet son.
It is certainly right that we should
     serve you.
All those who serve you well
will deserve joy without end.

God grant that I deserve it!

X. Las, ainz nul bien ne deservi,   Alas, I never deserved any reward,
56 Quar si petit ai Dieu servi   for I have served God so little
    M'ame a mort deservie.   that my soul deserves death.
    Dame, or m'apren si a servir   Lady, teach me how to serve
    La joie puisse deservir   so that I may deserve the joy[ful place]
60 Ou d'angres ies servie.   where angels serve you.

XI. Douce dame, sanz finement   Sweet lady, without end
     Servir te doit on finement.   One should serve you purely.
     Com ors ies afinee.   You are as pure as gold.
64   Les tiens afines com or fin   You purify your own like pure gold
     Et si leur donnes a la fin   and give them at the end
     Joie qui n'iert finee.   never-ending joy.

XII. Celui pri je au definer   I pray, in conclusion, to the one
68   Qui por nous vout en croiz finer,   who for us wished to meet his end on
     Qui tout commence et fine,   the cross,
     Qui commencemenz est et finz,   who begins and ends everything,
     Touz nous face a la fin si fins   who is the beginning and the end,
72   Qu'aions la joie fine. Amen.   that he make us all at the end so pure
                                                 that we attain pure joy. Amen.

Rejected readings (hereafter RR): 4 enchantent – 19 la – 20 d. ce qu'il –
30 pitieuse – 48 descontee

Roÿne celestre
Gautier de Coinci

1. Ro - ÿ - ne cel - es - tre,
2. Buer fus - ses tu ne - e,
3. Quant porte et fe - nes - tre
4. Du ciel es nom - me - e.
5. Tant es de haut es - tre,
6. pu - ce - le sa - cre - e,
7. Qu'el ciel a sa des - tre
8. T'a Diex cou - ron - ne - e.
9. Car de ta ma - me - le
10. Qui tant est en - mie - le - e,
11. Fu sa bou - che be - le

12. Pe - üe et a - be - vre - e.

13. Hau - te de - moi - se - le,

14. Vir - ge be - ne - ü - re - e.

15. Touz li mons ra - pe - le,

16. Par tout ies re - cla - me - e.

17. Hau - te pu - ce - le pure et mon - de,

18. De toi sourt la rou - se - e

19. Dont as tou - te la riens du mon - de

20. Nor - rie et a - rou - se - e.

21. Ro - ÿne en - nou - re - e,

22. Buer fus - ses en - gen - re - e,

34.Mes qui te sert,

35.Dieu en de - sert.

36.Que buer fus - ses tu ne - e.

ME: 14/7 note missing

Roÿne celestre

I. Roÿne celestre,   Celestial queen,
    Buer fusses tu nee,   how fortunate that you were born,
    Quant porte et fenestre   as you are called the door
4   Du ciel es nommee.   and window to heaven.
    Tant es de haut estre,   You are from such a high place,
    Pucele sacree,   holy maiden,
    Qu'el ciel a sa destre   that in heaven at his right side
8   T'a Diex coronnee,   God has crowned you,
    Car de ta mamele,   for at your breast,
    Qui tant est enmielee,   which is so sweet,
    Fu sa bouche bele   his beautiful mouth was fed
12 Peüe et abevree.   and satiated.
    Haute damoisele,   Esteemed maiden,
    Virge beneüree,   fortunate Virgin,
    Touz li mons rapele,   everyone keeps you in mind,
16 Partout ies reclamee.   you are beckoned from everywhere.
    Haute pucele, pure et monde,   Esteemed maiden, pure and immacu-
    De toi sourt la rousee   late,
    Dont as toute la riens du monde   from you flows the dew
20 Norrie et arousee.   from which you nourished and
    Roÿne ennouree,   watered
    Buer fusses engenree,   everything in the world.
    Car plus ies douce et plus plesanz   Honoured queen,
24 Et plus sade cent mile tans   how fortunate you were conceived,

Que mieuz en fresche ree.
Riens qu'a saveur,
Sans ta faveur,
28 Ne m'est asavouree.
Certes qui ne bee
De toute sa pensee
A toi servir tout en apert,
32 Puis bien dire que s'ame pert
Et qu'ele en iert dampnee;
Mais qui te sert
Dieu en desert.
36 Que buer fusses tu nee!

since you are sweeter and more
pleasant
and more delectable a hundred times
more
than fresh rays of honey.
Nothing that has taste
except your favour
is tasty to me.
For certain, he who does not turn
all of his thoughts
to serving you openly,
I can well say that he loses his soul
and it will be damned for it;
but he who serves you
deserves God.
How fortunate you were born!

II.   Fontaine de grace,
Mere Dieu, Marie,
Queque chascuns die,
40 Fouz est qui t'oublie.
Tourne nous ta face,
Qui tant est polie.
De nous tous efface
44 Toute vilanie.
Embasmee rose,
De nouvel espanie,
Touz li mons t'alose
48 Et vers toi s'umilie,
Car en toi repose
Et en toi se recrie
Cil qui toute chose
52 De nïent forme et crie.
Qui de bon cuer a toi s'otroie,
Qui t'aime, sert et prie,
Tu l'as tost mis a bone voie
56 Et retrait de folie.
En toi n'a boidie,
Barat ne loberie,
Tricherie ne fauseté.

Fountain of grace,
mother of God, Mary,
no matter what each person says,
the one who forgets you is foolish.
Turn to us your face,
which is so lovely.
From all of us erase
all baseness.
Sweet-smelling,
newly bloomed rose,
all praise you
and humble themselves before you,
for in you rests
and in you takes comfort
he who formed and created
everything from nothing.
The one who gives himself over wholeheartedly,
who loves, serves, and prays to you,
you put that one immediately on the
right path
and away from folly.
In you there is no perfidy,

60 Por ce a cil bien son sort jeté
    Qui a toi se marie.
    Tu as biauté
    Et loiauté,
64 Valeur et cortoisie.
    Ne foloie mie
    Qui de toi fait s'amie,
    Car cil qui t'aime de cuer fin
68 Ne puet faillir a fine fin
    N'a pardurable vie.
    Por ce t'enclin,
    Por ce m'aclin
72 A toi, virge Marie.

neither ruse nor deception,
neither trickery nor falseness.
For this, he has cast his lot well,
the one who marries you.
You have beauty
and loyalty,
merit and grace.
That person is no fool,
the one who takes you as beloved,
for he who loves you with a perfect
    heart
cannot fail to find a fine finish
and everlasting life.
For this, I bow to you.
For this, I devote myself
to you, Virgin Mary.

III. Rose fresche et clere,
    De Saint Espir plaine,
    Tu iez fille et mere
76 Au filz Dieu demaine.
    Tant fu ta matere
    Nete et pure et saine
    Qu'en toi prist tes pere
80 Forme et char humaine.
    Dame, qui tant sainte
    Et qui tant fus eslite
    Que grosse et enceinte
84 Fus du Saint Esperite,
    Oies ma complainte
    Et envers moi t'apite.
    Ma lampe est estainte,
88 M'ame en enfer escripte.
    Dame, [de moi] pitiez te
      preingne,
    Se deslace la corde,
    Que deable plus ne m'estraigne
92 Qui m'enlace et encorde.
    Ainz que mors me morde,
    Fai que me desamorde

Fresh and lovely rose,
full of the Holy Spirit,
you are the daughter and mother
of the son of God himself.
So immaculate and pure and clean
was your body
that in you your father
took flesh and human form.
Lady, who is so holy,
and who was so esteemed
that you became pregnant and
    impregnated
with the Holy Spirit,
hear my prayer
and take pity on me.
My lamp is extinguished,
my soul registered in hell.
Lady, you would show me mercy,
if you untied the rope
that ties and binds me,
so that the Devil may no longer
    strangle me.
Before death bites me,

De vilennie et de pechié.

96 Las! las! chetis! tant ai pechié
Que ma vie est trop orde.
Cuer ai de fer.
Du feu d'enfer
100 Ja ne cuit que j'estorde.
Mere de concorde,
Fai ma pais et m'acorde.
Pechiez m'a tout taint et nerci.
104 Doiz de douceur, merci! merci!
A ton doz fil m'acorde.
Mainte descordé
As recordé,
108 Fons de misericorde.

make it so that I liberate myself
from baseness and sin.
Alas, wretch, afflicted one! I have
    sinned
so much that my life abounds in filth.
I have a heart of iron.
From the fires of hell,
I do not think I can escape.
Mother of harmony,
make my peace and reconcile me.
sin has completely tainted and
    blackened me.
Source of sweetness, mercy! mercy!
Reconcile me with your sweet son.
You have remembered
many who have fallen out of favour,
fountain of mercy.

RR: 27 saveur – 35 sert – 45 rousee – 46 espinie – 82 fu – 91 estingne – 100 je restordre

D'une amour quoie et serie
Gautier de Coinci

1. D'une a - mour quoie et se - ri - e

2. Chan - ter vueil se - ri - e - ment.

3. Gart vi - lains ne m'es - cout mi - e

4. Seur es - com - mun - i - e - ment.

5. Nus qui aint vi - lain - ne - ment

6. Ces - te chan - çon ne com - ment.

7. N'est pas di - gnes qu'il en di - e

8. Nes le re - frait seu - le - ment:

9. *Vi - lai - ne genz,*

10. *Vous ne les sen - tez mi - e*

11. *Les dous maus que je sent.*

D'une amour quoie et serie

I.   D'une amour quoie et serie   Of a quiet and serene love
      Chanter vueil seriement.   I wish to sing serenely.
      Gart vilains ne m'escout mie   Beware that the lowly not listen to me
   4 Seur escommuniement.   on [the pain of] excommunication.
      Nus qui aint vilainnement   No one who loves basely
      Ceste chançon ne comment.   begins this song.
      N'est pas dignes qu'il en die   He is not even worthy to say
   8 Nes le refrait seulement: just the refrain:
      Vilaine genz,   *Base people,*
      Vous ne les sentez mie   *you do not feel them at all,*
      Les douz maus que je sent.   *the sweet pains that I feel.*

II.   D'amours la joians joie   In love's joyful joy
      M'esjoist joieusement   I rejoice joyfully.
      Toute joie est esjoie   Every joy is enjoyed
      Par son esjoissement   through its enjoyment.
  16 Joïssons la durement   Let us enjoy it thoroughly
      Et se l'amons doucement.   and let us love her sweetly.
      Qui sa douceur a sentie   The one who has felt her sweetness
      Dire puet bien vraiement: may well say:
  20 *Vilaine genz ...*   *Base people ...*

III. N'a pas Marot mes Marie   Her name not Marot but Mary,
  24 Cele a non que respesent   the one of whom I speak.
      Marot l'ame mesmarie   The soul makes a bad marriage in
      Marie en fet Dieu present   Marot;
      Sachent futur et present: Mary makes God's presence [felt].
  28 Nus ne l'aime ou tens present   Let all future and present [people]
      Quant il part de ceste vie   know:
      Qu'a son douz fil nel present   there is no one who serves her now
      Vilaine genz ...   that she will [fail to] present to her
                                               sweet
                                          son when that person leaves this life.
                                          Base people ...

IV.   Amons la rose espanie   Let us love the blooming rose
      Ou Diex prist aumbrement   Where God took shelter.
  36 Qui ne l'aime ne gart mie   The one who does not love her cares
      Le ciel ne le firmament.   not

Qui bien ne l'aime erraument
Crit li merci, si l'ament.
40 Qui ne l'aime gart ne rie
Mais touz tens pleurt et lament.
Vilaine genz ...

at all for heaven or paradise.
Should the one who does not love her
  immediately
cry to her for mercy, she improves his
  state.
The one who does not love her neither jokes nor
laughs, but rather constantly cries and
  laments.
Base people ...

V. Amons tuit la vraie amie
Qui la voie ou ciel aprent.
Laissons l'amie ennemie
48 Qui l'ame engigne et souprent.
Qui fole amour entreprent
Ades peche, ades mesprent,
Ades sert et ades prie,
52 Assez donne et petit prent.
Vilaine genz ...

Let us all love the faithful beloved
who points out the path to heaven.
Let us leave the enemy's beloved
who traps and ambushes the soul.
The one who undertakes foolish love
sins and commits error,
serves and begs,
gives much and receives little.
Base people ...

RR: 3 v. me e. – 6 nen – 23 M. lame m. – 30 Quant son d. fol. n. presens – 45 A la t. la

De chanter ne me puis tenir
Thibaut de Champagne

De chanter ne me puis tenir

I.   De chanter ne me puis tenir
    De la tres bele esperitaus,
    Cui rien du mont ne puet servir
4 Cui ja viegne honte ne maus;
    Que li rois celestïaux,
    Qui en le daigne venir,
    Ne porroit mie soffrir
8 Qui la sert, q'il ne fust saus.

I cannot keep myself from singing
about the most beautiful, spiritual lady
whom no one could serve and
receive shame or misfortune;
for the celestial king
who deigned to come into her
could never allow one
who has served her to not be saved.

II. Quant Deus tant la volt obeïr,
     qui n'estoit muables ne faus,
     bien nos i devons tuit tenir.
12   Dame, reïne naturaux,
     Cil qui vos sera feiaus,
     Vos li savrez bien merir;
     Devant vos porra venir
16   Plus clers qu'estoile jornaus.

When God, neither unchangeable nor
     false,
wishes to obey her,
well should we all cling to her.
Lady, queen of nature,
you know well how to repay
the one who will be faithful to you;
you are brighter
than the morning star.

III. Vostre biautez, qui si resplaint,
      Fet tot le monde resclarcir.
      Par vos vint Dex entre sa gent
20   En terre por la mort sosfir
      Et a l'enemi tolir
      Nos et giter de torment.
      Par vos avons vengement
24   Et par vos devons garir.

Your resplendent beauty
illuminates the entire world.
Through you God came among his
     people
on earth to suffer death
and save us from the enemy
and from torment.
Through you we are avenged
and through you we must be saved.

IV. David le sot premierement
     Que de li devïez issir,
     Quant il parla si hautement
28   Par la bouche dou saint Espir.
     Vos n'iestes mie a florir,
     Ainz avez flor si puissant:
     C'est Deus qui onques ne ment
32   Et par tot fet son plaisir.

David knew it first,
that from him you were to come forth,
when he spoke so clearly
with the voice of the Holy Spirit.
You are barely in bloom,
yet you have such a powerful flower:
it is God who never lies
and does everything according to his
     will.

V. Dame plaine de grant bonté,
    De cortoisie et de pitié,
    Par vos est toz renluminé
36 Li mondes, neis li renoié.
    Quant il seront ravoié
    Et creront que Dex soit nez,
    Seront sauf, bien le savez,
40 Dame, aiez de nouz pitié!

Lady full of great goodness,
of graciousness and compassion,
the whole world is illuminated
through you, even the renegade.
When they come back onto the path
and believe that God was born,
they will be saved, you know it well.
Lady, have pity on us!

VI. Douce dame, or vos pri gié   Sweet lady, I pray to you now for
     Merci, que me deffendez   compassion, that you prevent me
     Que je ne soie dampnez   from being damned
44   Ne perduz par mon pechié.   and lost through my sins.

RR: 8 qui ne fust – 17 V. grant b. – 38 crieront – 41je

Dou tres douz non a la virge Marie
Thibaut de Champagne

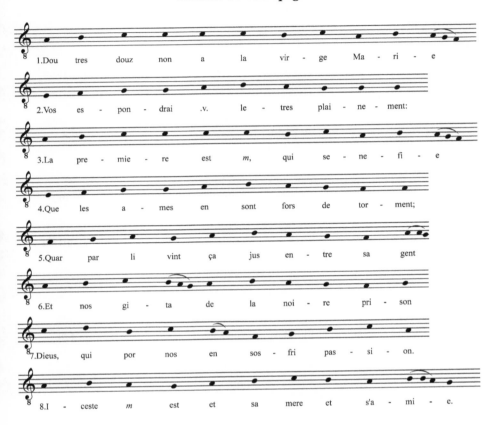

1.Dou tres douz non a la vir - ge Ma - ri - e

2.Vos es - pon - drai .v. le - tres plai - ne - ment:

3.La pre - mie - re est *m*, qui se - ne - fi - e

4.Que les a - mes en sont fors de tor - ment;

5.Quar par li vint ça jus en - tre sa gent

6.Et nos gi - ta de la noi - re pri - son

7.Dieus, qui por nos en sos - fri pas - si - on.

8.I - ceste *m* est et sa mere et s'a - mi - e.

Dou tres douz non a la virge Marie

I. Dou tres douz non a la virge
    Marie
    Vos espondrai .v. letres plaine-
    ment:
    La premiere est *m*, qui senefie
4   Que les ames en sont fors de tor-
    ment;
    Quar par li vint ça jus entre sa
    gent

I will clearly explain to you the five
letters
of the most sweet name of the Virgin
Mary.
The first is *m*, which means
that through her souls are freed from
torment;
for through her God came down here
among

Et nos gita de la noire prison
Dieus, qui por nos en sosfri
   passion.

his people, suffered for us, and turned
   us out
of the black prison.

8 Iceste *m* est et sa mere et s'amie.

This *m* is both his mother and his
   much-loved.

II.   *A* vient aprés; droiz est que je vos
     die
     Qu'en l'abecé est tot premiere-
     ment;
     Et tot premiers, qui n'est plains
     de folie,
12 Doit on dire le salu doucement
     A la dame qui en son biau cors
     gent
     Porta le roi cui merci atendon.
     Premiers fu *a* et premiers devint
     hom,
16 Que nostre lois fust fete
     n'establie.

A comes next; it is right that I tell you
   that
in the alphabet it comes first;
and – this is not foolish! – we should
   first
greet with a sweet Hail Mary
the woman, whose beautiful, noble
   body
bore the king from whom we await
   mercy.
First came *a* and first came man,
so that our law might be made and set
   down.

III.   Aprés vient *r*; ce n'est pas con-
     trovaille,
     Qu'erre savons que mult fait a
     prisier,
     Et s'el veons chascun jor, tot sanz
     faille,
20 Quant li prestres le tient en son
     mostier;
     C'est li cors Dieu, qui toz nos
     doit jugier,
     Que la dame dedens son cors
     porta.
     Or li prions, quant la mort nos
     vendra,
24 Que sa pitiez plus que droiz nos i
     vaille.

After comes *r*; it is no lie
that we know that *r* is praiseworthy,
and we see it every day, without fail,
when the priest holds it [up] in his
   church;
it is the body of God, who will judge us
   all,
that the lady carried in her body.
Let us pray now that we deserve more
pity than his justice when death comes
   for us.

IV.   *I* est toz droiz, genz et de bele
     taille.

I is upright, noble, and of gracious
   form.

Teus fu le cors, ou il n'ot
    qu'enseignier,
De la dame qui por nos se tra-
    vaille:
28 Biaux, droiz et gens, sanz tache et
    sanz pechier.
Por son douz cuer et por enfer
    brisier
Vint Deus en li, quant ele
    l'enfanta.
Biaus fu et bel, et bien s'en
    delivra;
32 Bien fist semblant Deus que de
    nos li chaille.

V.   *A* est de plaint: bien savez, sanz
    doutance,
Quant on dit *A*, qu'en s'en plait
    durement;
Et nos devons plaindre sans
    demorance
36 A la dame qui ne va el querant
Que pecherres viegne a amende-
    ment.
Tant a douz cuer, gentil et
    esmeré,
Qui l'apele de cuer sans fausseté,
40 Ja ne faudra a avoir repentance.

VI.   Or li prions merci por sa bonté
Au douz salu qui se commence
    Ave
Maria. Deus nos gart de
    mescheance!

Such was the body, and no proof is
    needed,
of the lady who takes great pains for
    us:
beautiful, upright and noble, without
blemish or sin. Because of her sweet
    heart and to
destroy hell, God came through her
    when she
gave birth. Beautiful and gracious, she
    gave
birth; God showed that he truly cares
    for us.

A is a lament: you know well, without a
    doubt,
when on says *Ah*, that one is in great
    pain;
and we should appeal without delay
to the lady who seeks only
that sinners come to repent.
She has such a sweet, noble, and pure
    heart,
the one who calls to her without guile
will never fail to obtain forgiveness.

Let us pray for her mercy in her good-
    ness
with the sweet greeting that begins
    Ave
Maria. God keep us from misfortune!

RR: 17 Puis vient – 18 s. qui m. – 19 Et ses – 32 de vos li c. – 33 A est est – 34 on dira quen sen deit – 40 a voire

Mauvez arbres ne puet florir
Thibaut de Champagne

1.Mau - vez ar - bres ne puet flo - rir,

2.Ainz se - che toz et va cro - lant;

3.Et hom qui n'ai - me, sanz men - tir,

4.Ne por - te fruit, ainz va mo - rant.

5.Fleur ne fruit de coin - te sem - blant

6.Por - te cil en qui naist a - mors.

7.En ce fruit a tant de va - lor

8.Que nus ne.l por - roit es - li - gier,

9.Que de toz maus peut al - le - gier.

10.Fruit de na - tu - re l'a - pele on;

11.Or vos ai de - vi - sé son non.

Mauvez arbres ne puet florir

I.   Mauvez arbres ne puet florir,
      Ainz seche toz et va crolant;
      Et hom qui n'aime, sanz mentir,
4 Ne porte fruit, ainz va morant.
      Fleur ne fruit de cointe semblant
      Porte cil en qui naist amors.
      En ce fruit a tant de valor
8 Que nus ne.l porroit esligier,
      Que de toz maus puet allegier.
      Fruit de nature l'apele on;
      Or vos ai devisé son non.

The bad tree does not bloom,
but rather it dries up completely and
    withers;
and the man who does not love, no lie,
does not bear fruit, rather he pro-
    ceeds to die.
Flower and fruit of fair demean
bears the one in whom love was born.
In this fruit there is so much worth
that no one could buy it,
for it alleviates all pains.
It is called the fruit of nature;
I have now explained its name to you.

II.   De ce fruit ne puet nus sentir,
      Se Dieus ne le fait proprement.
      Qui a Dieu amer et servir
      Done cuer et cors et talent,
16 Cil queut dou fruit trestot avant,
      Et Dieus l'en fait riche secors.
      Par le fruit fu li premiers plors,
      Quant Eve fist Adan pechier;
20 Mes qui dou bon fruit veut
        mengier,
      Dieu aint et sa mere et son non,
      Cil quiaudra le fruit de saison.

No one can taste of this fruit
if God has not formed him properly.
The one who gives his heart, body,
    and will
to love and serve God,
this one gathers the fruit first,
and God gives him abundant aid.
The first tears came through fruit,
when Eve made Adam sin;
but the one who wants to eat of the
    good
fruit, loves God, his mother, and his
    name,
this one will gather the fruit in season.

III.   Seignor, de l'arbre dit vos ai
24 De nature, de qu'amours vient;
      Du fruit meür conté vous ai
      Que cil quiaut qui a Dieu se tient
      Mes du fruit vert me resovient
28 Qui ja en moi ne meürra:
      C'est li fruiz en qu'Adans pecha.
      De ce fruit est plains mes vergiers;
      Des que ma dame vi premiers,

Lords, I have told you of the tree of
of nature, from which love procedes;
I have told you about the ripe fruit
that the one who cleaves to God
    gathers.
But I remember the green fruit
that will never ripen in me:
it is the fruit by which Adam sinned.
My orchard is full of this fruit;

32 Oi de s'amor plain cuer et cors
   Ne ja nul jor n'en istra fors.

from the moment I saw my lady,
of her love is my heart and body
and it will never leave me.

IV. Bien cuit dou fruit ne gosteré
    Que je cueilli, ainçois m'avient
36 Si com a l'enfant, bien le sé,
    Qui a la branche se sostient
    Et entor l'arbre va et vient
    Ne ja amont ne montera;
40 Ainsi mez cuers foloiant va.
    Tant par est granz mes desirriers
    Que je en tieng mes grans maus
       chiers;
    Si sui afinez com li ors
44 Vers li, cui est toz mes tresors.

I truly believe that I will not taste the
   fruit
that I picked; I am like
a child, I know it well,
who hangs from a branch
and comes and goes around a tree
but never climbs up;
in this way my foolish heart goes on.
My desire is so great
that my faults are dear to me;
I am purified like gold before her,
who is all my treasure.

V. Dieus, se je pooie cueillir
    Dou fruit meür de vos amer,
    Si com vos m'avez fait sentir
48 L'amor d'aval et comparer,
    Lors me porroie saouler
    Et venir a repentement.
    Par vostre douz commandement
52 Me donez amer la meillor;
    Ce est la precïeuse flor
    Par qui vos venistes ça jus,
    Dont li Deablez est confus.

God, if I could pick
the ripe fruit of loving you,
just as you made me taste
earthly love and pay for it,
then I could take my fill
and come to repentance.
Through your sweet commandment
give me the best lady to love;
she is the precious flower
through whom you came down here,
and by whom the Devil is foiled.

VI. Mere Dieu, par vostre douçor
57 Dou bon fruit me donez savor,
    Que de l'autre ai je senti plus
    C'onques, ce croi, ne senti nus.

Mother of God, through your sweetness
give me good fruit to taste,
for of the other I have tasted more of
   it,
I think, than any man who has ever
   tasted it.

VII. Phelipe, laissiez vostre errour!

Philip, leave your erroneous ways!

61 Je vos vi ja bon chanteor.
   Chantez, et nos dirons desus
   Le chant *Te Deum laudamus.*

I have already seen what a good singer
   you are.
Sing, and we will sing on high
   the song, *Te Deum laudamus.*

RR: 8 alegier – 28 meurera – 38 va viant – 56 Pere
Textual notes (hereafter TN): Second envoi missing from all manuscripts
except *S* (Paris, BnF fr. 12581).

De grant travail et de petit esploit
Thibaut de Champagne

1.De grant tra - vail et de pe - tit es - ploit

2.Voi le sie - cle char - gié et en - con - bré,

3.Que tant son - mes plain de mal - e - ûr - té

4.Que nus ne pense a fe - re ce q'il doit;

5.Ainz a - vons si le de - ab - le trous - sé

6.Qu'a li ser - vir chas - cuns pense et es - sai - e.

7.Et Deus, qui ot pour nos la cru - ĕl plai - e,

8.Av - ons mes tuit ar - rie - re dos bou - té:

9.Mult est har - diz qui pour mort ne s'es - mai - e.

ME: 4/9 d is repeated

De grant travail et de petit esploit

I.   De grant travail et de petit esploit
    Voi le siecle chargié et enconbré,
    Que tant sonmes plain de maleürté
4 Que nus ne pense a fere ce q'il doit;
    Ainz avons si le deable troussé
    Qu'a li servir chascuns pense et essaie.
    Et Deus, qui ot pour nos la cruël plaie,
8 Avons mes tuit arriere dos bouté:
    Mult est hardiz qui pour mort ne s'esmaie.

I see the world burdened and encumbered
with great hardship and few deeds;
for we are so full of wickedness
that each one thinks only of doing what he must;
we have so aligned ourselves with the Devil
that each one plans and tries to serve him.
And God, who suffered a cruel wound for us,
we have turned out backs on him:
the one who fears not death is indeed bold.

II.   Dex, qui tout set et tout puet et tout voit,
    Nos avroit tost un entre .ii. geté
12 Se la Dame, plaine de grant bonté,
    Qui est lez lui, pour nous ne li prioit.
    Si tres douz moz plesanz et savoré
    Le grant coroz du grant Seigneur rapaie.
16 Mult par est fous qui autre amor essaie,
    'Qu'en cestui n'a barat ne fausseté,
    'Ne es autres ne merci ne manaie.

God, who knows, sees, and can do all,
would have cut [each one of] us in two
if the Lady of great goodness, who is beside him, had not pleaded our case to him.
Her exceedingly sweet, pleasant, and delicate
words soothe the great ire of the great Lord.
Foolish is the one who tries another love,
for in this one there is neither guile nor falseness,
[and] neither compassion nor aid in the others.

III. La soriz qiert, por son cors garantir
20 Contre l'iver, la noiz et le forment,
    Et nous, chetis! n'alons mes riens querant

In order to save its body from the winter,
the mouse gathers nuts and grain,
and us, wretched ones! we gather nothing
that might help us when we die;

Quant nos morrons, ou nos puis-
   sons guerir;
Nous ne cerchons fors qu'enfer le
   puant.
24 Ore esgardez q'une beste sauvage
Porvoit de loing encontre son
   damage;
Et nous n'avons ne sens ne
   escïent.
Il m'est avis que plain sonmes de
   rage.

we seek out nothing but stinking hell.
Now consider that wild animals
provide for hardship long in advance;
and we have neither sense nor wisdom.
It is my opinion that we are completely mad.

IV. Li Deable a geté pour nous ravir
   .iiii. aimeçons aoschiez de torment:
Couvoitise lance premierement
Et puis Orgueil pour sa grant rois
   emplir;
32 Luxure va le batel trainant,
Felonie les gouverne et les nage.
Ensi peschent et viennent au
   rivage,
Dont Dex nos gart par son com-
   mandement,
36 En qui sainz fonz nous feïsmes
   honmage.

In order to catch us, the Devil has cast
   out
four hooks baited with torment:
he throws out Couvetousness first
And then Arrogance to fill up his
   huge net;
Lust pulls the boat,
Wickedness steers and guides them.
They fish in this way and make shore,
from which God keeps us through his
commandment, in whose sacred fount
   we did homage.

V. Les preudonmes doit on tenir
   mult chiers,
La ou il sont, et servir et amer,
Mais a paines en puet on nus
   trouver,
40 Car il sont mes si com li faus
   deniers
Que on ne puet en trebuchet
   verser,
Ainz le gete on sans coing et sanz
   balance.
Tors et pechiez en eus fine et ven-
   jance.

One should greatly admire the valiant,
wherever they are, and serve and love
   [them],
but one can find them only with difficulty
for they are mixed in like a counterfeit
   penny
that one cannot toss into the balance,
so one throws it out without biting or
   weighing it.
Evil and sin and revenge end in them.
False traitors, you should keep in
   mind that

44 Faus triceour, bien vos devroit
  membrer
 Que Dieus prendra de vos crüel
  vanjance.

God will cruelly avenge himself on
 you!

VI. A la Dame qui touz les biens
  avance
 T'en va, chanson! S'el te veut
  escouter,
48 Onques ne fu nus de meilleur
  cheance.

To the Lady who increases all goods
 go, song! If she wishes to listen to you
 never will anyone have been so
 fortunate.

RR: 3 sont mes – 12 dame p plaine – 23 ne nee / pullant
TN: Verses 44–8 missing from *K*.

Seignor, sachiés qui or ne s'en ira
Thibaut de Champagne

1.Sei - gnor, sai - chiés qui or ne s'en i - ra

2.En ce - le terre ou Dex fu mors et vis,

3.Et qui la crois d'Ou - tre - mer ne pen - ra,

4.A pai - nes mais i - ra en pa - ra - dis.

5.Qui a en soi pi - tié ne ra - mem - bran - ce

6.Au haut sei - gnor doit quer - re sa ven - jan - ce

7.Et de - liv - rer sa terre et son pa - ïs.

Seignor, sachiés qui or ne s'en ira

I.   Seignor, sachiés qui or ne s'en ira
En cele terre ou Dex fu mors et vis,
Et qui la crois d'Outremer ne penra

Lords, know that the one who does not go
into that land where God died and lived,
and who will not take the crusading cross

4 A paines mais ira en paradis.
  Qui a en soi pitié ne ramem-
    brance
  Au haut seignor doit querre sa
    venjance
  et delivrer sa terre et son païs.

II. Tuit li mauvés demorront par
    deça,
  Qui n'aiment Dieu, bien ne
    honor ne pris;
  Et chascuns dit: 'Ma feme, que
    fera?
  Je ne lairoie a nul fuer mes amis.'
12 Cil sont cheoit en trop fole aten-
    dance
  Qu'il n'est amis fors que cil, sans
    doutance,
  Qui por nos fu en la vraie crois
    mis.

III. Or s'en iront cil vaillant bacheler
16 Qui aiment Dieu et l'eneur de
    cest mont,
  Si sagement vuelent a Dieu aler;
  Et li morveux, li cendreux demor-
    ront:
  Avugle sont, de ce dout je mie.
20 Qui un secors ne fait Dieu en sa
    vie,
  Et por si pou pert la gloire dou
    mont.

IV. Diex se lessa en crois por nos
    pener
  Et nos dira au jor ou tuit ven-
    dront:
24 'Vos qui ma crois m'aidastes a
    porter,
  Vos en irez la ou mi angle sont;
  La me verrez et ma mere Marie.

will not go at all to paradise.
The one who has compassion and
  remembers
the great Lord must seek to avenge
  him and
deliver his land and his country.

All the evil ones will stay behind,
those who love not God, goodness,
  honour,
and worth. Each one says: 'What will
  my
wife do? I would never leave my
  friends.'
They have fallen into foolish concerns, for
there is no friend except him,
  without a
doubt, who was put on the true cross
  for us.

Now the valiant young men will go
  forth,
those who love God and worldly
  glory,
so wisely do they wish to go to God;
and the snivelling, cowardly ones will
  remain:
they are blind, of this I have no doubt.
The one who never helps God in his
  life,
loses worldly glory for so little.

God let himself suffer on the cross for
  us
and will say on the day when all will
  come:
'You who helped me carry my cross,
you will go there where my angels are;
there you will see me and my mother
  Mary.

Et vos par cui je n'oi onques aïe
28 Descendrez tuit en enfer le parfont.'

And you through whom I never
received aid
will all descend into the depths of
hell.

V. Chascuns cuide demorer toz
haitiez
Et que jamés ne doie mal avoir;
Ainsi les tient anemis et pechiez
32 Que il n'ont sen, hardement ne
pooir.
Biaus Sire Diex, ostés leur tel
pensee
Et nos metez en la vostre contree
Si saintement que vos puisons
veoir!

Each one believes that he will remain
healthy and that never will evil befall
him;
in this way the enemy and sin seize
them
until they have neither sense, bold-
ness, nor
strength. Beautiful Lord God, remove
such
thoughts from them and put us in
your country
so saintly that we might see you!

VI. Douce Dame, roïne coronee,
37 proiez por nos, virge bien aüree!
Et puis aprés ne nos puet mescheoir.

Sweet Lady, crowned queen,
pray for us, fortunate virgin!
And then no evil can ever befall us.

RR: 25 ou tuit

Dame, einsi est qu'il m'en couvient aler
Thibaut de Champagne

1.Dame, ein - si est qu'il m'en cou - vient a - ler

2.Et de - par - tir de la dou - ce con - tre - e

3.Ou tant ai max sos - frez et en - du - rez;

4.Quant je vos lais, droiz est que je m'en he - e

5.Dex, por quoi fu la ter - re d'Ou - tre - mer,

6.Qui tant am - anz a - vra fait des - se - vrer

7.Dont puis ne fu l'am - ors re - con - for - te - e

8.Ne ne po - rent la joi - e re - mem - brer?

ME: 6/3 an extra b is written before this note

Dame, einsi est qu'il m'en couvient aler

I.   Dame, einsi est qu'il m'en cou-
        vient aler
     Et departir de la douce contree
     Ou tant ai maus sosfrez et
        endurez;

Lady, since it is fitting that I leave
and depart from the sweet country
where I have suffered and endured
   such pain;
as I leave you, it is right that I hate

4 Quant je vos lais, droiz est que je
    m'en hee.
  Dex, por quoi fu la terre d'Out-
    remer,
  Qui tant amanz avra fait dessevrer
  Dont puis ne fu l'amors reconfor-
    tee
8 Ne ne porent la joie remembrer?

myself.
God, why does it exist, the Holy
  Land
that will separate so many lovers
who will then find no comfort in
  love
and not be able to remember their joy?

II. Ja sanz amors ne porroie durer,
    Tant par i truis fermement ma
      pensee,
    Ne mes fins cuers ne m'en lait
      retorner,
12 Ainz sui a lui, la ou il velt et bee.
    Trop ai apris durement a amer;
    Por ce ne voi comment puisse
      durer
    Sanz joie avoir de la plus desirree
16 C'onques nus hom osast merci
      crïer.

I could never last without love,
so firmly is my thought engrained in
  it,
and my true heart does not let me
  renounce it,
rather I belong to it, where it wishes
  and desires.
I learned all too well and cruelly about
  love;
for this I do not see how I can endure
without having the joy of the most
  desirous
one to whom a man ever dared to cry
  for mercy.

III. Je ne voi pas, quant de li sui
      partiz,
    Que puisse avoir bien ne solas ne
      joie,
    Car onques rien ne fis si a envis
20 Com vos laissier, se je jamés vos
      voie.
    Trop par en sui dolens et esbahiz.
    Par maintes foiz m'en serai
      repentiz,
    Quant onques vols aler en ceste
      voie
24 Et je recort vos debonaires dis.

I do not see, when I am separated
  from her,
how I can have good, solace, or joy,
for never have I done anything so
  reluctantly
as leave you, if I might never see you.
I am so very saddened and dismayed
  by it.
Many a time will I repent my decision
of ever wanting to take this path
when I remember your gracious
  words.

IV. Biaus sire Dex, vers vos me sui
      ganchiz;

Good Lord God, I turn to you;
I leave to you all that I loved so much.

Tot laiz por vos ce que je tant
  amoie.
Li guerredons en doit estre floris,
28 Quant por vos per et mon cuer et
  ma joie.
De vos servir sui toz prez et garnis;
A vos me ren, biau pere Jhesucris!
Si bon seignor avoir je ne porroie:
32 Cil qui vos sert ne puet estre traïz.

V. Bien doit mes cuers estre liez et
    dolenz:
    Dolens de ce que je part de ma
    dame,
    Et liez de ce que je sui desirrans
36 De servir Dieu, cui est mes cors et
    m'ame.
    Iceste amors est trop fine et puis-
    sanz;
    Par la covient venir les plus
    sachanz:
    C'est li rubinz, l'esmeraude, la
    dame
40 Qui tost garist des vix pechiez
    puans.

VI. Dame des ciex, grant reïne puis-
    sant,
    Au grant besoing me soiez sec-
    oranz!
    De vos amer puisse avoir droite
    flamme!
44 Quant dame par, dame me soit
    aidanz.

The reward for this should be flowery,
when for you I lose both my heart and
  joy.
I am ready and prepared to serve you;
I surrender myself to you, good father
  Jesus!
I could never have a better lord:
the one who serves you cannot be
  betrayed.

My heart should be happy and saddened:
saddened that I am leaving my lady,
and happy in my desire
to serve God, who is my body and
  soul.
This love is exceedingly noble and
  powerful;
by this path it is fitting that the wise
  come:
it is the ruby, the emerald, the lady
who cleanses everyone from vile, reeking sin.

Lady of heaven, great, powerful
  queen,
be of help to me in my great need!
May I be inflamed with love for you!
When I leave a lady, by a lady may I be
  helped.

RR: 1 est qui men – 6 aurai – 14 ce nen voi – 15 De joie – 22 mainte – 23 ionques – 44 d me me soit

Commencerai a fere un lai
Thibaut de Champagne

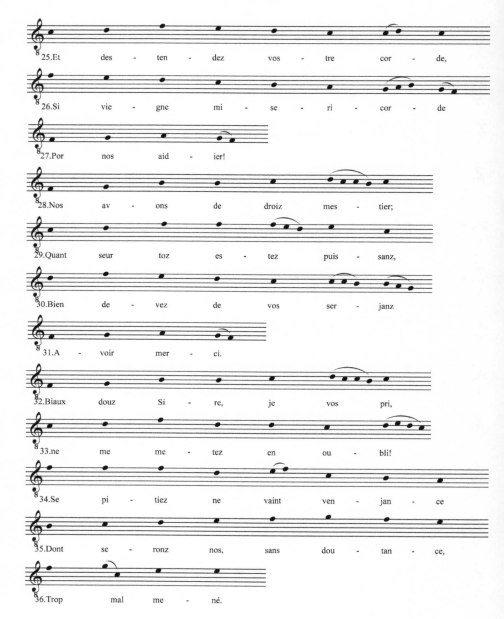

37. Da - me ple - ne de bon - té,

38. Vos - tre douz moz sa - vo - ré

39. Ne soi - ent pas ou - bli - é!

40. Proi - ez por nos!

41. Ja - més ne se - rons res - couz

42. Se ne le so - mes par vos,

43. De voir le sai.

44. Ci lais - ser - ai;

45. Et Diex nos doint sans de - lai

46. A - voir son se - cors ver - ay!

Commencerai a fere un lai

Commencerai	I will begin
A fere un lai	to compose a *lai*
De la meillor.	about the best one.
4 Forment m'esmai,	I am greatly distressed
Que trop par ai	For I have caused
Fet de dolor,	too much pain,
Dont mi chant torront a plor.	for which my songs will turn to tears.
8 Mere, Virge savoree,	Mother, pleasing Virgin,
Se vos faitez demoree	If you delay
De proier le haut Seignor,	before pleading [my case] to the
Bien doi avoir grant paor	noble Lord,
12 Du Deable, du Felon,	I should indeed greatly fear
Qui en la noire prison	the Devil, the Wicked One,
Nos velt mener,	who wants to lead us
Dont nus ne puet eschaper;	into the dark prison,
16 Et j'ai forfet, douce Dame,	from which no one can escape.
A perdre le cors et l'ame,	And I have erred, sweet lady,
Se ne m'aidiez.	to the point of losing body and soul,
Douz Diex, aiez	if you do not help me.
20 Merci de mes vix pechiez!	Sweet God, have
Ou sera merci trovee,	mercy on my vile sins!
S'ele est de vos refusee,	Where will mercy be found,
Qui tant valez?	if you, who is so worthy,
24 Sire, droiture oublïez,	you refuse it [to me]?
Et destendez vostre corde,	Lord, forget justice,
Si viegne misericorde	and loosen the cord [of your bow],
Por nos aidier!	and let mercy
28 Nos avons de droit mestier;	come to our aid!
Quant seur toz estez puissanz,	We have need of justice;
Bien devez de vos serjanz	when you hold power over all,
Avoir merci.	you should indeed have mercy
32 Biaux douz Sire, je vos pri,	on your soldiers.
ne me metez en oubli!	Good, sweet Lord, I implore you,
Se pitiez ne vaint venjance,	do not forget me!
Dont seronz nos, sans doutance,	If pity does not vanquish vengeance,
36 Trop mal mené.	then we will be, without a doubt,
Dame plene de bonté,	in a bad way.
Vostre douz moz savoré	Lady full of goodness,

Ne soient pas oublié!   may your sweet, gracious words
40 Proiez por nos!   not be forgotten!
Jamés ne serons rescouz   Pray for us!
Se ne le somes par vos,   We will never be helped
De voir le sai.   if it is not through you,
44 Ci laisserai;   I know this truly.
Et Diex nos doint sans delai   I leave off [my song];
Avoir son secors veray!   and may God grant that we have
                                         true help without delay.

RR and TN: 11 doit – 12 du du deable – 23 line missing from *Mt* (provided from MS. *O*, BnF fr. 846, fol. 23r)

Chanter m'estuet de la virge puchele
Anonymous

10Des fe - lons Ju - ïs pour le mon - de sau - ver.

11.*Pri - és   vos - tre...*

III.

13.Tres dou - ce da - me, ro - ï - ne cou - ron - ne - e,

14.Ro - se ver - mel - le, tres dou - ce rou - se - e,

15.Vo chars fu mout bien de Jhe - su a - our - ne - e;

16.Tout li pech - e - our vous doi - vent re - clam - er.

17.*Pri - és...*

IV.

19.Ro - se ver - melle, o - dour qui sou - ef flai - re,

20.On doit bien pour vous chan - sons et ri - mes fai - re,

21.Car en vo dous cors fist Jhe - sus son re - pai - re:

22.Ce fu pour le mont de tor - men - te je - ter.

23.Pri - és...

V.

25.Ches - te   mi - racle   est   a - per - te   pro - ve - e:

26.Ja   Ju - ï - se   n'iert   de   son   fruit   de - li - vre - e

27.Se   la   me - re   Dieu   n'est   a - vant   re - cla - me - e;

28.Por   ce   l'aim - me   je   et   la   voel   tous   jours   a - mer.

29.Pri - és   vos - tre   fil   dou - ce   vir - ge   Ma - ri - e

30.Qu'il   nous   doinst...

Textual and musical notes (hereafter MN): Järnström and Långfors give 'Qu'i' in verse 3 and in the refrain's second verse. One stanza is written in the left margin, and Järnström and Långfors place it in second position (Tischler omits the stanza altogether from his edition without comment). Furthermore, although the song appears composed in chanson style, that is, the melody is the same for all stanzas, musical notation accompanies the entire song. For this reason, Järnström and Långfors speculate that the song might belong to another lyric genre, an opinion with which Tischler obviously concurs, as he includes the song among the *lais* of his complete comparative edition, for *lais* are usually entirely notated in their manuscripts. The preserved melody, while easily schematized as A (aa) B(bb′) R(bb′) on a large scale, also contains many minor differences, and providing the entire melody seems, therefore, the best approach.

Chanter m'estuet de la virge puchele

I. Chanter m'estuet de la virge
        puchele
    Que Jhesus trouva et tant nete et
        tant bele
    Qu'il se soola du lait de sa
        mamele
4   Et dedens son cors se degna
        reposer.
    Priés vostre fil, douce virge Marie,
    Qu'il nous doinst sa grace et s'amor
        conquester.

II. On doit bien avoir tel dame en
        ramembrance
8   Qui porta le fruit qui se mist en
        balance
    Et ens el costé fu ferus de la
        lanche
    Des felons Juïs pour le monde
        sauver.
    Priés vostre ...

III. Tres douce dame, roïne couron-
        nee,
    Rose vermelle, tres douce rousee,
    Vo chars fu mout bien de Jhesu
        aournee;
16 Tout li pecheour vous doivent
        reclamer.
    Priés ...

IV. Rose vermelle, odour qui souef
        flaire,
20 On doit bien pour vous chansons
        et rimes faire,
    Car en vo dous cors fist Jhesus son
        repaire:

I must sing of the virgin maiden
that Jesus found so clean and so beau-
    tiful
that he satiated himself with her
    breast milk
and daigned to rest in her body.
Pray to your son, sweet Virgin Mary,
that he grant us his grace and love.

One should indeed have such a lady in
    mind,
she who bore fruit that put let himself
    be judged
and pierced in the side with a lance
by the felonous Jews to save the world.
Pray to your ...

Ever so sweet lady, crowned queen,
red rose, exceedingly soft dew,
your flesh was well adorned with
    Jesus;
all sinners should call to you.
Pray ...

Red rose, sweet-smelling fragrance,
one should indeed compose songs
    and poems for you,
since Jesus made your sweet body his
    abode:
it was to save the world from torment.

Ce fu pour le mont de tormente   *Pray ...*
   jeter.
Priés ...

V.   Cheste miracle est aperte provee: This miracle is clearly proven:
     Ja Juïse n'iert de son fruit delivree   never will the Jewess be delivered of
     Se la mere Dieu n'est avant rec-   her fruit
        lamee;   if the mother of God is not first beck-
  28 Por ce l'aimme je et la voel tous   oned;
        jours amer.   for this I love her and want to love her
     Priés vostre fil douce virge Marie   always.
     Qu'il nous doinst ...   *Pray to your son, sweet Virgin Mary,*
                                                that he grant us ...

Du douz Jhesu souvent devons chanter et lire
Anonymous

Du dous Jhesu souvent devons chanter et lire

Du douz Jhesu souvent devons chanter
et lire.

I.   Chanter m'estuet, quar volenté
m'en prie,

We should often sing and read of sweet
Jesus.

I must sing, for my will urges me to do
so,

Du rossignollet qui d'[amours
  s'escrie].

4 [Quant pens au] dous Jhesu,
  Qui est monté lassus,
  Et nous sommes ça jus,
  Tous li cuers m'en souspire.
8 Du dous Jhesu devons adez bien
  dire.
  *Du douz Jhesu souvent devons
  chanter et lire.*

II. Rossignolet, bien faites vostre
  office,
  Les fins amans bien aprenez a
  vivre;
12 Ditez: Fuiez, fuiez,
  Tout le monde laissiez,
  Ne vous i apuiez,
  Quar trop i a de guile.
16 Li dist Jhesu sont vrai com evan-
  gile.
  *Du douz Jhesu souvent devons
  chanter et lire.*

III. Rossignolet, par vo grant cortoisie
  Menez m'ou bois o vous en la
  gaudie.
20 La serons en deduit
  Et le jour et la nuit,
  Et si l'orons, celui
  Qu'amours firent ocirre.
24 Folz est li cuers qui Jhesum ne
  desirre.
  *Du douz Jhesu souvent devons
  chanter et lire.*

IV. De li loer ne se devroit nus taire.
  Merveilles fist quant vint en no
  repaire:
28 Povres volt devenir

of the little nightingale who cries out
  lovingly.

When I think of sweet Jesus,
who ascended there above,
and we are down here,
all my heart longs for him.
Of sweet Jesus we should always speak
  well.
*We should often sing and read of sweet
  Jesus.*

Little nightingale, you perform your
  duty well,
you teach perfect lovers how to live;
you say: flee, flee,
leave behind the entire world;
do not trust in it,
for there is so much falseness.
Jesus' words are the gospel truth.
*We should often sing and read of sweet
  Jesus.*

Little nightingale, through your great
  nobility
lead me to the woods with you in joy.
There we will delight
day and night
and we will pray to him
that love pressed on to death.
Foolish is the heart that does not
  desire Jesus.
*We should often sing and read of sweet
  Jesus.*

No one should ever leave off praising
  him.
He performed marvels when he came
  among us:

Et en la crois mourir.
Merveilles fu a faire:
Diex du ciel vint pour nous
    d'enfer retraire.
32 *Du douz Jhesu souvent devons*
    chanter et lire.

he agreed to become poor
and die on the cross.
It was a marvellous deed:
God came from heaven to pull us out
    of hell.
We should often sing and read of sweet
    Jesus.

V.   Rossignolet, pour Dieu, quar me
    conseille.
    Ou est li hons qui feïst tel
    merveille,
    Qui souffrist mort et si grant
    vilennie
36 Pour rendre a nous qu'avions
    perdu la vie?
    Jhesus est Diex et filz dame
    Marie.
    Du douz Jhesu souvent devons
    chanter et lire.

Little nightingale, for [the love of]
    God, tell me.
Where is the man who performed
    such marvels,
who suffered death and such great
    humiliation
to return to us life which we had lost?
Jesus is God and the son of lady
    Mary.
We should often sing and read of sweet
    Jesus.

VI. Rossignolet, Jhesu de piteus estre,
40 Assié nous tous delez toy a ta
    destre
    En ce biau paradis,
    Qui est parez tous dis;
    La sont joie et deliz.
44 Diex! tant i fait bon estre.
    Li douz Jhesus siet du pere a la
    destre.
    Du douz Jhesu souvent devons
    chanter et lire.

Little nightingale, humiliated Jesus,
seat all of us at your right hand
in that beautiful paradise,
which is forever adorned;
joy and delight joy there.
God! It is such a good place.
Sweet Jesus sits at the right hand of
    the Father.
We should often sing and read of sweet
    Jesus.

VII. La verront cil Marie
48 Qui l'averont servie
    De cuer et en purté;
    La seront a seurté
    En pardurable vie;
52 Bele est la compaignie.

There they will see Mary,
they who will have served her
from the heart and purely;
There they will be safe
in everlasting life;
the company is beautiful.

Jhesus nous doint que nous n'i
   faillons mie.
Du douz Jhesu souvent devons
   chanter et lire.
Amen.

Jesus grant that we not miss out at all
   on it.
We should often sing and read of sweet
   Jesus.

TN: The editors, Järnström and Långfors, hypothesize, based on the piece's metre, that a verse between 28 and 29 is missing. However, as they point out, because no lacuna is indicated in the manuscript and, more important, the entire text displays great metrical heterogeneity, I see no reason to concur.

Li solaus qui en moy luist est mes deduis
Anonymous

Li solaus qui en moy luist est mes deduis

Li solaus qui en moy luist est mes deduis, | The sun that shines within me is my delight,
Et Diex est mes conduis. | and God is my guide.

I.   Et que me deman[dez vous], amis | What do You ask of me, gracious
     mi[gnoz]? | friend?

4 [Quar a vous] ai tout donné, et
    cuer et cors.
  Et que voulez vous de moy?
    Voulez ma mort,
  Savoreus Jhesucrist?
  Li solaus [qui en moy luist est mes
    deduis
8 *Et Diex est mes conduis].*

For I have given my all to You, both
    heart and body.
And what do You want from me? Is it
    my death,
sweet Jesus Christ?
The sun that shines within me is my
    delight,
and God is my guide.

II. Je li feray une tour a mon
       cuerçon,
     Ce sera ou plus biau lieu de ma
       maison;
     Il n'en istra ja nul jour, mon ami
       douz,
  12 Ains sera en deduit.
     Li soulaus [qui en moy luist est mes
       deduis
     Et Diex est mes conduis].

I will build Him a tower in my little
    heart,
it will be in the finest place in my
    house;
my sweet beloved will never leave it,
rather, He will live there in delight.
The sun that shines within me is my
    delight,
and God is my guide.

III. Diex! or ardent cilz bisson par
         paradis;
   16 Amours les font jubiler et tres-
         saillir.
      Fins amans ont tout le temps en
         Jhesucrist,
      Quar c'est tout leur desir.
      Li solaus [qui en moy luist est mes
         deduis
   20 *Et Diex est mes conduis].*

God! How these bushes are burning in
    paradise;
love makes them exult and sparkle.
Their true love is ever Jesus Christ,
for He is all they long for.
The sun that shines within me is my
    delight,
and God is my guide.

IV. Hé mi, lasse! que feray? N'i puis
        aler.
     Esperance et fine amour, quar
        m'i portez,
     Qu'aprez ceste mortel vie i puisse
        aler:
  24 Ce sont tous mes deduis.
     Li solaus [qui en moy luist est mes
        deduis
     Et Diex est mes conduis].

Oh, wretched me! What will I do? I
    cannot get there.
Hope and true love, please carry me
    there,
so that after this mortal life I may go
    there;
that is all my delight.
The sun that shines within me is my
    delight,
and God is my guide.

V.   Dame Marie, priez a vostre fil

28 Qe tant com vivons en ce mortel essil,

Sa grace nouz doint, par quoy soions si fil,

Et en son livre escrit.

Li solauz [qui en moy luist est mes deduis

32 *Et Diex est mes conduis].*

Lady Mary, entreat your Son

that, as long as we live in this mortal exile,

he grant us His grace, by which we may be his children,

and be written in His book.

The sun that shines within me is my delight,

and God is my guide.

Li debonnaires Dieus m'a mis en sa prison
Anonymous

Li debonnaires Dieus m'a mis en sa prison

Li debonnaires Dieus m'a mis en sa prison.

The gracious Lord has put me in His prison.

I.   Vous ne savez que me fist
Jhesucrist, li miens amis,
4 Qu[ant] jacobine me fist
Par grant amours.
Li debonnaires [Dieus m'a mis en sa prison].

You do not know what Jesus Christ,
my beloved, did to me,
when He made me a Jacobin
through His great love.
The gracious Lord has put me in His prison.

II. Il m'a si navré d'un dart,
  8 M[ais que] la plaie n'i pert.
     Ja nul jour n'[en] guariré
     Se par li non.
     Li debonn[aires Dieus m'a mis en sa
        prison].

He has struck me with His arrow,
though the wound cannot be seen.
I will never be cured
if not by Him.
The gracious Lord has put me in His
   prison.

III. Dieus, son dart qui m'a navré,
      Comme il est dous et souefz!
      N[uit] et jour mi fait penser
      Con Dieus [est] douz.
  16 *Li debonnaires [Dieus m'a mis en sa*
         prison].

God, the arrow that struck me,
how sweet and gentle it is!
Night and day it reminds me of
how sweet God is.
The gracious Lord has put me in His
   prison.

IV. Quant regart par paradis,
     Dont [li] rois est mes amis,
     De larmes [et] de soupirs
  20 Mes cuers font to[us].
     Li debonnaires [Dieus m'a mis en sa
        prison].

When I look toward heaven,
where my beloved is king,
my whole heart melts
into tears and sighs.
The gracious Lord has put me in His
   prison.

V. Se je souvent plouroie
    Et tre[s] bien Dieu amoie,
  24 Il me donr[oit] sa joie,
    Autrement non.
    Li debo[nnaires Dieus m'a mis en sa
       prison].

If I were to weep often
and love God perfectly,
he would give me His joy,
otherwise not.
The gracious Lord has put me in His
   prison.

VI. Quant je pense a Marie,
  28 Qui fu [de] nete vie,
     J'ai une jalousie
     Que [...] bon.
     Li debonn[aires Dieus m'a mis en sa
        prison].

When I think of Mary,
who led a pure life,
I am jealous
that [...] good.
The gracious Lord has put me in His
   prison.

VII. Prions [a] la pucele,
      Qui fu saint[e et] honneste,
      Qu'en paradis nous [mete]:
      C'est mout biau don.
  36 *Li debonn[aires Dieus m'a mis en sa*
         prison].

Let us pray to the maiden,
who was holy and honorable,
to lead us to paradise:
it's a glorious gift.
The gracious Lord has put me in His
   prison.

Ave Maria, j'aim tant
Anonymous

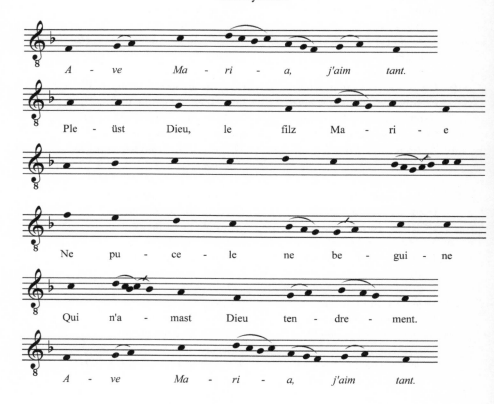

A   -   ve   Ma   -   ri   -   a,   j'aim   tant.

Ple   -   üst   Dieu,   le   filz   Ma   -   ri   -   e

Ne   pu   -   ce   -   le   ne   be   -   gui   -   ne

Qui   n'a   -   mast   Dieu   ten   -   dre   -   ment.

A   -   ve   Ma   -   ri   -   a,   j'aim   tant.

Ave Maria, j'aim tant

| *Ave Maria, j'aim tant.* | *Hail Mary, I am so in love.* |

I.   Pleüst Dieu, le filz Marie,   May it please God, Mary's son,
     ....
  4 Ne pucele ne beguine   neither maiden nor beguine
     Qui n'amast Dieu tendrement.   who did not love God tenderly.
     Ave Maria, j'aim tant.   *Hail Mary, I am so in love.*

II. La beguine s'est levee,   The beguine got up,

8 De vesture bien paree,
  Au moustier s'en est alee,
  Jhesucrist va regretant.
  Ave Maria, j'aim tant.

dressed herself well,
and went to the church,
longing all the while for Jesus Christ.
Hail Mary, I am so in love.

III. Quant ele vint a l'esglise,
    Jus contre terre s'est mise,
    Si vit Dieu, le filz Marie,
    En crois pendant laidement.
16 *Ave Maria, j'aim tant.*

When she came to the church,
she sat down on the ground,
and beheld God, Mary's son,
hanging gruesomely on the cross.
Hail Mary, I am so in love.

IV. Aprés ce s'est relevee
    Et l'ymage a regardee
    Et les plaies ravisee;
20 A poy le cuer ne li fent.
    Ave Maria, j'aim tant.

After this, she got back up
and looked at the statue
and studied the wounds;
her heart nearly broke.
Hail Mary, I am so in love.

V. Aprés si s'est escrïee:
    'Ha, lasse, mal eüree,
24 Qui recevra tel colee
    Con le jour du jugement!
    Ave Maria, j'aim tant.

She then cried out:
'Ha, wretched, unfortunate one,
who will receive such a blow
on the day of judgment!
Hail Mary, I am so in love.

VI. Prestre, clerc et chevalier,
28 Damoiseles, escuier,
    Bourgois et gent de mestier
    I seront tuit en present.
    Ave Maria, j'aim tant.'

Priests, clerics, and knights,
ladies, squires,
merchants and workers
will all be there assembled.
Hail Mary, I am so in love.'

Lasse, que devendrai gié
Anonymous

I. AA

1.Las - se, que de - ven - drai gié,
7.Filz, on - ques ne fus es - tous,

2.Que cil Ju - If en - ra gié
8.Mes plus sou - ef et plus dous

3.Ont mon fil tant out - ra - gié
9.Que n'est lais ne miaus ne mouz;

4.Qu'a un mort le mont chan - gié,
10.Tant mar fu vos - tre biau voz.

5.Et sans nul for - fait
11.Diex, pour - coy mou - ri

6.M'ont si grant tort fait?
12.Flours qui si flo - ri?

II. B

13.On - ques ne cuid - ai sa - voir

14.Que deulz est; or le sav - rai.

15.Main - tes joi - es seul a - voir

16.Ne sai se plus en av - rai.

17.Bien dit l'es - crip - t[u - re] voir

18.Par tans m'en a - per - ce - vrai

19.Que j'av - oie a re - ce - voir

B' 20.Un glaive; or le re - ce - vrai.

21.Biaus fix tu fus con - ce - us

22.Et tres glo - ri - eu - se - ment.

23.Des bes - tes fus con - ne - uz

24.En la crei - che tout pre - mie - re - ment

25.Et des rois a - per - ce - us

III. C 26.Qui t'of - ri - rent leur dons dou - ce - ment.

27.Tou - te riens fu es - bau - di - e

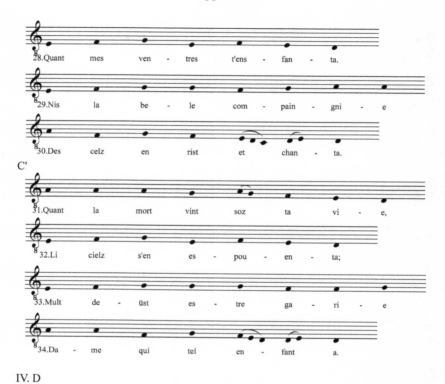

28. Quant mes ven - tres t'ens - fan - ta.

29. Nis la be - le com - pain - gni - e

30. Des celz en rist et chan - ta.

C'

31. Quant la mort vint soz ta vi - e,

32. Li cielz s'en es - pou - en - ta;

33. Mult de - üst es - tre ga - ri - e

34. Da - me qui tel en - fant a.

IV. D

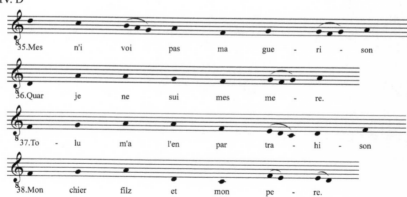

35. Mes n'i voi pas ma gue - ri - son

36. Quar je ne sui mes me - re.

37. To - lu m'a l'en par tra - hi - son

38. Mon chier filz et mon pe - re.

D'
39. Or si l'a mis en sa pri - son,

40. La mort dure et a - me - re.

41. Li pro - phe - te que nous li - son

42. Y pri - rent leur ma - te - re.

V. E
43. Biau douz filz, [vous me plong - iez

44. En] dou - lour par - fon - de.

45. Cist deulz dont vous ne pais - siez,

46. Cri - eng ne me con - fon - de.

E'
47. Tou - te joie est a - bais - sié,

48. Et dou - leur ha - bun - de

49. Quant li ar - bres est plais - siez

50. Qui pas - soit tout le mon - de.

VI. FF

51.Nu — le rien que diez cri - a
55.Li folz qui mon fil li - a

52.Ne me pour - roit a pais - ier.
56.Et li fist le sanc rai - er;

53.Las - se, com mal deulz ci a;
57.Ce sa - chiez, Diex l'ou - bli - a;

54.Mult se doit or es - mai - er
58.Mau jour li a - jour - na hier.

VII. GG

59.On - ques ne sen - ti dou - lour,
63.Li cors qui de tel sei - gnour

60.Biau filz, quant vous fus - tes nez,
64.a - voit es - té [es - tre - nez.]

61.Ne ne mu - ay la cou - lour:
65.Or ai duel; nus n'ot grei - gnor

62.Ne pou - oit estre es - gen - ez
66.Dont vous es - tes si men - es.

VIII. H

67.Biau filz, je vous a - lai - tai;

68.Mors es - tes, do - lente en sui.

IX. I

I'

J

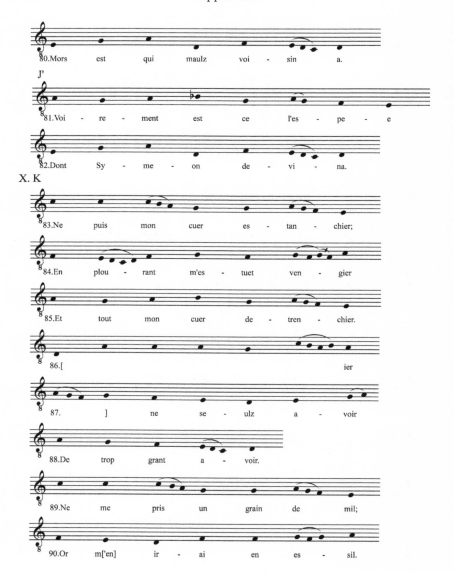

80.Mors   est   qui   maulz   voi - sin   a.

J'

81.Voi - re - ment   est   ce   l'es - pe - e

82.Dont   Sy - me - on   de - vi - na.

X. K

83.Ne   puis   mon   cuer   es - tan - chier;

84.En   plou - rant   m'es - tuet   ven - gier

85.Et   tout   mon   cuer   de - tren - chier.

86.[ier

87.   ]   ne   se - ulz   a - voir

88.De   trop   grant   a - voir.

89.Ne   me   pris   un   grain   de   mil;

90.Or   m['en]   ir - ai   en   es - sil.

91.A Dieu com - man - de mon fil

92.Qui fu a - buv - res d'ai - sil

93.Et mis [en] la crois.

94.Ci me faut la vois.

MN: Lyrics or notes in brackets indicate that they are missing from the manuscript. The lyrics provided within brackets are hypothesized. Due to excessive marginal trimming, clefs are not always visible. My edition assumes that the clef does not change in those regions.

Lasse, que devendrai gié

I.   Lasse, que devendrai gié,
       Que cil Juïf enragié
       Ont mon fil tant outragié
4 Qu'a un mort le mont changié,
       Et sans nul forfait
       M'ont si grant tort fait?
       Filz, onques ne fus estous,
8 Mes plus souef et plus dous
       Que n'est lais ne miaus ne mouz;
       Tant mar fu vostre biau voz.
       Diex, pourcoy mouri
12 Flours qui si flori?

    Alas, what will become of me,
    for these enraged Jews
    have so disgraced my son
    that one death has changed the world
    and have done me such wrong
    without any reparation?
    Son, never were you arrogant
    but rather more delicate and sweeter
    than flowers or honey or moss;
    how unfortunate your beautiful voice
       has
    been. God, why did the flower
    that bloomed so well die?

II.   Onques ne cuidai savoir
       Que deulz est; or le savrai.
       Maintes joies seul avoir
16 Ne sai se plus en avrai.

    Never before did I think that I knew
    what pain is; now I will know.
    I am used to experiencing many a joy;
    I do not know if I will have any more.

Bien dit l'escript[ure] voir
Par tans m'en apercevrai
Que j'avoie a recevoir
20 Un glaive; or le recevrai.
Biaus fix, tu fus conceus
Et tres glorieusement.
Des bestes fus conneuz
24 En la creiche tout premierement
Et des rois aperceus
Qui t'ofrirent leur dons douce-
    ment.

III. Toute riens fu esbaudie
28 Quant mes ventres t'ensfanta.
Nis la bele compaingnie
Des celz en rist et chanta.
Quant la mort vint soz ta vie,
32 Li cielz s'en espouenta;
Mult deüst estre garie
Dame qui tel enfant a.

IV. Mes n'i voi pas ma guerison
36 Quar je ne sui mes mere.
Tolu m'a l'en par trahison
Mon chier filz et mon pere.
Or si l'a mis en sa prison,
40 La mort dure et amere.
Li prophete que nous lison
Y prirent leur matere.

V. Biau douz filz, [vous me plongiez
44 En] doulour parfonde.
Cist deulz dont vous ne paissiez,
Crieng ne me confonde.
Toute joie est abaissié,
48 Et douleur habunde
Quant li arbres est plaissiez
Qui passoit tout le monde.

Scripture says it truly well
that by and by I would realize
that I had to receive a blow
from a sword; now I will receive it.
Beautiful son, you were conceived
and ever so gloriously.
You were known to the livestock
in the manger first
and shown to the kings
who gently offered you their gifts.

Everything was made better
when my womb gave birth to you.
Even the beautiful company
of heaven delighted in and sang about
    it.
When death came over your life
heaven was horrified;
the woman who has such a child
should be healed indeed.

But I do not see my cure
for I am no longer a mother.
They have robbed me of my son
and my father through treachery.
Merciless and bitter death
has but him in his prison.
The prophets that we read
took their words from there.

Beautiful sweet son, you plunge me
into profound pain.
I fear that this pain of which you are
    not
recovering will befuddle me.
All joy is diminished,
and pain abounds
when the tree that overtook
everyone is cut down.

VI. Nule rien que diez cria
52 Ne me pourroit apaisier.
Lasse, com mal deulz ci a;
Mult se doit or esmaier
Li folz qui mon fil lia
56 Et li fist le sanc raier;
Ce sachiez, Diex l'oublia;
Mau jour li ajourna hier.

VII. Onques ne senti doulour,
60 Biau filz, quant vous fustes nez,
Ne ne muay la couleur:
Ne pouoit estre esgenez
Li cors qui de tel seignour
64 avoit esté [estrenez.]
Or ai duel; nus n'ot greignor
Dont vous estes si menes.

VIII. Biau filz, je vous alaitai;
68 Mors estes, dolente en sui.
Mainte fois vous afaitai
Ou berçuel si comm je dui.
Pour Herode vous guetai
72 Et jusq'en Egypte en fui.
Onques ne m'en deshaitai
Autretant comm je faiz hui.

IX. A martire sui livree;
76 Ne sai qui ce destina.
Li Juïf m'ont desertee;
Onques nus d'euz ne fina
D'avoir vers mon fil mellee;
80 Mors est qui maulz voisin a.
Voirement est ce l'espee
Dont Symeon devina.

X. Ne puis mon cuer estanchier;
84 En plourant m'estuet vengier

Nothing that God created
could soothe me.
Alas, what bitter pain is this;
Well should that one despair, the
foolish one who hung my son on the
    cross
and made his blood flow forth;
know this, God has forgotten him;
a bad day did he spend yesterday.

Never did I feel pain,
good son, when you were born,
nor did I change colour:
The body that had
contained such a lord
could never be worsened.
Now I feel pain; never did I have worse
than [now] when you are treated so.

Beautiful son, I nursed you;
you are dead, I am grieved by it.
Many a time did I care for you
in the cradle as I had to.
I hid you from Herod
and fled as far as Egypt.
Never have I been as disheartened
as I am now.

I am left to martyrdom;
I do not know who decided this.
The Jews have deserted me,
Never did any of them stop
challenging my son;
dead is the one with an evil neigh-
    bour.
Truly this is the sword
that Simeon prophesied.

I cannot stop my heart from bleeding,
crying, I must avenge myself

Et tout mon cuer detrenchier.   and bind my heart.
[. . . . . (ier)   . . . .
. . .] ne seulz avoir   . . . . . not used to having
88 De trop grant avoir.   too many possessions.
Ne me pris un grain de mil;   I do not care a grain of millet;
Or m['en] irai en essil.   I now march into exile.
A Dieu commande mon fil   I commend my son to God
92 Qui fu abuvres d'aisil   who was given vinegar to drink
Et mis [en] la crois.   and put on the cross.
Ci me faut la vois.   Here my voice falls silent.

TN: 80 This verse paraphrases Proverbs 16:29: 'A violent man entices his neigh-bour and leads him into the way that is not good' (Vir iniquus lactat amicum suum et ducit eum per viam non bonam) – 92. This verses alludes to the branch of hyssop upon which a vinegar-soaked sponge was raised to Jesus' lips while he hung on the cross (John 19:29).

Grant talent ai k'a chanteir me retraie
Jacques de Cambrai

I.   Grant talent ai k'a chanteir me
     retraie;
  Si me covient per chanteir esjoïr.
  Loiaul amor droituriere et veraie
4 Me fait ameir de cuer et obeïr
  A la millor ke nuls hom puist veïr.
  He! franche riens, qui aveis sig-
     norie
  La sus el ciel, soiés de ma partie
8 Quant en dous pairs me conven-
     rait partir.

I have an ardent desire to sing;
it is fitting that I rejoice in song.
Loyal, righteous, and true love
makes me love wholeheartedly and
   obey
the best woman that any man could
   see.
Oh! honest one, who has authority
above in heaven, be on my side
when I must split into two halves.

II.   Dame poissans, ceu m'ocist et
     esmaie
  K'en pechiet maing, et si n'en
     puis issir,
  Maix li grans biens de vos mes
     mals apaie;
12 Por ceu vos veul honoreir et
     servir:
  Il ne m'en puet se grans bien non
     venir;
  Car ki a vos ait s'amor otroïe
  En dous leus puet demoneir bone
     vie,
16 Si et en ciel pou aprés le morir.

Powerful lady, it kills and dismays me
that I proceed into sin, and I cannot
   get out,
but your great goodness soothes my
   pain;
for this I wish to honour and serve
   you:
nothing but good can come to me
   from it;
for the one who has given his love to
   you
can lead a good life in a lovely place,
here and in heaven shortly after
   death.

III. He! tres douls cuers, se mercis me
     delaie,
  Je ne saurai ou aleir ne foïr.
  Et c'il vos plaist, douce dame, ke
     j'aie
20 La vostre amor, riens ne me puet
     nuisir.
  Doneis la moi, s'il vos vient a
     plaixir

Oh! very sweet heart, if mercy is
   delayed,
I will not know where to go or flee.
And if it pleases you, sweet lady, that I
   have
your love, nothing can harm me.
Give it to me, if it pleases you
or otherwise joy will disappear from
   me.

Ou atrement joie m'iert defaillie.
Dame, mercit a jointes mains vos
    prie
24 Por celi Deu ki de vos volt
    nasquir.

Lady, I pray to you with joined hands
In the name of God who wished to be
    born in you.

Ausi conme unicorne sui
Thibaut de Champagne
(model for Jacques's Haute dame com rose et lis)

Ausi conme unicorne sui

I.   Ausi conme unicorne sui
    Qui s'esbahist en regardant
    Quant la pucele va mirant.
4 Tant est liee de son ennui,
    Pasmee chiet en son giron;
    Lors l'ocit on en traïson
    Et moi ont mort d'autel senblant.
8 Amors et ma dame, por voir,
    Mon cuer ont, n'en puis point
      avoir.

I am like the unicorn
that becomes entranced
when it looks at the young girl
   [virgin].
It is so happy in its torment
that it faints in her lap.
Then they kill it treacherously.
They killed me also in the same way.
Love and my lady, in all honesty,
they have my heart, and I cannot
   recover it.

II.   Dame, quant je devant vos fui
    Et je vos vi premierement,
12 Mes cuers aloit si tresaillant
    Qu'il vos remest quant je m'en
      mui.
    Lors fu menés sans raençon
    En la douce chartre en prison,
16 Dont li piler sont de talent
    Et li huis sont de biau veoir
    Et li anel de bon espoir.

Lady, when I came before you
and I saw you for the first time,
my trembling heart leapt forth so far
that it stayed with you when I left.
It was then taken away – there was no
   offer
of ransom – to the sweet prison,
of which the pillars are made of
   desire,
the doors of fair looks,
and the rings of hope.

III. De la chartre a la clef Amors,
20 Et si i a mis trois portiers:
    Biau Semblant a non li premiers,
    Et Biautez ceus en fait seignors;
    Dangier a mis a l'uis devant,
24 Un ort felon, vilain puant,
    Qui mult est maus et pautonniers.
    Cist troi sont et viste et hardi;
    Mult ont tost un home saisi.

The key to this prison, Love holds it
and there are three guards:
the first is named Fair Seeming,
and Beauty is her lord;
in front of the gate stands Refusal,
a filthy traitor, a repulsive rustic,
who is evil and most malicious.
These three are both alert and bold;
many a man have they seized.

IV. Qui porroit soufrir la tristors
    Et les assaus de ces huissiers?
    Oncques Rollans ne Oliviers
    Ne vainquirent si fors estors;

Who could endure the vexations
and the assaults of these guards?
Never would have Roland or Oliver
triumphed in such fierce battles;

32 Il vainquirent en conbatant,   they triumphed in warfare,
    Mais ceus vaint on humiliant.   but one vanquishes these guards by
    Soufrirs en est gonfanoniers,   humbling oneself.
    En cest estor dont je vos di,   Patience bears our standard
36 N'a nul secors que de merci.   in this battle of which I am telling you,
                                          there is no aid but in mercy.

V. Dame, je ne dout mes riens plus   Lady, there is nothing that I fear more
    Fors tant que faille a vos amer.   than not obtaining your love.
    Tant ai apris a endurer   I have learned so well how to endure
40 Que je sui vostres tout par us;   that I am yours by custom;
    Et se il vos en pesoit bien,   even if that were to grieve you,
    Ne m'en puis je partir por rien   I cannot leave for anything
    Que je n'aie le remenbrer   without remembering,
44 Et que mes cuers ne soit adés   without leaving my heart forever
    En la prison et de moi pres.   in the prison and me next to it.

VI. Dame, quant je ne sai guiler,   Lady, since I don't know how to feign,
    Merciz seroit de saison mes   it is now time to pity me
48 De soustenir si grevain fes.   who shoulders such a heavy burden.

De fin cuer et d'aigre talent attributed to Pierre de Gand (another contrafactum of Thibaut's 'Ausi conme unicorne sui')

I.   De fin cuer et d'aigre talent   With a fine heart and ardent desire
     Vuil un servantois commencier   I want to begin a 'servantois'
     Pour löer et pour regracier   to praise and thank
4   La roïne dou firmament;   the queen of heaven;
     De sa löenge et de son non   all of my poetry and all my songs
     Muevent tuit mi lai et mi son.   are infused with her praise and her
     Ensi vuil user mon jouvent   name.
8   En li servir en bon espoir,   In this way I want to spend my youth:
     De tant com j'avrai de savoir.   serving her in good faith
                                          as long as I am able.

II. Gabrïel gloriousement   Gabriel went in glory
     Ala cest dame noncier   to this lady to announce

12   Qu'en li se devoit herbergier
     Et prendre charnel vestement
     Cil qui fist Adam dou limon.
     La virge, qui fu en friçon,
16   Lo creï; et fu erranment
     Parole chars et conçut l'oir
     Qui puissance a a son voloir.

that in her should find shelter
and take carnal form
the one who made Adam from earth.
The virgin, shivering with fright,
believed him; and immediately was
the word made flesh and the heir con-
     ceived
who has power at his will.

III. Nesque salemandre n'esprent,
20   Quant ele gist ou brasier,
     Ne mua ele a l'enchargier
     Ne au naistre de son enfant.
     Virge porta son enfançon,
24   Virge le tint en son geron,
     .... (ant)
     Virge le vit mort recevoir
     Et virge en paradis seoir.

Just as the salamander does not burn
when it lies in the fire,
she changed neither at the concep-
     tion
nor at the birth of her child.
She bore her child as a virgin,
as a virgin she sat him in her lap,
....
as a virgin she saw him die
and, still a virgin, saw him seated in
     paradise.

IV. S'en ceste dame eüst noient
     Qui trop en feïst a proisier,
     Ja cil qui tout puet justicier
     N'i fust enclos si longuement.
32   Mes se tuit ierent Salemon,
     Home et oixel, beste et poisson,
     Et la loassent bonnement,
     Ne porroient dire le voir
36   De s'onnour et de son pooir.

If in this lady there were anything
that one could not praise exceedingly,
never would the one who governs all
have been enclosed in her so long.
But if all creatures were [wise as]
     Solomon –
men and birds, beasts and fish –
and praised her earnestly,
they could not tell the whole truth
about her honour and her power.

V.   Tres douce dame, a vos me rens;
     Se vos me volez conseillier,
     Je me guarde de periller
40   D'aversité ne de torment.
     Mere a l'aignel, mere au lyon,
     Mere et fille au vrai Salemon,
     Mere si que nule ensement,

Very noble lady, to you I surrender
     myself;
if you wish to advise me,
I will keep myself from the peril
of adversity and torment.
Mother of the lamb, mother of the
     lion,

44 Menez vos a vostre manoir,
    Ou nus mauvais ne puet manoir.

mother and daughter of the true
    Solomon,
mother without equal,
lead us to your home,
where no evil one may dwell.

Haute dame, com rose et lis
Jacques de Cambrai

I.   Haute dame, com rose et lis
    Ont sormonteit toute color
    Et ke li blans prent resplandor
4 Ou vermeil k'est en li espris,
    Tout aussi prist li sovrains rois
    Colour dedens le lis cortois
    En patience et per amor,
8 Et soffri mort ou fust croixiet
    Por vaincre le vilain pechiet.

Noble lady, like a rose and lily
[that] have surpassed all colour
and in which the white becomes
    resplendent
or the red that is taken in it,
in that same way did the sovereign
    king take
on colour in the gracious lily
patient and loving,
and suffered death and was crucified
to vanquish vile sin.

II.   Dame, se tu portais la flor
    De ton peire ki est tes fils,
12 Il ne m'en doit pais estre pis
    Quant tu ais sormonteit valor.
    Cil ki tous biens ait embraisiciés
    Vint en ton cors par amistiés
16 Por moi, s'en dois avoir merci
    Et conforteir, ceu est tes drois,
    Por eil ne pendi Deus en croix.

Lady, if you carried the flower
of your father who is your son,
it should not seem bad to me
that you have surpassed worth.
He who has embraced all goodness
came to your body out of friendship
for me, so I should be grateful
and comforted; this is your right;
God hung on the cross for no other
    [reason].

III. Bien ait son cuer d'amerous prix
20 Sil ki son cors livre a dolor;
    On le tenroit or a folor,
    Maix tuit fuissiens a noient mis,
    Se ne fust cil ki fut en croix;
24 En enfer o les Abejois
    Alaist chascuns sens nul retor,
    Aincor nos serait reprochie

His heart is full of loving worth,
He who gives over his body to pain;
one might nowadays consider this
    folly,
but all would have been reduced to
    nothing
if it were not for he who was on the
    cross;

Quant li mal fait seront jugie.

into hell with the Albigensians
each one would have gone with no
    escape;
we will still be reproached for it
when evil actions will be judged.

IV. Cil ki est appelleis David
    Et compareis a pellican,
    A droit ait a nom Habrahan
    Et tous biens est en ces brais mis.
32 Li douls fenis sens compaignon,
    Li doulz aignias, li fiers lion
    Nos abovrait tous de son sanc.
    Humiliteis nos ot besoing,
36 Mas la fierteit forment resoing.

He who is called David
and compared to the pelican,
rightly does he have the name of
    Abraham
and all goodness is placed in his arms.
The sweet phoenix without equal,
the sweet lamb, the proud lion
will quench our thirst with his blood.
We are in need of mercy,
but I fear greatly [Jesus'] pride.

V. Dame, tu es Ave per san
    Et Eva fut nos anemis;
    Tu es porte de paradis
40 Jheremie en trais a tesmoing:
    Cinc mille ans et neuf cens de
      loing
    Davant vos et aprés Adam
    Dist ke aincor vanroit li hon
    Ki nos metroit hors de prixon.

Lady, you are rightly hailed
and Eve was our enemy;
you are the door to paradise
Jeremiah testifies to it:
he said that five thousand and nine
hundred years after Adam and before
    you
a man would yet come
who would pull us out of prison.

Kant je plus pens a commencier chanson
Jacques de Cambrai

I. Kant je plus pens a commencier
    chanson,
    Et plus me plaist celle ou j'ai mon
    cuer mis,
    K'ains de millor n'oï parleir nuls
    hom:
4 Ki s'amor ait en honor et en pris,
    Serait sauveis el grant jor del juïs,

It is when I think about beginning a
    song
that she in whom I placed my heart
    pleases me
most, for no man has ever heard of
    better:
the one who obtains her love through
    honour and

Et qui ne l'ait, Deus! si mar ains
    fut neis
Ke sens mercit serait mors et
    dampneis.

merit will be saved on the great judg-
    ment day,
and he who does not have it, God!
    cursed be his
birth for he will die and be damned
    mercilessly.

II.   Dame, ki pues et ki dois per
      raixon
    Estre por nos et proier ke tes fils
    Per sa pitié nos face vrai pardon
    Car autrement ne doit estre
      requis;
12 Or le fait dont, franche dame
      gentis;
    Si voirement k'en tes beneois leis
    Fut li vrais Deus conceüs et
      porteis.

Lady, who can and must by reason
be there for us and pray that your son
through his mercy forgive us truly
for otherwise it cannot be acquired;
do it now, honest, gentle lady;
as truly as in your blessed womb [lit.
    sides]
the true God was conceived and
    carried.

III. Sires, ki es et vrais Deus et vrais
      hons,
16 Et ki por nos fut en la croix occis,
    Quant tu por nos donais si riche
      don
    Com ton saint cor, ki tant est de
      haut prix,
    Bien nos puet estre otroiés para-
      dis,
20 Car tu vals muels ke paradis
      aisseis;
    He! veuilliés dont ke il nos soit
      doneis.

Lord, who is truly God and truly man,
and who died on the cross for us,
Since you gave us a gift as precious
as your saintly body, which is of such
    high
value, well do we deserve paradise,
for you are worth much more than
    paradise;
Oh! wish then that it be given to us.

Loeir m'estuet la roïne Marie
Jacques de Cambrai

I.   Loeir m'estuet la roïne Marie
    En cui tant ait de bien et de vail-
      lance,

I must praise Mary the queen
in whom there is such goodness and
    courage

Ke nuit et jor por les pechëors
  prie
4 A son chier fil k'il ait en remen-
  brance
De nos aidier et de nos warantir
Vers l'anemin ke tant devons
  cremir,
C'adés non veult engingnier et
  honir.
8 Ne plaice a Deu ke jai en ait pous-
  sance!

that night and day for sinners she
prays to her dear son that he keep us
  in mind
to help us and keep us safe
from the enemy whom we should
  greatly fear,
for right now would he trap and dis-
  honour us.
May it not please God that he ever be
  able to do it!

II. Dame, tous biens et toute courtoisie
Est dedans vos et maint a
  remenance,
Nuls n'en diroit la centisme
  partie.
12 Maix, a mon greit, vos fais grant
  honorance
Quant Meire Deu vos appel, et
  plaixir
Vos doit forment, car je ne puis
  veïr
C'on vos peüst si bel juël offrir;
16 Por ceu en fais moult souvent
  recordence.

Lady, all goodness and all grace
is in you and remains there,
none could describe a hundredth of
  it.
But I willingly do you great honour
when I call you the Mother of God,
  and it
should please you greatly, for I cannot
  see
how one could offer you a more precious jewel;
for this I often remind you.

III. He! Maire Deu, roïne coronee,
Por la pitiet k'eüs dou roi celestre
Quant tu veïs sa chair en croix
  levee
20 Entre les Juis ki sont de malvaix
  estre,
Belle dame, ke tant fais a
  proixier,
Proie ton fil ke il me veille aidier
A cest besoing, ke j'en ai grant
  mestier,
24 Ou autrement mar me vi onkes
  naistre.

Oh! Mother of God, crowned queen,
for the sorrow you felt for the celestial
  king
when you saw his body lifted on the
  cross
among the Jews who are of a poor
  estate,
beautiful lady, who does such great
  deeds,
pray to your son that he wish to help
  me
in my need, for I have great need of it,
or otherwise cursed be that I ever saw
  day.

Meire, douce creature
Jacques de Cambrai

I. Meire, douce creature,
   Ou li fils Deu volt venir
   Et prendre humainne nature
4 Por sa deïteit couvrir
   Et morir
   Por l'anemin retolir
   La proie de sa pasture
8 K'en hidouse fosse obscure
   Les menoit poene soffrir;
   Plus ne le volt consentir,
   Vos douls fils, plains de droiture,
12 Ains vint lou sien cors offrir
   Et por nos la mort soffrir.

Mother, sweet creature,
in whom the son of God wished to
   come
and take human form
to cover his divinity
and die
to take back from the enemy
the prey of his pasture
whom he was leading to suffer pain
in a dark and hideous pit;
he did not wish any longer to consent
   to this,
your sweet son, full of righteousness,
rather he came to offer his own body
and suffer death for us.

II. Ensi com sor la verdure
   Descent rosee des ciels,
16 Vint en vo cors, Virge pure,
   De paradis vos douls fiels;
   Vos cors pues,
   Ke tant est frans et gentiels,
20 Ainz n'an senti blesseüre,
   Maix se nos dist l'escripture
   Ke per droit en valut muels:
   Quant li fins airgens soubtuels
24 Est avuec l'or en jointure,
   Dont di je, se m'aïst Deus,
   Ki li airgens en valt muels.

Just as on the pasture
dew descends from heaven,
your sweet friend came from paradise
to your body, pure Virgin,
your holy body,
which is so simple and gracious,
suffered no injury from it,
scripture tells us, in fact,
that its value is rightly augmented:
when fine, refined silver
is joined with gold;
so I say to you, so help me God,
the silver is more valuable.

III. Dame, vos iestes la pree
28 Veritablement lou di,
   Ou la tres douce rousee
   De paradis descendi,
   Ki rendi
32 Por la dolor k'il soffri,
   Vie, sentei et duree

Lady, you are the meadow,
truly do I speak,
on which the very sweet dew
descended from paradise,
[and] who returned,
through the pain that he suffered,
life, health, and time

K'Adam nos avoit enblee   that Adam had taken from us
Par l'ennort de l'anemi;   at the the enemy's behest;
36 Maix li sires ki naski   but the lord to whom you gave birth,
De vos, pucelle honoree,   honoured maiden,
Paiait par un Vendredi   paid back on one Friday
Ceu ke Adam despendit.   that which Adam spent.

IV. Ha! loiaus Virge honouree, Oh! loyal, honoured Virgin,
Fontaine sour douc gravier, fountain on soft sand,
Sourgons de miel et de ree source of honey and nectar
Pour les durs cuers restancier to stop hardened hearts
44 De pechier,   from sinning,
Ki se veut en vous ploncier the one who wishes to submerge him-
Par repentance enbrasee,   self
Vostre amours li est dounee, in you through sincere repentance,
48 Ki bien le puet avancier that person receives your love,
Et en paradys lancier which can help him
En la joie desiree and lift him into paradise
U Diex nous vaut tous hucier, into the desired joy(fulness)
52 Quant se fist en crois drechier. where God wished to bring us,
   when he let himself be put upon the
   cross.

V. Tres douce loiaus roïne, Very sweet loyal queen,
Deseur toutes es li flors, over all others you are the flower,
De tous maus es medecine for all maladies and for criminal sin
56 Et de pechié crimineus; you are the medicine;
Li hideus, the hideous one,
Ki tant est fel et morteus who is so foul and deadly
Et plains de male querine, and full of evil hatred,
60 Dame, ne fera saisine Lady, will not seize
Ki vous sert, cors prescïeux; the one who serves you, precious
Mais la sus ert ses osteus body,
U joie est ki ne define; but there above was his place
64 S'il vous plaist, faites nous tels where there is never-ending joy;
Ke ce soit vostre catels. if it pleases you, make us such
   according to your goodness.

O Dame, ke Deu portais
Jacques de Cambrai

I. O Dame, ke Deu portais
 Et norris et alaitais,
 Per ta grant misericorde
4 A ton chier fil me racorde,
 Ke trop seux hontous et mas
 Des grans pechiés ou je maing:
 Ne aincor pais ne me fraing!
8 Ma vië est vis et orde;
 Sires Deus, a vos me plaing
 Ke vos m'osteis cest mahaing!

O Lady, who carried and nourished
and nursed God,
through your great mercy
reconcile me to your dear son,
for I am so ashamed of and humiliated by
the great sins that I commit:
let them not break me yet!
My life is vile and filthy;
Lord God, I beseech you
that you pull me out of this wretched
 state!

II. Honis seux, c'est veriteis,
12 Se la sainte deïteis
 Et la virge nete et pure
 De moi aidier ne prent cure
 Tant ke je soie laveis.
16 He! sires Deus Jhesucris,
 Ki por moi la mort souffris,
 Oste moi de cette ordure.
 He! dame de paradis,
20 Proiés en vostre chier fil!

I am shamed, it's the truth,
if the saintly divinity
and the pure and immaculate virgin
do not undertake to help me
until I am washed clean.
Oh! Lord Jesus Christ,
who suffered death for me,
deliver me from this filth.
Oh! lady of paradise,
pray to your dear son!

Retrowange novelle
Jacques de Cambrai

I. Retrowange novelle
 Dirai et bonne et belle
 De la virge pucelle
4 Ke meire est et ancelle
 Celui ki de sa chair belle
 Nos ait raicheteit,
 Et ki trestout nos apelle
8 A sa grant clairteit.

I will declaim a new *rotrouenge*
both good and beautiful
of the virgin maiden
who is mother and handmaiden
to the one who with his beautiful flesh
bought us back,
and who calls us all
to his great light.

II. Se nos dist Isaïe
        En une profesie:
        D'une verge delgie,
   12 De Jessé espanie,
        Istroit flors, per signorie,
        De tres grant biaulteit.
        Or est bien la profesie
   16 Torneie a verteit.

Thus Isiah says
in a prophecy:
from a thin rod
grown from Jesse
would come forth a noble flower
of very great beauty.
Now has the prophecy
well come true.

III. Celle verge delgie
        Est la virge Marie;
        La Flor nos senefie,
   20 De ceu ne douteis mie,
        Jhesucrist ki la haichie
        En la croix souffri,
        Tout por randre ceaus en vie
   24 Ki ierent peri.

That thin rod
is the Virgin Mary;
the flower represents for us,
have no doubt about it,
Jesus Christ who suffered
pain on the cross,
all to return to life
those who had perished.

C'est de Notre Dame
Rutebeuf

I. Chanson m'estuet chanteir de la
        meilleur
        Qui onques fust ne qui jamais
        sera;
        Li siens douz chanz garit toute
        doleur:
   4 Bien iert gariz cui ele garira.
        Mainte arme a garie;
        Huimais ne dot mie
        Que n'aie boen jour,
   8 Car sa grant dosour
        N'est nuns qui vous die.

I must sing of the best woman
who ever was and who will ever be;
her sweet song cures every pain:
he who is cured by her is well cured.
She has cured many a soul;
I now no longer fear
that I will not see good days,
for her sweetness is such
that no one could tell you [about it].

II. Mout a en li cortoizie et valour;
        Bien et bontei et charitei i a.
   12 Con folz li cri merci de ma folour:
        Foloié ai, s'onques nuns foloia.
        Si pleur ma folie

There is in her graciousness and
    merit;
in her is goodness, righteousness, and
    charitableness.
Like a fool, I beg that she have mercy

Et ma fole vie;
16 Et mon fol senz plour
   Et ma fole errour
   Ou trop m'entroblie.

on my folly:
I have behaved foolishly, like no other
   fool.
I cry over my foolishness
and my foolish life;
and I decry my foolish sense
and my foolish behaviour
or I will stray too far.

III. Quant son doulz non reclain-
     ment picheour
20 Et il dient son *Ave Maria*,
   N'ont puis sans doute dou Maufei
     tricheour
   Qui mout doute le bien qu'en
     Marie a,
   Car qui se marie
24 En teile Marie,
   Boen marriage a:
   Marions nos la,
   Si avrons s'aïe.

When sinners proclaim her sweet
   name
and they say the *Ave Maria*,
they no longer fear the treacherous
   Evil one
who fears Mary's goodness so much,
for he who marries
this Mary,
has a good marriage;
let us marry her,
and we will have her help.

IV. Mout l'ama cil qui, de si haute
     tour
   Com li ciel sunt, descendi juque
     ça.
   Mere et fille porta son creatour
   Qui de noiant li et autres cria.
32 Qui de cuer s'escrie
   Et merci li crie
   Merci trovera:
   Jamais n'i faudra
36 Qui de cuer la prie.

He loved her much, he who from a
   tower
as high as the heavens, descended to
   here.
Mother and daughter, she carried her
   creator
who from nothingness created her
   and all others.
He who cries out from the heart
and begs her for mercy
will find mercy:
she will never fail the one
who prays to her from the heart.

V. Si com hom voit le soloil toute jor
   Qu'en la verriere entre et ist et
     s'en va,
   Ne l'enpire tant i fiere a sejour,
40 Ausi vos di que onques n'empira

Just as we see the sun every day
pass through the window, enter, and
   leave,
without damaging it no matter how
   long it stays,

La Vierge Marie:
Vierge fu norrie,
Vierge Dieu porta,
44 Vierge l'aleta,
Vierge fu sa vie.

Explicit.

I tell you that similarly she was never
    damaged,
the Virgin Mary:
she was raised a virgin,
she carried God a virgin,
she nursed him a virgin,
she was all her life a virgin.

La Repentance/Mort Rutebeuf
Rutebeuf

I.   Lessier m'estuet le rimoier,
     Quar je me doi moult esmaier
     Quant tenu l'ai si longement.
  4 Bien me doit le cuer lermoier,
     C'onques ne me poi amoier
     A Dieu servir parfetement,
     Ainz ai mis mon entendement
  8 En geu et en esbatement,
     Qu'ainz ne daignai nés saumoier.
     Se por moi n'est au Jugement
     Cele ou Diex prist aombrement,
 12 Mau marchié pris au paumoier.

I must leave aside poetry making,
for I should be greatly dismayed
after having clung to it so long.
Well should my heart weep,
for never have I been able
to serve God perfectly;
rather I have occupied myself
with gambling and amusements,
and never did I deign to read my
    psalms.
If at my side on the Day of Judgment
she in whom God took refuge is not
    there,
I will have made an unwise wager.

II. Tart serai més au repentir,
     Las moi, c'onques ne sot sentir
     Mes fols cuers quels est repen-
         tance
 16 N'a bien fere lui assentir!
     Comment oseroie tentir
     Quant nes li juste avront dou-
         tance?
     J'ai toz jors engressié ma pance
 20 D'autrui chatel, d'autrui sub-
         stance:
     Ci a bon clerc, au miex mentir!

It is very late for me to repent,
poor me, for never did my foolish
    heart
feel repentance
or resolve to do good.
How dare I plead
when even the just will fear?
All my days I filled my stomach
with the property, the things of others:
what a good cleric I am, thanks to my
    lying!
If I say: 'It is due to ignorance

Se je di: 'C'est par ignorance,
Que je ne sai qu'est penitence,'
24 Ce ne me puet pas garantir.

that I do not know what penitence is,'
it will not save me.

III. Garantir? Las! en quel maniere?
Ne me fist Diex bonté entiere
Qui me dona sens et savoir
28 Et me fist a sa forme chiere?
Encor me fist bonté plus chiere,
Que por moi vout mort recevoir.
Sens me dona de decevoir
32 L'Anemi qui me veut avoir
Et metre en sa chartre premiere,
La dont nus ne se puet ravoir
Por priere ne por avoir:
36 N'en voi nul qui reviegne arriere.

Save me? Alas, how?
Did not God show me great goodness,
he who gave me sense and wisdom
and who made me in his precious
    image?
He showed me even more goodness
when he willingly died for me.
He gave me intelligence to trick
the Devil who seeks me out and wishes
to put me first and foremost in his
    prison,
there from where no one can escape
through either entreaty or through
    bribery:
I see no one return from there.

IV. J'ai fet au cors sa volenté,
J'ai fet rimes et s'ai chanté
Sor les uns por aus autres plere,
40 Dont Anemis m'a enchanté
Et m'ame mis en orfenté
Por mener a felon repere.
Se Cele en qui toz biens resclere
44 Ne prent en cure mon afere,
De male rente m'a renté
Mes cuers ou tant truis de con-
    traire:
Fisicien n'apoticaire
48 Ne me pueent doner santé.

I fully satisfied my body's desires,
I composed songs and I sang
about certain people to please others;
thus has the Devil beguiled me
and rendered my soul an orphan
in order to lead it to a foul place.
If she in whom all things delight
does not take up my case,
my heart, which I find so contrary,
will have made a bad investment:
neither physician nor apothecary
can restore my health.

V. Je sai un fisicienne
Que a Lions ne a Viane
Ne tant comme li siecles dure
52 N'a si bone serurgiene.
N'est plaie, tant soit anciene,
Qu'ele ne netoie et escure,
Puis qu'ele i veut metre sa cure.
56 Ele espurja de vie obscure

I know a physician;
in Lyons or in Vienna
and until the end of time,
you will find no better surgeon.
There is no wound, no matter how
    old,
that she could not clean and heal
were she to tend to it.

La beneoite Egypciene:
A Dieu la rendi nete et pure.
Si com c'est voirs, si praingne en
    cure
60 Ma lasse d'ame crestiene!

She brought forth from a life of dark-
    ness
the blessed Egyptian:
she gave her back to God clean and
    pure.
Just as that came to be true, let her
    take care
of my wretched Christian soul.

VI. Puis que morir voi foible et fort,
    Comment prendrai en moi con-
        fort
    Que de mort me puisse desfen-
        dre?
64 N'en voi nul, tant ait grant esfort,
    Que des piez n'ost le contrefort,
    Si fet le cors a terre estendre.
    Que puis je, fors la mort atendre?
68 La mort ne lest ne dur ne tendre
    Por avoir que l'en li aport;
    Et quant li cors est mis en cendre,
    Si covient a Dieu reson rendre
72 De quanques fist dusqu'a la mort.

I see both the strong and the weak die:
how will I find the strength
to defend myself from death?
I see no one, no matter how fast he
    stands,
whose feet are not taken out from
    under him
and laid out on the ground.
What can I do besides wait for death?
Death spares neither the cruel nor the
    kind
whatever sum they offer him;
and when the body is reduced to dust,
it must be that it accounts to God
for everything it did up until death.

VII. Or ai tant fet que ne puis més,
    Si me covient lessier en pés;
    Diex doinst que ce ne soit trop
        tart!
76 Toz jors ai acreü mon fés,
    Et oi dire a clers et a lés:
    'Com plus couve li feus plus art.'
    Je cuidai engingner Renart:
80 Or n'i valent engin ne art,
    Qu'asseür est en son palés.
    Por cest siecle qui se depart
    M'en covient partir d'autre part:
84 Qui que l'envie, je le lés.
        Ci faut la mort Rustebeuf.

I have done so much that I cannot go
    on,
and I must rest;
God grant that it is not too late!
Every day I have compounded my [sin-
    ful] acts,
and I overhear clerics and laypeople
    alike:
'The longer a fire smolders, the hotter
    it burns.'
I thought I was tricking Renard:
but trickery and ruses mattered none,
for he is safe and sound in his palace.
This world goes on,
but I must go another way:

[go on playing] if you wish, but I'm
leaving [the game].
Here ends the death of Rustebeuf

L'*Ave Maria* **Rustebeuf**
Rutebeuf

A toutes genz qui ont savoir
Fet Rustebués bien a savoir
    Et les semont:
4 Cels qui ont les cuers purs et
        mont
    Doivent tuit deguerpir le mont
        Et debouter,
    Quar trop covient a redouter
8 Les ordures a raconter
        Que chascuns conte;
    C'est veritez que je vous conte.
    Chanoine, clerc et roi et conte
12   Sont trop aver;
    N'ont cure des ames sauver,
    Més les cors baignier et laver
        Et bien norrir;
16 Quar il ne cuident pas morir
    Ne dedenz la terre porrir,
        Més si feront,
    Que ja garde ne s'il prendront
20 Que tel morsel engloutiront
        Qui leur nuira,
    Que la lasse d'ame cuira
    En enfer, ou ja nel lera
24   Estez n'yvers.
    Trop par sont les morsiaus divers
    Dont la char menjuent les vers
        Et en pert l'ame.
28 Un salu de la douce Dame,
    Por ce qu'ele nous gart de
        blasme,
        Vueil commencier,

To all people who have some wisdom
Rutebeuf would like to say
and to advise:
those whose heart is pure and clean
must leave the world
and reject it,
for it is only too right to suspect
the filthy tales that
everyone tells:
I am telling you the truth.
Canons, clerics, and kings and counts
are too greedy;
they do not care about saving souls,
but about bathing and cleaning
and feeding themselves well;
for they do not think about dying
and about rotting in the earth,
but they will do so,
for never do they think
that such morsels that they eat
will harm them,
that their wretched souls will burn
in hell unceasingly
in summer as in winter.
They are very dangerous, these
    morsels
that will lead worms to eat the flesh
and cause the perdition of the soul.
I wish to begin an address to
the sweet lady
so that she keep us from harm's way,
for in a worthy and dear place

Quar en digne lieu et en chier
32 Doit chascuns metre sans tencier
    Cuer et penssee.
    Ave, roïne coronee!
    Com de bone eure tu fus nee,
36   Qui Dieu portas!
    Theophilus reconfortas
    Quant sa chartre li raportas
        Que l'Anemis,
40 Qui de mal fere est entremis,
    Cuida avoir lacié et mis
        En sa prison.
    Maria, si com nous lison,
44 Tu li envoias garison
        De son malage,
    Qui deguerpi Dieu et s'ymage
    Et si fist au deable hommage
48   Par sa folor;
    Et puis li fist, a sa dolor,
    Du vermeil sanc de sa color
        Tel chartre escrire
52 Qui devisa tout son martire;
    Et puis aprés li estuet dire
        Par estavoir:
    'Par cest escrit fet a savoir
56 Theophilus ot por avoir
        Dieu renoié.'
    Tant l'ot deables desvoié
    Que il estoit toz marvoié
60   Par desperance;
    Et quant li vint en remembrance
    De vous, Dame plesant et
        franche,
        Sanz demorer
64 Devant vous s'en ala orer;
    De cuer commença a plorer
        Et larmoier;
    Vous l'en rendistes tel loier,
68 Quant de cuer l'oïstes proier,
        Que vous alastes,

must everyone put without protest
both heart and mind.
Hail, crowned queen!
At a happy hour were you born,
you who carried God!
You comforted Theophilus
when you returned the contract to
    him
that the enemy,
who tried to do evil,
thought he had snared and thrown
into his prison.
Mary, just as we read it,
you sent him the cure
for his illness:
he renounced God and his image
and did homage to the devil
in his foolishness;
and he [the devil] made him
    [Theophilus],
with pain and with his red blood
write out this contract
that dictated all conditions of his
    martyrdom;
and then afterwards he had to say
to fulfil the bargain:
'By this writing Theophilus makes it
    known
that for riches he has
renounced God.'
The devil had so bewildered him
that he became deranged
with despair;
and when he remembered
you, pleasing and honest Lady,
without hesitation
he went and prayed before you.
He started to cry and weep
from the heart;
you repaid him in such a way,

D'enfer sa chartre raportastes,
De l'Anemi le delivrastes
72   Et de sa route.
Gracia plena estes toute:
Qui ce ne croit il ne voit goute
Et li compere.
76 *Dominus* li sauveres Pere
Fist de vous sa fille et sa mere,
  Tant vous ama;
Dame des angles vous clama;
80 En vous s'enclost, ainz n'entama
  Vo dignité,
N'en perdistes virginité.
Tecum par sa digne pité
84   Vout toz jors estre
Lasus en la gloire celestre;
Donez le nous ainsinques estre
  Lez son costé.
88 *Benedicta* tu qui osté
Nous as del dolererus osté
  Qui tant est ors
Qu'il n'est en cest siecles tresors
92 Qui nous peüst fere restors
  De la grant perte
Par quoi Adam fist la deserte.
Prie a ton fil qu'i nous en terde
96   Et nous esleve
De l'ordure qu'aporta Eve
Quant de la pomme osta la seve,
  Par qoi tes fis,
100 Si com je suis certains et fis,
Souffri mort et fu crucefis
  Au Vendredi
(C'est veritez que je vous di)
104 Et au tiers jor, plus n'atendi,
  Resuscita.
La Magdelene visita,
De toz ses pechiez la cuita
108   Et la fist saine.
De paradis es la fontaine,

when you heard him pray from the
  heart,
that you went forth
and brought back the contract from
  hell.
From the enemy and his minions
you delivered him.
You are completely *full of grace*:
He who does not believe it sees
  nothing
and pays for it.
The Lord, the saving Father,
made of you his daughter and his
  mother,
he loved you so;
he proclaimed you Lady of the angels;
he enclosed himself in you, but he did
not compromise your dignity,
you did not lose your virginity.
With you, in his noble mercy
he wanted to be with you always
above in celestial glory;
grant that we too may be
at his side.
Blessed [*are*] you who
took us from that sorrowful place
that is so repugnant
For there is in this world no treasure
that could make restitution
for the great loss
that through Adam's sin we [rightly]
  deserved.
Pray to your son that he purify us
and lift us
from the filth that Eve brought about
when she tasted the juice of the apple,
for which reason your son,
of this I am certain and confident,
suffered death and was crucified
on Friday

In *mulieribus* et plaine
   De seignorie.
112 Fols est qui en toi ne se fie.
   Tu hez orgueil et felonie
     Seur toute chose;
   Tu es li lis ou Diex repose;
116 Tu es rosiers qui porte rose
     Blanche et vermeille;
   Tu as en ton saint chief l'oreille
   Qui les desconseilliez conseille
120   Et met a voie;
   Tu as de solaz et de joie
   Tant que raconter n'en porroie
     La tierce part.
124 Fols est cil qui pensse autre part
   Et plus est fols qui se depart
     De vostre acorde,
   Quar honesté, misericorde
128 Et pacience a vous s'acorde
     Et abandone.
   Hé! benoite soit la corone
   De Jhesuscrist, qui environe
132   Le vostre chief;
   Et benedictus de rechief
   Fructus qui soufri grant meschief
     Et grant mesaise.
136 Por nous geter de la fornaise
   D'enfer, qui tant par est pusnaise,
     Laide et obscure.
   Hé! douce Virge nete et pure,
140 Toutes fames por ta figure
     Doit l'en amer.
   Douce te doit l'en bien clamer,
   Quar en toi si n'a point d'amer
144   N'autre durté:
   Chacié en as toute obscurté.
   Par la grace, par la purté
     Ventris tui,
148 Tuit s'en sont deable fuï;
   N'osent parler, car amuï

(I am telling you the truth)
and on the third day, he no longer
   waited,
he rose from the dead.
He visited the Magdalene,
from whom he removed all sin
and whom he made pure.
You are the fountain of paradise
among women and full
of nobility.
Foolish is the one who does not trust
   in you.
You hate arrogance and cruelty
over all things;
you are the lily in whom God finds
   rest;
you are the rose bush that brings forth
red and white roses;
in your saintly head is the ear [*lit.*]
that counsels the ones who have
   strayed
and puts [them] on the right path;
you are solace and joy
so much so that I could not tell
a third of it.
Foolish is the one who thinks otherwise
and more foolish is the one who
   departs from
your friendship,
for honesty, mercy,
and patience abide in you
without limits.
Ah! blessed be the crown of
Jesus Christ that encircles
your head;
and blessed once again
the fruit that suffered great anguish
and great pain
in order to wrench us out of the oven

Sont leur solas.
Quant tu tenis et acolas
152 Ton chier filz, tu les afolas
      Et maumeïs.
   Si com c'est voirs que tu deïs,
   'Hé! biaus Pere qui me feïs,
156   Je suis t'ancele.'
   Toi depri je, Virge pucele,
   Prie a ton Fil qu'il nous apele
      Au jugement,
160 Quant il fera si aigrement
   Tout le monde communement
      Trambler com fueille,
   Qu'a sa partie nous acueille!
164 Disons *Amen*, qu'ainsi le veuille!
      *Explicit l'*Ave Maria *Rustebeuf*

TN: Verses 154–5 are inverted in ms.
   A.

of hell, which is so foul,
ugly, and dark.
Ah! sweet, immaculate, and pure
   Virgin,
because of you[r face] we should
love every woman.
It is right to call you sweet,
for in you there is no bitterness
or harshness of any kind:
you have driven away all darkness,
through your grace, through the
   purity
of your womb,
all demons have fled;
they dare not speak, for their solace
has vanished.
When you held and embraced
your dear son, you wounded them
and reduced them to a sorry plight.
It was the truth when you spoke:
'Ah! good Father who made me.
I am your handmaiden.'
I implore you, Virgin,
pray to your son that he call to us
on the day of judgment,
when he will make everyone
gathered together
shake violently like leaves,
that he count us among his own!
Let us say *Amen*, may he wish it so!

La Repentance Théophile
Rutebeuf

I.   Ha! laz, chetiz, dolanz, que porrai
      devenir?
    Terre, coument me puéz porteir
      ne soutenir
    Quant j'ai Dieu renoié et celui
      vox tenir
  4 A seigneur et a maitre qui tant
      mal fait venir?

Alas, miserable and afflicted one, what
    will become of me?
Earth, how can you carry and support
    me
when I have renounced God and wish
    to take as
lord and master the one who causes
    all evil?

II.   Or ai Dieu renoié, ne puet estre
      teü:
    Si ai laissié le baume, pris me sui
      au seü.
    De moi a pris la chartre et le brief
      receü
  8 Mauffeiz, si li rendrai de m'arme
      le treü.

I have renounced God, that cannot be
    hidden:
I have rejected the balm and sucked
    on the elder.
The evil one has taken my contract
    and
received my letter, so I owe my soul as
    tribute.

III.   Hé! Diex, que feras tu de cest
      chetif dolant
    De cui l'arme en ira en enfer le
      buillant
    Et li maufei l'iront a lor piez
      defolant?
 12 Hai! terre, quar huevre, si me vai
      engoulant!

O God, what will you do with this tor-
    tured,
afflicted one whose soul will boil in
    hell
where demons will go to trample it
    under their
feet? Ah! Earth, open and swallow me
    up.

IV.   Sire Diex, que fera ciz dolenz
      esbahiz
    Qui de Dieu et dou monde est
      hüeiz et haïz
    Et des maufeiz d'enfer engigniez
      et traïz?
 16 Dont sui ge de trestouz chaciez et
      envaïz?

Lord God, what will you do with this
    pained,
deranged one, booed and hated by
    God and
the world, betrayed by hell's demons?
Am I then chased and attacked by
    everyone?

V.   Ha! las, com j'ai estei plains de
       grant nonsavoir
    Quant j'ai Dieu renoié por un
       petit d'avoir!
    Les richesces dou monde que je
       voloie avoir
20 M'ont getei en teil leu dont ne
       me puis raveir.

Ah! wretched one, how ignorant I was
when I renounced God for a little
    wealth!
The worldly riches that I desired threw
    me
into a place from which I cannot
    redeem myself.

VI. Sathan, plus de .vij. anz ai senti
      ton sentier;
    Mauz chanz m'ont fait chanteir li
      vin de mon chantier.
    Mout felonesse rente m'en ren-
      dront mi rentier;
24 Ma char charpenteront li felon
      charpentier.

Satan, more than seven years have I
    walked your path;
the wines of my stockroom have made
    me sing many evil songs.
My renters will render me a cruel
    payment;
cruel carpenters will strike at my
    body.

VII. Arme doit hon ameir: m'arme
      n'iert pas amee,
    N'oz demandeir la Dame qu'ele
      ne soit dampnee.
    Trop a mal semance en sa maison
      semee
28 De cui l'arme sera en enfer
      seursemee.

One should cherish the soul; I did not
    cherish my soul;
I dare not ask Our Lady that it not be
    damned.
He has sown bad seed when sowing,
he whose soul will perish in hell.

VIII. Ha! laz, con fou bailli et com fole
      baillie!
    Or sui je mau bailliz et m'arme
      mau baillie.
    S'or m'ozoie baillier a la douce
      baillie,
32 G'i seroie bailliez et m'arme ja
      baillie.

Alas, how foolishly I have behaved!
My soul and I are now in a bad way.
If I dared give myself over to the sweet
    governess,
I would be well governed and my soul,
    too.

IX. Ors sui, et ordeneiz doit aleir en
      ordure.
    Ordement ai ovrei, ce seit Cil qui
      or dure

I am filth and the filthy should rejoin
    filth.
I have acted filthily, this he knows, he
    who lasts

Et qui toz jors durra, s'en avrai la
  mort dure.

36 Maufeiz, com m'aveiz mort de
  mauvaise morsure!

and will last forever. I will endure a
  harsh death.

Evil one, how you have bitten me with
  an evil bite.

X. Or n'ai je remanance ne en ciel
  ne en terre.
  Ha! laz, ou est li leuz qui me
  puisse sofferre?
  Enfers ne me plait pas ou je me
  volz offerre;

40 Paradix n'est pas miens, que j'ai
  au Seigneur guerre.

There is now no place for me in
  heaven or earth.

Ah! wretched one, what place would
  suffer me?

Hell to which I am pledged does not
  please me;

heaven is not for me, for I am at war
  with God.

XI. Je n'oz Dieu reclameir ne ces
  sains ne ces saintes,
  Las, que j'ai fait homage au
  deable mains jointes.
  Li Maufeiz en a lettres de mon
  aunel empraintes.

44 Richesce, mar te vi! J'en avrai
  doleurs maintes.

I do not dare invoke God or his saints,
  alas, for I paid homage to the devil
  with joined hands.

The evil doer has a letter with my seal.

Riches, I curse the day I saw you! I will
  suffer greatly for it.

XII. Je n'oz Dieu ne ces saintes ne ces
  sainz reclameir,
  Ne la tres douce Dame que chacuns doit ameir.
  Mais por ce qu'en li n'a felonie
  n'ameir,

48 Se ge li cri merci nuns ne m'en
  doit blasmeir.
  Explicit.

I do not dare invoke God or his saints,
  or the sweetest Lady that everyone
  should love.

But because there is nothing cruel or
  bitter in her,

if I cry to her for mercy, no one could
  blame me.

La Prière Théophile
Rutebeuf

I.   Sainte Marie bele,
        Glorieuze pucele,
        Dame de grace plainne
    4 Par cui toz bienz revele,
        Qu'au besoing vous apele
        Delivres est de painne;
        Qu'a vous son cuer amainne
    8 En pardurable rainne
        Avra joie novele.
        Arousable fontainne
        Et delitable et sainne,
   12 A ton Fil me rapele!

Saintly, beautiful Mary,
glorious virgin,
Lady full of grace
in whom all goodness is revealed,
whoever calls to you in need
is delivered from suffering;
he who leads his heart to you
will have renewed joy
in the everlasting kingdom.
Sparkling, delectable,
and pure fountain,
intercede for me with your son.

II. En vostre doulz servise
        Fu ja m'entente mise,
        Mais trop tost fui tenteiz.
   16 Par celui qui atize
        Le mal et le bien brize;
        Sui trop fort enchanteiz.
        Car me desenchanteiz,
   20 Que vostre volenteiz
        Est plainne de franchize,
        Ou de granz orfenteiz
        Sera mes cors renteiz
   24 Devant la fort justise.

In your sweet service
I had once put my energy,
but I was quickly tempted.
By the one who stirs up
evil and destroys goodness
I am bedevilled.
Break the spell,
for your will
is full of generosity,
or the worse of abandonments
will be my payment
before [God's] terrible judgment.

III. Dame sainte Marie,
        Mon corage varie
        Ainsi que il te serve,
   28 Ou jamais n'ert tarie
        Ma doleurs ne garie,
        Ains sera m'arme serve.
        Ci avra dure verve
   32 S'ainz que la mors m'enerve
        En vous ne se marie
        M'arme qui vous enterve.
        Soffreiz li cors deserve
   36 Qu'ele ne soit perie.

Saintly Lady Mary,
change my heart
so that it serves you,
or my pain will never be lessened
or cured,
and my soul will be oppressed.
It will be a hard message to bear
if before death takes hold of me
my soul cannot marry you
to whom it aspires.
Grant that the body deserve
that it [my soul] not perish.

IV. Dame de charitei   Lady of charity,
    Qui par humilitei   who in humility
    Portas notre salu,   carried our salvation,
40 Qui toz nos a getei   who freed us
    D'enfer et de vitei   from hell and baseness
    Et d'enferne palu,   and from the pit of hell,
    Dame, je te salu!   Lady, I hail you!
44 Ton saluz m'a valu,   Your *Hail Mary* has aided me,
    Jou sai de veritei.   I know [it] truly.
    Gart qu'avec Tentalu   Watch that my destiny not
    En enfer le jalu   be with Tentalus
48 Ne preigne m'eritei!   in coveteous hell.

V. En enfer ert offerte,   My soul is pledged to hell,
    Dont la porte est overte,   to which the door is open,
    M'arme par mon outrage.   thanks to my arrogance.
52 Ci avra dure perte   It will be a harsh loss
    Et grant folie aperte   and a great folly,
    Se la prent habergage.   if it finds a home there.
    Dame, or te fas homage: Lady, I now do you homage:
56 Torne ton dolz visage;   turn [to me] your sweet face;
    Por ma dure deserte,   even if I deserve it [hell],
    Envers ton Filz lou sage,   in the name of your wise son,
    Ne soffrir que mi gage   grant not that the bets I laid
60 Voisent a tel poverte!   lead me to such impoverishment!

VI. Si come en la verriere   As sunlight enters and pierces
    Entre et reva arriere   the window
    Li solaux que n'entame,   without breaking it,
64 Ausi fus virge entiere   thus you remained a virgin
    Quant Diex, qui en cielz iere,   when God, who is in heaven,
    Fit de toi mere et dame.   made you [his] mother and wife.
    Ha! resplendissans jame,   Ah! splendid jewel,
68 Tantre et piteuze fame,   tender and compassionate woman,
    Car entent ma proiere   hear my prayer
    Que mon vil cors et m'ame   and make my vile
    De pardurable flame   body and my soul turn back
72 Fai retourner arriere.   from everlasting fire.

VII. Roïne debonaire,   Generous queen,
     Les yex dou cuer m'esclaire   uncover the eyes of my heart,

Et l'ocurtei efface,

76 Si qu'a toi puisse plaire
    Et ta volentei faire:
    Car m'en done la grace.
    Trop ai eü espace
80 D'estre en ocure trace;
    Ancor m'i cuident traire
    Li serf de pute estrace;
    Dame, ja toi ne place
84 Qu'il fassent teil contraire!

VIII. En viltei, en ordure,
      En vie trop oscure
      Ai estei lonc termine:
88   Roïne nete et pure,
      Quar me pren en ta cure
      Et si me medicine.
      Par ta vertu devine
92   Qu'adés est enterine
      Fai dedens mon cuer luire
      La clartei pure et fine
      Et les iex m'enlumine,
96   Que ne me voi conduire.

IX.   Li proierres qui proie
      M'a ja pris en sa proie:
      Pris serai et preeiz,
100   Trop asprement m'asproie.
      Dame, ton chier Filz proie
      Que soie despreeiz.
      Dame, car lor veeiz,
104   Qui mes meffeiz veeiz,
      Que n'avoie a lor voie.
      Vous qui la sus seeiz,
      M'arme lor deveeiz
108   Que nuns d'eulz ne la voie.
      Explicit.

and dissipate the shadows
so that I may please you
and do your will:
bestow upon me your grace.
I have too long
followed the dark path;
they think that they still guide me,
the serfs of a filthy race;
Lady, may it never please you
that they commit such an offence.

In baseness, in filth,
in a life too dark
have I lingered:
immaculate and pure queen,
put me in your care
and cure me.
By the divine virtue
that resides wholly in you
make shine in my heart
pure and perfect light
and render to me my sight
without which I cannot see my way.

The predator that preys
has me already in his clutches:
I will be preyed upon and taken,
it torments me so bitterly.
Lady, pray to your dear son,
that I be delivered.
Prevent them, Lady,
you who see my faults,
from leading me along their path.
You, seated there above,
keep my soul from them,
let none of them discover it.

RR: 5 besoig – 33 ne ce m. – 44 Tes

Un dist de Nostre Dame
Rutebeuf

De la tres glorieuse Dame
Qui est saluz de cors et d'ame
Dirai, que tere ne m'en puis;
4 Més l'en porroit avant un puis
Espuisier c'on poïst retrere
Combien la Dame est debonaire.
Por ce si la devons requerre
8 Qu'avant qu'elle chaïst sor terre
Mist Diex en li humilité,
Pitiez, dousors et chairitez,
Tant que ne sai ou je commance:
12 Besoignex sui par abondance.
L'abondance de sa loange
Remue mon corage et change
Si qu'esprover ne me porroie,
16 Tant parlasse que je voudroie.
Tant a en li de bien a dire
Que trop est belle la matiere.
Se j'estoie bons escrivens,
20 Ainz seroie d'escrire vains
Que je vous eüsse conté
La terce part de sa bonté
Ne la quarte ne redeïsme:
24 Ce set chacuns par lui meïsme.

Qui orroit comment elle proie
Celi qui de son cors fist proie
Por nous toz d'enfer despraer;
28 C'onques ne vost le cors
    despraer,
Ainz fu por nos praez et pris,
Dou feu de charité espris!
Et tot ce li ramantoit elle
32 ....
   ....
La douce Virge debonaire:
'Biaus filz, tu suis fame et home,
36 Quant il orent mors en la pome,

About the most glorious Lady
who is the salvation of both body and
   soul
I will tell, for I can keep quiet no
   longer;
but one could run a well dry
before one could tell
of this Lady's generosity.
For this we should implore her,
for even before she came down to
   earth
God put in her humility,
compassion, sweetness, and charita-
   bleness,
so much so that I know not where to
   begin:
I have overwhelmed by abundance.
The abundance of her praiseworthi-
   ness
moves and stirs my heart
so much so that I could never exhaust
myself no matter how long I talked.
There is so much good to say about
   her
that the subject is exceedingly beautiful.
If I were a good writer,
I would tire of writing
before I would have told
a third of her goodness
or even a fourth or a hundredth:
Everyone knows this by himself.

One should hear how she prays
to the one who offered his body
to save us all from hell;
Never did he wish to save himself,
rather he was for us seized and taken,

Il furent mort par le pechié
Dou Maufez est toz entechiez,
En enfer il dui descendirent
40 Et tuit cil qui d'enfer yssirent.
Biax chiers fis, il t'en prist pitiez
Et tant lor montras d'amistiez
Que pour aus decendis des ciaus.
44 Li dessandres fu bons et biax:
De la fille feïs ta mere,
Tiex fu la volanté dou Pere.
De la creche te fit on couche:
48 Sans orguel est qui la se couche.
Porter te convint en Egypte;
La demorance i fu petite,
Car aprés toi ne vesqui gaires
52 Tes anemis, li deputaires
Herodes, qui fist decoler
Les inocens et afoler
Et desmenbrer par chacun
    menbre,
56 Si com l'Escriture remenbre.
Aprés ce revenis arriere;
Juï te firent belle chiere,
Car tu lor montroies ou Temple
60 Maint bel mot et maint bel
    example.
Mont lor plot canques tu deïs
Juqu'a ce tens que tu feïs
Ladre venir de mort a vie.
64 Lors orent il sor toi envie,
Lors fus d'aus huiez et haïz,
Lors fus enginiez et traïz
Par les tiens et a aus bailliez,
68 Lors fus penez et travillez
Et lors fus lïez a l'estache:
N'est nus qui ne le croie et sache.
La fus batuz et deplaiez,
72 La fus de la mort esmaiez,
La te convint porter la croiz
Ou tu crias a haute voiz
Au Juïs que tu soif avoies.

full of the fire of charity!
She reminded him of all of this
....
....
the sweet and gracious Virgin:
'Good son, you follow[ed] woman and
    man
after they bit into the apple
and died because of sin,
for which the Evil One is responsible.
The two descended into hell
as well as all who [later] left hell.
Dear, good son, pity took hold of you
and you showed them such love
that you descended from heaven for
    them.
The descent was good and beautiful:
You made your daughter your mother,
such was the will of the Father.
They made you a bed out of the
    manger:
he who sleeps there is without
    arrogance.
You had to be taken to Egypt;
the stay there was short,
for after your birth he lived only
    shortly,
your enemy, the despicable
Herod, who had innocent children
decapitated, killed and
torn apart piece by piece,
just as scripture testifies.
After this you came back;
the Jews delighted in you
because you explained in the temple
many fine words and many fine
    stories.
What you said pleased them
until the time when you made
Lazarus rise from the dead.

76 La soif estoit que tu savoies
   Tes amis mors et a malaise
   En la dolor d'enfer punaise.
   L'ame dou cors fu en enfer
80 Et brisa la porte d'enfer.
   Tes amis tressis de leans,
   Ainc ne remest clerc ne lai anz.
   Li cors remest en la croiz mis;
84 Joseph, qui tant fu tes amis,
   A Pilate te demanda:
   Li demanders mout l'amanda.

   Lors fus ou sepucre posez;
88 De ce fu hardiz et osez
   Pilate qu'a toi garde mist,
   Car de folie s'entremist.
   Au tiers jor fus resucitez:
92 Lors fus et cors et deïtez
   Ensanble sans corricion,
   Lors montas a l'Ascension.

   Au jor de Pentecouste droit,
96 Droit a celle hore et cel androit
   Que li apostre erent assis
   A la table, chacuns pencis,
   Lors envoias tu a la table
100 La toe grace esperitable
   Dou saint Esperit enflamee,
   Que tant fu joïe et amee.
   Lors fu chacuns d'aus si hardiz,
104 Et par paroles et par diz,
   C'autant prisa mort comme vie:
   N'orent fors de t'amor envie.
   Biax chers fiz, por l'umain
      lignage
108 Jeter de honte et de domage
   Feïs tote ceste bonté
   Et plus assez que n'ai conté.
   S'or laissoies si esgaré
112 Ce que si chier as comparé,
   Ci avroit trop grant mesprison,

Then they became envious of you,
then they booed and hated you,
then you were caught and betrayed
by your friends and delivered to them,
then you were tortured and tor-
   mented
and you were tied to the pillar:
there is no one who does not believe
   and know it.
There you were beaten and wounded,
there you were troubled by death,
there you had to carry the cross
upon which you cried out loudly
to the Jews that you were thirsty.
Your thirst was knowing
that your friends were dead and tor-
   mented
in the pain of reeking hell.
Your soul [left] its body and went to
   hell
and broke the door to hell.
You ushered your friends from
   therein,
and neither cleric nor layperson
   remained.
Your body remained on the cross;
Joseph, who loved you so,
asked Pilate [for it]:
he granted his wish willingly.

Then you were laid in the tomb;
Pilate was rash and bold when
he set up guards around you,
because this is folly.
On the third day you were resur-
   rected:
then you were flesh and divinity
together without corruption,
then you rose to heaven on the
   Ascension.

S'or les lessoies en prison
Entrer, don tu les as osté,
116 Car ci avroit trop mal hosté,
Trop grant duel et trop grant
        martire,
Biau filz, biau pere, biau doz sire.'
Ainsi recorde tote jor
120 La doce Dame, sans sejor;
Ja ne fine de recorder
Car bien nous voudroit racorder
A li, don nos nos descordons
124 De sa corde et de ses cordons.
Or nous acordons a l'acorde
La Dame de misericorde
Et li prions que nos acort
128 Par sa pitié au dine acort
Son chier Fil, le dine Cor Dé:

Lors si serons bien racordé.
Explicit de Notre Dame

TN: The divisions in the text are
determined by where small initials
would have been placed, had the
manuscript been finished.

On the day of Pentecost,
right at the moment and in the place
that the apostles were seated
at table, each one pensive,
you sent to their table
your spiritual grace
enflamed with the Holy Spirit,
that was so enjoyed and loved.
Then each one was so emboldened
in words and speech,
that life and death were equal to
    them:
they wanted nothing save your love.
Handsome, good son, in order to rid
humanity of shame and hurt,
you did all these good things
and more that I did not say.
If now you were to let get away
that for which you paid so dearly,
it would be a grave error.
If you were to let them enter into the
prison, from which you delivered them,
it would be a most inhospitable
    shelter,
excessively painful and full of suffer-
    ing,
dear son, dear father, dear, good
    lord.'
Thus every day the Sweet Lady
reminds him, without rest;
she never stops reminding
because she so wants to reconcile us
    with
him from whose cord and ties we
dissociate ourselves.
Let us now accept the reconciliation
[brought about by] the Lady of mercy
and let us pray that she accord us
through her pity a worthy accord
with her dear son, the worthy heart of
    God:
then we will be well reconciled.

Notes

Introduction

1 For an excellent example of the influence of religious poetry on secular song, see Margaret Switten's 'Modèle et variation,' in which she discusses questions of intertextuality pertaining to 'Ave, Maris Stella,' 'O Maria Deu maire,' and 'Reis glorios.' See also Joan Tasker Grimbert's 'Songs by Women and Women's Songs,' for criticism of Bec's approach to register. Grimbert's comments are especially germane to devotional song.

2 Epstein edits the religious songs found in trouvères mss. *V* (Paris, BnF fr. 24406 (*Chansonnier de la Vallière*) and *X* (Paris, BnF Nouvelles acquisitions françaises 1050 (*Chansonnier de Clairambault*) for which the texts but not the melodies were published by Edward Järnström and Arthur Långfors in their *Recueil de chansons pieuses*.

3 Lyric songs are identified by their Raynaud-Spanke number in the text and in the table provided at the beginning of the appendix. Gautier's songs are equally identified by the numbers provided in Koenig's edition for the ease of those studying Gautier's songs in the context of his *Miracles de Nostre Dame*. The roman numeral refers the reader to the pertinent book of the *Miracles*; the abbreviation that follows designates the genre: 'Ch' for 'chanson,' and 'Pr' for 'prologue'; the arabic numeral provides the number of the piece within the book; and, finally, the numbers after the colon refer to verses. Thus, II Ch 3: 1–3 refers to verses 1 to 3 of the song that comes in third position of the second book.

4 Cathyrnke Dijkstra faces similar difficulties in her study of another hybrid genre: the crusade song. Dijkstra employs the philosophical notions of *intentio* and 'necessary condition' for separating crusade songs from lyrics that

merely include one or more motifs common to the crusade song (*La Chanson de croisade* 52).

5 In the first book, Augustine distinguishes between things to be enjoyed in and of themselves and things to be utilized: 'It is to be understood that the plenitude and the end of the Law and of all the sacred Scriptures is the love of a Being which is to be enjoyed and of a being that can share that enjoyment with us, since there is no need for a precept that anyone should love himself. That we might know this and have the means to implement it, the whole temporal dispensation was made by divine Providence for our salvation. We should use it, not with an abiding but with a transitory love and delight like that in a road or in vehicles or in other instruments, or, if it may be expressed more accurately, so that we love those things by which we are carried along for the sake of that toward which we are carried' (I:35) [Ut intellegatur Legis et omnium divinarum Scripturarum plenitudo et finis esse dilectio rei qua fruendum est, et rei quae nobiscum ea re frui potest, quia ut se quisque diligat praecepto non opus est. Hoc ergo ut nossemus atque possemus, facta est tota pro nostra salute per divinam providentiam dispensatio temporalis qua debemus uti, non quasi mansoria quadam dilectione et delectatione, sed transitoria potius tamquam viae, tamquam vehiculorum vel aliorum quorumlibet instrumentorum, aut si quid congruentius dici potest; ut ea quibus ferimur propter illus ad quod ferimur diligamus.]

6 See *Truth and Method* (hereafter *TM*) 328 or *Wahrheit und Methode* (hereafter *WM*) 311 for Gadamer's reasons for extending this legal concept into the field of general hermeneutics.

7 Reading music and text together has been the subject of many studies in the troubadour and trouvère repertories. My 'Text and Melody in Early Trouvère Song' provides both a model of this approach built upon much of the musicological and philological research of the past three decades and a bibliographical overview of that work.

Chapter 1

1 Its architecture also varies from codex to codex, an observation that forms the central thesis of the excellent PhD dissertation by Kathryn A. Duys. Based on codicological evidence gleaned from all available manuscripts, she draws out the rules of a complex literary game at work in the *Miracles* that she calls 'literary literacy' and defines as 'the practices and concepts that informed the compilation, circulation, and use of verbal art in writing' (4–5). Her work serves to bridge the gap left by past critics who concentrate either entirely on the songs or on his narratives; she also provides nuance to the

comments of critics like Mariella Vianello Bonifacio, who calls Gautier the 'autore di miracoli drammatici dedicati alla Vergine, *Les miracles de Nostre Dame*, nei quali si alternano orazioni e canzoni alla maniera dei romans à refrains' (458). The *Miracles* hardly resemble *romans à refrains* such as the *Roman de la Rose* [*ou de Guillaume de Dole*]. The architectural design that I employ for my analysis is based on the 'reconstruction' of the *Miracles'* original arrangement as posited by V.F.W. Koenig.

2 See Duys' analysis of II Ch 36 as a mnemonic for the Marian psalter (93–100).

3 As Hans-Robert Jauss puts it in his analysis of Christian poets' appropriation and reformulation of the classical doctrine of catharsis, the movement from *compassio* to *imitatio* lies at the centre of the Christian aesthetic experience: 'The true *compassio* (Augustine still uses the term *misericordia*) with which Christian poetry wants to break through the "Pleasure in pain," i.e. the aesthetic objectification of a sympathetically enjoying attitude, must prove itself as readiness for *imitatio*' (*Aesthetic Experience and Literary Hermeneutics* 104).

4 See Duys 134–5 for the centrality of the Leocadia narrative and lyric sequence in the Petersburg codex (Ms. *R*; St Petersburg, National Library of Russia, Fr. F. v. XIV 9).

5 Stadtmüller provides a longer, more detailed listing of the themes and motifs that Gautier takes from Marian literature in Latin and secular love poetry. Flory makes the use of love vocabulary a central issue in his discussion of Gautier's representation of Mary. In the twelfth century, Bernard of Clairvaux, the *doctor Mariae*, wrote several sermons on Mary. For its homiletic production, its scholastic treatises on Marian theology, and its musical sequences in the twelfth century, the abbey at St Victor could be considered a centre for Marian theological activity. In the plastic arts, Mary began appearing above church entrances, a movement studied in 'Religious Image: Iconography of the Virgin Mary,' chapter 2 of Gold, *The Lady and the Virgin*. In vernacular poetics, Wace wrote his life of the Virgin. Of course, the bibliography of the first troubadours and trouvères is vast, and readers are directed to the bibliographies compiled by Margaret Switten and Eglal Doss-Quinby as well as Dragonetti's *La Technique poétique des trouvères*.

6 Bibliography on these questions as well as the cult of the Virgin in general is vast. The recent anthology of essays edited by Russo Palazzo, *Marie: le culte de la Vierge dans la société médiévale*, provides detailed studies of the cult in its wider societal context from the early through the late Middle Ages. Readers can find a concise chronology of the cult of the Virgin in the appendix to Marina Warner, *Alone of All Her Sex*. Along the same lines as Warner's feminist reading of the cult of Mary is Sarah Jane Boss's *Empress and Handmaid*. Bernard of Clairvaux (1091–1153) meditated upon the Annunciation with

great fervour in his four sermons *In Laudibus Virginis Matris* (c.1125). See Gold for interest in the Coronation of Mary, especially the chapter cited in the preceding note. Finally, in his *Epistola de virginitate beatae Mariae*, Hugh of Saint Victor struggled to reconcile the seeming paradox between perpetual virginity and conjugal duty due to Mary as the wife of Joseph. See Edward Schillebeeckx's fundamental study of the theology of marriage for more on the question of terrestrial versus spiritual marriage.

7 While playing 'Eva' off of 'Ave' was widely exploited throughout the Middle Ages, one recent article proves that more has yet to be said about the figure: see Ansermet and André's psychoanalytic reading of late medieval paintings entitled, 'Eve dans Marie.'

8 See Taylor for chess imagery in Gautier.

9 See Ducrot-Granderye (140–71) for her comments on Gautier's life, his work, and his public. See also Koenig (xviii–xxx) and Duys (12–31).

10 See Diehl's analysis of the 'container contained' topos in medieval religious lyric (204–8).

11 See Warner's chapter 'The Milk of Paradise' (192–205) for a history of Mary's milk as both topos and relic.

12 To the best of my knowledge, the figure is unique to Gautier at the beginning of the thirteenth century. Rutebeuf uses it towards the end of the century in his 'C'est de Notre Dame.' Consecrated virgins, male or female, traditionally married Christ, not Mary, and by the thirteenth century, the concept of the *sponsa* was used only for women. Gautier's 'La Fontenele i sourt clere,' which is appended to Gautier's sermon on chastity (II Chast 10), speaks most extensively about spiritual marriage and is composed in the voice of the nuns of Soissons and not in that of the sexless, universal 'I.' For a discussion of the *sponsa Dei* motif in the Middle Ages, see Bugge 80–110. Finally, Gautier's moralistic *queues*, although occupying the final verses of his miracles, are their heuristic centre. For a study that centralizes his *queues* in a discussion of the representation and function of children in the *Miracles*, see my 'Reading Children in Gautier de Coinci's *Miracles de Nostre Dame*.'

13 See *Songs of the Women Trouvères* for examples of commentary, and bibliography on the form. Passing reference to the genre is also made throughout the recent anthology of essays, *Medieval Woman's Songs: Cross-Cultural Approaches*.

14 Duys addresses the problem in her codicological analysis. See also under 'Studies and Secondary Sources' Auerbach, Bonifacio, Colombani, Drzewicka, Larmat, and Stadtmüller, for other work on the combination of sacred and profane poetics in the work of Gautier de Coinci and others. Chailley assumes that all of Gautier's melodies are borrowed, but a number of models have yet to be identified (49).

15 See Duys 126–32.

16 See Drzewicka 192–7 for a study of the refrains Gautier borrows. Both Drzewicka and Duys might overstate the case for seeing Gautier's attachment of refrains to melodies that previously lacked refrains as a paradigm-shifting amalgamation of songs from the *registre aristocratisant* and the *registre popularisant* (Bec, *La Lyrique française* I:33–5). Refrains are more common in popular songs; however, they are common enough in aristocratic love songs to prohibit too sweeping a generalization. The significance of Gautier's stitching together of melodies lies more in the choice among particular songs and not among registers or genres. Nevertheless, we might see Gautier's seeming negligence of generic boundaries as an even more serious transgression of the law they uphold.

17 See Drzewicka, 'La fonction des emprunts,' for a nuanced analysis of this Gautier's contrafactum on Blondel's song.

18 The melodies used are by no means stable among the extant manuscripts. Duys goes to great lengths to demonstrate the large-scale *mouvance* in the melodies. Gautier's songs are textually stable and submit to few alterations from manuscript to manuscript, but their position in the cycles and the melodies attached to them are quite variable. Nevertheless, the cycle arrangement Koenig, Chailley, and Duys employ is the most common and complies with the arrangements found in the most complete and artful compilations.

19 Carruthers puts it most succinctly in her introduction: 'The key lies in the imposition of a rigid order to which prepared pieces of textual content are attached' (8).

20 Duys expertly demonstrates the extent to which memory is a concern to Gautier in songs like 'Entendez tuit ensemble,' which functions as a mnemonic system for the Marian psalter (93–9). On a larger scale, in the compilation of Gautier's manuscripts, Duys shows how certain melodies recur at key moments in order to prompt an audience's memory and make links between various points in the *Miracles.*

21 After Gautier, the vernacular poet most famous for his use of *annominatio* is Rutebeuf; Nancy Freeman Regalado's analysis of the figure in her important work, *Poetic Patterns in Rutebeuf*, remains the best treatment to date of the figure both in Rutebeuf and in general. See especially 205 ff. Regalado defines *annominatio* as the 'repetitions of various forms of a word, words based on the same root, homonyms, or words that are identical except for a letter or two' (191 n.5).

22 Diehl cites Matthew de Vendôme's *ars poetica* as representative of the medieval authors who subscribe to the preeminence of metaphor (203). See Gadamer's interpretive analysis of the doctrine of the Trinity in the Middle

Ages and of the human word as the counterpart to the Word of God (*TM* 418–28 and *WM* 395–404). See Diehl and Epstein for lists of traditional Marian metaphors. Gautier uses some while leaving others aside.

23 I have consulted both volumes of Järnström's *Recueil* as well as Epstein's more recent edition of songs from mss. *X* and *V*. I can find no other poet who uses *annominatio* in devotional lyrics. Rutebeuf, of course, uses the figure widely, but his compositions are lyric in a different sense.

24 By comparison, in the first song of the cycle that opens the second book, both the individual rhymes and the root words used for *annominatio* change from stanza to stanza.

25 In *La faiblesse chez Gautier de Coinci,* Cazelles believes that Gautier's use of *annominatio* is anchored in roots with both positive and negative significations that bolster the central dualism of good versus evil. It should be noted that Cazelles focuses first and foremost on Gautier's narratives. Nevertheless, among her examples she cites one that appears in the song currently under analysis: 'chant.' Cazelles takes the figure from the *queue* of I Mir 14 and believes that it signifies in the miracle's *queue* 'ensorcellement et enchantement' (106). However, it also signifies 'songs' (both secular and religious) and the morpheme '[I] sing.' While I think that Cazelles's theory is ingenious, by tying the figure to the binarism good/evil she excessively restricts its function.

26 Because I cite so many expressions from this song in so short a space, I refer to the verse numbers only in this passage instead of using the usual formula, i.e., I Ch 3: 3.

27 Throughout this study, I use the pitch nomenclature that corresponds to line two of example 1 in the article 'Pitch nomenclature' of the *New Grove Dictionary of Music*: 'c' denotes 'middle C,' 'c'' an octave above, and 'C' an octave below.

28 Generically speaking, the *lai*'s section tends to be longer that the *chanson*'s stanza. Nevertheless, Gautier's thirty-six-verse sections are longer than most examples of the genre.

29 See Regalado for a brief sketch of this *annominatio* in vernacular Marian literature (*Poetic Patterns* 213–15).

30 In *La Métaphore Vive* (in English, *The Rule of Metaphor*), Ricoeur borrows the idea from Mary Hesse's work on Aristotle's *Poetics*.

31 I quote Ricoeur's essay from *A Ricoeur Reader*.

32 This refrain, number 1840 in Boogaard's index, is extant in seven other contexts: a *chanson avec des refrains* by Colart le Boutellier (RS 839, stanza VI), two motets – 'Vilene gens/Honte et dolor/Haec dies' (Ludwig and Gennrich no. 125) and 'Trop font vilenie/Reg(nat)' (Ludwig and Gennrich no. 447a) –

three *dits*: *Li Confrere d'Amors*, Baudouin de Condé's *La Prison d'Amours*, and the *Salut d'Amours* found in Paris, BnF fr. 837 (fols. 269b–71a), and the fourteenth-century Catalan devotional work *Llibre d'amoretes*. For an account of how this refrain interacts in its different contexts, see my 'Old French Refrains in Song, Verse, and Prose: A Case Study (forthcoming).'

33 For Chrétien's romance, I cite David Hult's edition based on ms. *P* (Paris, BnF fr. 1433) found in the volume of Chrétien's work edited by Michel Zink et al.

34 See Dyggve's introduction to Gilles's works in *Trouvères et protecteurs dans les cours seigneurials de France* and Duys (72) for comments and bibliography concerning this trouvère and his tumultuous poetic career.

35 'Dans la métaphore, au contraire, la perception d'une incompatibilité est essentielle, comme on l'a vu, à l'interprétation du message' (*La Métaphore vive* 236).

36 'Es besteht wirklich eine Polarität von Vertrautheit und Fremdheit, auf die sich die Aufgabe der Hermeneutik gründet, nur daß diese nicht mit Schleiermacher psychologisch als die Sprannweite, die das Geheimnis der Individualität birgt, zu verstehen ist, sondern wahrhaft hermeneutisch, d.h. im Hinblick auf ein Gesagtes: die Sprache, mit der die Überlieferung uns anredet, die Sage, die sie uns sagt. Auch hier ist eine Spannung gegeben. Die Stellung zwischen Fremdheit und Vertrautheit, die die Überlieferung für uns hat, ist das Zwischen zwischen der historisch gemeinten, abständigen Gegenständlichkeit und der Zugehörigkeit zu einer Tradition. *In diesem Zwischen ist der wahre Ort der Hermeneutik*' (*WM* 279).

Chapter 2

1 Emmanuèle Baumgartner provides a nuanced reading of Thibaut's work in the context of *O*, arguing that each illuminated capital represents a 'lettre 'historiée' that comments most often on the song it illustrates, most often by Thibaut (40–1). She also makes comments pertaining to the author-centred anthologies similar to my own analysis, provided above. Of course, her work is a general survey of Thibaut's work in manuscript, and so she provides few details regarding the place of any genre, let alone the devotional corpus specifically, among various compilations (39–40).

2 It is even possible that Thibaut himself had a hand in compiling his songs, as is attested in the *Grandes Chroniques*. See Sylvia Huot for more comments on this possibility in the context of other single-authors compilations (*From Song to Book* 64–6).

3 I use the term 'sirventois' to denote the political or satiric song, known in Occitan as the 'sirventes.' Wallensköld's term 'serventois religieux' notwith-

standing, the label 'serventois' is reserved for the devotional lyric genre that flourished in fourteenth-century *puys.*

4 Elizabeth Kuhs cites Thibaut's text as an early example of vernacular poetry derived from its written form, but she also focuses on how written and spoken language come together in Thibaut's song: 'Durch Homophonieüberschneidungen werden die Buchstabennamen in engen Sinnzusammenhang mit einem gleichklingenden Wort gebracht, so daâ dem ganzen Namen MARIA schlieâlich die Einzelbedeutungen der homophonen Wörter inhärent zu sein scheinen' (22–3) (Though homophonic overlap, the letter [names] are closely linked semantically to similar sounding words, so that the particular meanings of the homeophonic words seem inherent to the whole name MARIA).

5 An associated passage is Mark 12: 20–5 where the disciples spot the withered fig tree that Jesus had previously cursed because it bore no fruit. He draws a teaching similar to the passages cited above: a tree that bears no fruit shall be cut down and thrown upon the fire.

6 One should note that Mary appears in the majority of Rutebeuf's crusade pieces, which are not included in Bédier's anthology, probably because they did not have musical accompaniment. However, Mary's presence in Rutebeuf's crusade poems is purely incidental and not functional. Crusade songs have enjoyed more recent critical attention since the Bédier/Beck edition. See Siberry's article 'Troubadours, trouvères, minnesingers and the crusades' for a reading of vernacular crusade songs as valuable historical documents and Dijsktra's *La chanson de croisade: Etude d'un genre hybride* for a general discussion of the genre.

7 A similar contrast occurs among Thibaut's *jeux-partis*: in 'Sire, ne me celez mie,' Thibaut defends the position that it is better to enjoy physical pleasure than the game of courting, but in 'Sire, loez moi a choisir' Thibaut defends the pleasure of seeing his beloved over physical pleasure without seeing her.

8 See Brahney's introduction as well as Dolly and Cormier for their discussion of memory in Thibaut's lyric production.

9 Dijkstra's reading concurs with my interpretation of the 'guerredons floriz' ('Troubadours, trouvères, and crusade lyrics' 177).

10 The manuscript witnesses to Thibaut's piece pose several difficulties pertaining to the work's genre and its form. Music survives in *MtOV,* but not in *T.* Most disconcerting in the witnesses is the seeming lack of any kind of textual organization: puncta are used irregularly after rhyme words in the text of *O, T,* and *V.* In *Mt,* puncta are seldom used: we find them at the bottom of each column and only three times within the second column of text. In *MtOV,* there are no corresponding *virgules* in the music, even if the scribe of *Mt*

occasionally uses them in transcribing the melodies of Thibaut's other works. The scribe of *V* puts a stem on nearly every note whereas the use of stems in *Mt* is erratic. On the other hand, the scribe of *O* would seem to have transcribed the melody in the first rhythmic mode with liberal use of *fractio* and *extensio modii*. In short, the scribal habits at use in preserving this piece are particularly erratic and provide no help in discerning an overall organizational principle. Editorial reactions have ranged from agonizing over the piece's metrical irregularities (Jeanroy and Aubry) to asserting simply that the *lai* is metrically irregular as a rule (Wallensköld and Brahney).

11 Richard Baum's survey of criticism of the *lai* demonstrates how little consensus has been achieved concerning the genre's characteristics ('Les troubadours et les lais'), and attempts to describe the genre are plagued with qualifiers such as 'generally,' 'largely,' and 'usually.' Jean Maillard has called the *lai* a 'composition poétique de caractère personnel, traitant généralement de problèmes amoureux ou religieux, et essentiellement destinée à être mise en musique (voix ou instrument)' (*Evolution et esthétique du lai lyrique* 93).

12 In order to achieve regularity, Alfred Jeanroy hypothesizes that the copyist interpolated parts of verses 19–20 and verse 32, skipped a seven-syllable verse (presumably verse 41), and omitted three syllables in the third-to-last verse (Jeanfroy, Aubry, and Brandin 100–1). Such changes would bring about a regular rhythm of a single quadrisyllable followed by three seven-syllable verses after verse 13. Subsequent editors such as Axel Wallensköld and Kathleen Brahney prefer a more conservative approach and make no such textual emendations in their editions. Wallensköld proposes a scheme apparently according to syntax, where hard stops – places where he places a period, question mark, an exclamation point, and sometimes, but not always, a semi-colon – separate groupings and, in so doing, only better demonstrates the syntactic and metrical heterogeneity of Thibaut's *lai*.

Chapter 3

1 As no complete and satisfactory edition of 'Lasse' exists, I offer a new edition of both text and melody in the appendix. Tischler publishes the *planctus* in his *Trouvère Lyrics with Melodies* (no. L25) with mensural notation, as does Yvonne Rosketh in her partial edition from earlier in the twentieth century. Recueil is edited by Järnström and Långfors.

2 Sylvia Huot follows a similar logic in her review of *SWT* for *Speculum*: 'Many readers will be surprised by the absence of the *chanson de toile*, excluded on the grounds that such songs have a male narrator; in fact, the gender of the

narrative voice is indeterminate in many *chansons de toile* and could be considered female as easily as male. The editors' point, however, is that they have included only songs that either bear a female attribution or have a voice that is clearly gendered feminine. In the absence of explicit attribution, a gender-neutral voice is not good enough to meet that criteria' (874).

3 Järnström and Långfors make some comments on the manuscript in the second volume of the *Recueil* (17–23), but more recently Duys has offered a more complete codicological analysis of the codex in chapter 4 of her PhD dissertation.

4 Långfors noticed the marginal expressions 'Quid'' for 'Quidam' when a known work is being cited and 'Ros'' for 'Rosarius' at those moments where the compiler seems to abandon his models to versify freely. Zetterberg and Sandqvist apparently concur (9), citing Faral and Bastin who note a similar practice in the manuscripts transmitting Rutebeuf's works (24).

5 The manuscript shows affinities with the devotional books described by Huot in 'A Book Made for a Queen.'

6 Although this manuscript has garnered considerable attention from scholars for over a century, the reconstruction of the *Rosarius* chapters is a long, complicated, and arduous task, as there is no complete edition of the codex. Moreover, the manuscript itself is only partially preserved and the part that survives is badly damaged – past marginal trimming has made reading text along the edges, at times, impossible. For this reason, hypothesized parts of both melody and text are put in brackets. Arthur Långfors published a detailed description of the manuscript but only portions of the text in his *Notice du manuscrit français 12483 de la Bibliothèque Nationale*. As indicated above, he published the text of the songs in the *Recueil de chansons pieuses* with Edward Järnström. Alfred Jeanroy studies the song texts in his 'Les chansons pieuses du ms. fr. 12483 de la Bibliothèque Nationale.' The music of some of the songs is published in *SWT* and the others can be found in Tischler's *Trouvère Lyrics with Melodies*. In the case of those found in the latter publication, I have reedited the melodies from the manuscript for reasons explained in the introduction to my appendix. The 'plantaire' material from the work's various chapters was published by Mary Alberta Savoie; the bestiary and lapidary materials appear in Sven Sandqvist's *Le Bestiaire et le lapidaire du* Rosarius; Sandqvist finished the work of Anders Zetterberg, who died prematurely, and assured the publication of the other chapters on inanimate objects in *Les Propriétés des choses selon le* Rosarius *(B.N.fr. 12483)*. Critical editions of the compilation's narrative miracles can be found in Pierre Kunstmann, ed., *Miracles de Notre-Dame tirés du* Rosarius *(Paris, ms. B.N.fr. 12483)*. The *contes dévots* that are not miracles *in stricto sensu* are found among compi-

lations of *contes* and fabliaux such as Jubinal's *Nouveau recueil de contes, dits, fabliaux, et autres pièces inédites des XIIIe, XIVe et XVe siècles, I–II* and the *Recueil général et complet des fabliaux des XIIIe et XIVe s.* edited by Anatole de Montaiglon and Gaston Raynaud. In the individual readings below, I indicate from which edition I am citing materials. My citations from the chapter on the falcon come from Sandqvist, *Le Bestiaire* 143–52, and the numbers in parentheses indicate verse numbers from his edition.

7 Boynton, like many scholars before her, takes recourse to scenes of musical performance in fictional works like the *Guillaume de Dole* or *Flamenca*, which provide intriguing, if elusive, information about performance practices: 'Some genres (such as the *canso*) could be performed by women or men, without any inherent link between the voice of the poem and the sex of the singer. Even genres closely associated with performance by women, such as the *chanson de toile* and the *rondet de carole*, could apparently be sung by men or women, as seen above in the *Guillaume de Dole*. The appropriation of a song's voice by a singer seems often to have been considered an integral part of the song, which was then interpreted as a personal statement by the performer' (61). Ardis Butterfield relies on Jean Renart's *Rose* for her 'contextual' (her term) study of poetry and music of the thirteenth and fourteenth centuries. According to Christopher Page, gleaning evidence of performance practice from fictional works is possible, but one must tread very carefully: 'A passage in an epic or romance cannot prove anything by itself, although it may possess a kind of metaphorical realism whereby contemporary interests and preoccupations are brought onto the stage of the narrative in the garb provided for them by the story-materials and conventions available to the narrator' (*The Owl and the Nightingale* 192).

8 Matilda Tomaryn Bruckner carefully argues that trobairitz song is neither the same nor a mere inversion of male troubadour song in her introduction to *Songs of the Women Troubadours* as well as in her recently republished article 'Fictions of the Female Voice,' and in her 'Na Castelloza, *Trobairitz*, and Troubadour Lyric.' Similarly, Burns has argued: 'We do not yet have an adequate conceptual framework for understanding the *chanson de toile* as a form of lyric composition distinctly different from the songs of the trouvères or the troubadours to which they are poetically indebted and closely linked – much less as a genre that could effectively stage alternate subject positions for its female protagonists' ('Sewing Like a Girl' 104).

9 I cite the cantiga from volume 1 of Walter Mettman's edition. The translation is my own.

10 I take my citations of surrounding chapter context of '*Du dous Jhesu*' from Sandqvist *Le Bestiaire*, but my citations of the song from Järnström. Järnström

provides only a few comments on the text itself, but Wendy Pfeffer reads the song more carefully in her article, '"Mourir comme le rossignol,"' much of which gets reincorporated into her monograph, *The Change of Philomel.*

11 I take my references for the commentary on the camel from Sandqvist's *Le Bestiaire.* I take my references for the song, however, from *SWT.* The numbers is parentheses is both cases refer to verse numbers.

12 Unfortunately, Pfeffer misreads this stanza and fails to see that Jesus and the nightingale are one. Nevertheless, her reading, which calls our attention to how the bird's song, usually associated with secular lovers, becomes transformed in its religious context, is overall correct: the nightingale calls lovers to turn towards God and the joy that can only be derived from communion with him.

13 For a detailed examination of the tension among medieval religious orders, see chapter 10, 'Cura mulierium,' of McNamara, *Sisters in Arms.* A thorough, but uncritical, history of the Dominican order can be found in Hinnebusch's *The History of the Dominican Order.*

14 I take my citations for the song's surrounding context from Sandqvist's *Le Bestiaire* but for the song itself, I cite *SWT.*

15 Past editors have offered hypotheses for the lacuna in verse 30: Bartsch suggests 'Que ne m'est bon' while Järnström and Långfors propose 'Qu'art con charbon.'

16 Both Järnström and Bec point to the similarities between this song and *Bele Aeliz* (*Recueil,* volume 2:30, and *Lyrique Française,* volume 1:147–8, respectively). It may be true that the two songs share motifs, but Aeliz usually goes joyfully into some idyllic setting such as a meadow or forest; the beguine's rather somber experience in the church takes place presumably against an urban backdrop. The resulting contrast casts the beguine's sorrowful condition into stark relief, and so while Järnström and Bec's comments are not incorrect, they once again show how such comparisons should be the beginning, not the conclusion, of reading.

17 Scholarship on women's mysticism abounds, and I can delve deeply into neither the subject nor its bibliography here, but recent contributors include Monica Furlong, Jane Ellen McAvoy, Nathalie Fraise, and the collaborators Emilie Zum Brunn and Georgette Epiney-Burgard.

18 In his PhD dissertation, John R. Secor examines the *planctus* in Latin and a number of vernacular traditions, including French, and focuses especially on lexical 'borrowings' from the secular, courtly tradition. The results of his work in Occitan can be found in his article, 'The *Planctus Mariae* in Provençal Literature.' 'Je plains et plors come feme dolente' (*SWT* no. 38, RS 746a), another example of a *planctus,* dates from the twelfth century, and

so it antedates the period under study here. The editors of *SWT* suggest that the 'Je plains' is a religious paraphrase of a women's lament like the duchesse de Lorraine's 'Par maintes fois avrai esteit requise.' This is undoubtedly true; however, the editors make no mention of the nearly fifty Old French *planctus Mariae* from the twelfth to the sixteenth century (Secor 49).

19 For an extensive study of this relationship and its impact on the history of medieval theatre, see Sandro Sticca.

20 For example, in the debate poem between Mary and the cross found in Paris, BnF fr. 17068 and edited by Arthur Långfors in 'Notice du manuscrit français 17068 de la Bibliothèque Nationale,' the cross plays the optimistic foil to the Virgin's painful lamentations.

21 According to Sticca, some of the greatest theologians of the period, among whom figure Albert the Great (1193–1280), Peter Olivi (d. 1298), and Raymond Lull (c. 1231–1315), addressed the question of the coexistence of pain and joy felt by Mary at the foot of the cross (33–42).

Chapter 4

1 I cite Jean-Claude Rivière's edition of Jacques's texts. Dinaux published a short, anecdotal history of Bern, Stadtbibliothek 389 as well as two love songs, Jacques's *pastourelle*, and three 'chansons dévotes' in 1836. His *pastourelle* was also published by Bartsch in 1870, and all seven religious songs appear in Järnström and Långfors's *Recueil de chansons pieuses* (7). Rivière believes that charters and other documentary evidence will one day reveal more about Jacques (11). Indeed, a comprehensive history of medieval Cambrai has yet to be written. We do know that thirteenth-century Cambrai produced brilliant church administrators like Guiard de Laon who, according to Joseph Avril, was largely responsible for one of the earliest finished collections of synodal statutes. See Avril's *Les Statuts synodaux de l'ancienne province de Reims*. Another famous Cambrensien was Thomas de Cantimpré, who produced the *Bonum universale de apibus* and saints' lives of many of his female contemporaries, who were often beguines, as they were especially numerous in thirteenth-century Cambrai. The region also knew the rancour of the Inquisition in the sadistic practices of Robert le Bougre, as verses 28871–9025 of the *Chronique rimée de Philippe Mouskès* testifies.

2 Recent studies of this manuscript include Paola Moreno's work in *'Intavulare'* and Richard A. Schutz's PhD dissertation: 'The Unedited Poems of Codex 389.' Sylvia Huot compares the manuscript to the *Chansonnier Cangé* (Paris, BnF fr. 846) as manuscripts that order their pieces alphabetically by incipit (*From Song to Book* 46–7). Brief comments may be found in Järnström's

Receuil; diplomatic editions in Wackernagel as well as Brakelmann; and earlier descriptions in Hofmann's 'Altfranzösische Pastourelle aus der Berner Handschrift nr 389' and his 'Eine Anzahl altfranzösische lyrischer Gedichte aus Berner Codex 389.'

3 The ideal of the crusades remained strong later in Cambrai than in other regions. For general information on the contemporary religious climate, see E. de Moreau's article 'Belgique' and M. Chartier's article 'Cambrai' in the *Dictionnaire d'histoire et de géographie ecclésiastiques.*

4 It is tempting to see an influence of Jacques's urban environment here: by the third quarter of the thirteenth century, the mendicant orders who stressed Jesus' humanity were making rapid progress in urban centres like Paris and Arras. Sermons delivered by mendicant preachers might be one source, doubtless among many, for this thematic choice.

5 The best known authority on the Albigensian crusades remains the work of Joseph Strayer, entitled simply *The Albigensian Crusades.*

6 See Rivière's introduction for an overview of the different metres, etc., that Jacques's songs use. Rivière pays only cursory attention to Jacques's models.

7 The information in this table is derived from Hans Tischler's *Trouvère Lyrics with Melodies: A Complete Comparative Edition.*

8 Thibaut's song survives in no fewer than fifteen manuscripts and Gauthier's, in twelve.

9 I cite Rudolf's stanza from Tischler's *Trouvère Lyrics with Melodies,* in which it appears as one of the texts accompanying song no. 637.

10 The author wishes to express his gratitude to Gregory Heyworth for his aid in translating the stanza.

11 See my 'Revisiting *Mouvance* and Medieval Lyric Performance' for an in-depth analysis of the three extant versions of Jacques's song.

12 I cite Adam's text from Tischler's *Trouvère Lyrics with Melodies* in which it appears as one of the texts accompanying song no. 1206.

13 The author wishes to express his gratitude to Jan M. Ziolkowski for his aid in translating the stanza.

14 I cite Jehan's stanza from Tischler's *Trouvère Lyrics with Melodies* in which it appears as one of the texts accompanying song no. 434.

15 The two genres are difficult to summarize in any schematic way as they continually evolved. Gros studies them very carefully in *Le Poème du Puy marial.* In *Le Poète, la Vierge, et le Prince du Puy,* more information about the inner workings of the *puys* themselves is given.

16 'Dans tous les cas, l'envoi de ces deux poèmes permet de deviner l'existence d'un Puy (probablement arrageois) où pouvaient s'exercer les amateurs de poésie religieuse, dès le troisième quart du XIIIe siècle' (*Le Poème du Puy*

marial 24). In a different publication, Gros indicates with a map where *puys* did exist and where they may have existed, Cambrai constituting one of his speculations (*Le Poète, la Vierge, et le Prince du Puy* 38). Unfortunately, Gros does not explain the reasons for this suggestion.

Chapter 5

1 Gros's article, 'La *semblance* de la *verrine*: Description et interprétation d'une image mariale,' constitutes an in-depth study of this figure.
2 I rely on Edmond Faral and Julia Bastin's edition of Rutebeuf for citations for all texts, except the Theophilus poems, which I reedit from ms. *C* and append to this work. A glance at some of the thematic categories into which the editors divide Rutebeuf's poetry reveals the omnipresence of religion in the poet's work: 'L'Eglise, les Ordres Mendiants, et l'Université,' 'Les Croisades,' and an entire section entitled 'Poèmes religieux.' Among the 'Pièces à Rire' we find the fabliau 'Frère Denise,' which opens with the lesson, 'Li abis ne fet pas l'ermite' (1). Even among what Faral and Bastin name 'Poèmes de l'Infortune,' religion is repeatedly evoked. And although only four of the 'Poèmes religieux' are designated as 'Pièces en honneur de la Vierge,' Mary plays a significant role in all of them. Mention is also made of Mary in two of the songs on the church, mendicant orders and university ('Les Ordres de Paris' [64, 107] and 'La Voie de Paradis' [557–60]), in several of the 'Poèmes de l'infortune,' ('La Griesche d'hiver' [91], 'Le Mariage Rutebeuf' [40, 77, 87], 'Le Dit d'Aristote' [20], 'La Mort (Repentence) Rutebeuf,' [11, 43–60]), and in the majority of Rutebeuf's crusade poetry ('La Complainte de Mgr Geoffroi de Sergines' [58], 'Le Dit de Pouille' [35, 45], 'La Complainte du Comte Eudes de Nevers' [14], 'La Complainte de Guillaume de Saint-Amour' [52, 193–4], 'La Disputasion du Croisé' [234], 'La Complainte du Roi de Navarre' [135–6], and 'La Nouvelle Complainte d'Outremer' [361–2]). Zink comments on the ominipresence of religion in the introduction to his *Oeuvres complètes* (23), and Miha Pintariè builds upon his comments in her 'Rutebeuf entre le temps de l'eglise et le le temps du marchand.'
3 David Flory offers a reading of the sacristan's tale in his *Marian Representations*.
4 See Mustanoja's for the question of attribution. Critics who have previously worked on Rutebeuf's Marian material stress his continuity with earlier poetic traditions, as I do; however, their conclusions stop short of revealing Rutebeuf's real contribution to the Marian tradition. Jean Dufournet's study of the representation of the Virgin in Rutebeuf's poetry stresses the extent to which Rutebeuf's portrait of the Virgin resembles those of past poets:

'Plus nous avancerons dans l'étude, plus nous nous rendrons compte que Rutebeuf, qui a chanté la Vierge dans tous les genres, n'a rien d'un nova-teur' ('Rutebeuf et la Vierge' 15). Faral and Bastin comment on the individ-ual motifs employed and reach a similar conclusion: 'Si sincères qu'aient pu être ses sentiments, il n'y a guère d'originalité dans son inspiration: il n'a fait que reprendre des lieux communs traités par une foule d'autres poètes' (235). Notwithstanding the accurate, though overly conservative conclusions of those studies, Rutebeuf's particular choice of figures from among the stock available to him, his recasting of traditional motifs into the new rhythm of spoken poetry, and the variety of speaking subjects make his Marian poetry deserving of in-depth study.

5 Nancy Freeman Regalado's fundamental study of Rutebeuf has shown that the poet adopted the voice of different noncourtly poetic personae in his oeuvre: the struggling jongleur, the outraged polemicist, the husband of an ugly, overbearing wife, etc. (*Poetic Patterns*). In his Marian works, much the same is true, but it has escaped the notice of most critics. Michel Zink describes the rise of a literary consciousness in the thirteenth century in his book, *La Subjectivité littéraire*.

6 Past generations of critics have, in fact, viewed such texts as autobiographi-cal, and as late as 1980, critics continued to try to glean autobiographical information from Rutebeuf's work. Faral and Bastin read Rutebeuf's poetry as autobiographical, an interpretation against which Regalado reads in her *Poetic Patterns*. Michel-Marie Dufeil's article (published in 1980, thus ten years after the appearance of Regalado's book), 'L'Œuvre d'une vie rhyth-mée: Chronographie de Rutebeuf,' tries again to read Rutebeuf's poetry as an ensemble of clues to the poet's life, resulting in an attempt to order and date the poems chronologically. In the introduction to his edition of Rute-beuf, Zink believes Dufeil's chronology to be ingenious if not definitive: 'Quelles que soient les incertitudes de détail, la chronologie proposée par Michel-Marie Dufeil emporte l'adhésion. L'idée que la vie et la carrière de Rutebeuf ont été marquées par une crise matérielle et morale liée à la défaite des séculiers dont il avait embrassé la cause, éclaire de façon saisis-sante son oeuvre dans sa cohérence et dans ses ruptures. Mais dans la mesure assez large où cette reconstitution se fonde sur la critique interne des poèmes, elle pose la question de leur valeur référentielle. Dufeil paraît admettre au point de prendre pour argent comptant, comme l'avaient fait Edmond Faral et Julia Bastin, les confidences du *Mariage* et de la *Complainte Rutebeuf*. Cette interprétation, c'est le moins qu'on puisse dire, ne va pas de soi. On ne peut savoir comment lire Rutebeuf et comment le croire tant que l'on n'est pas au clair touchant sa poétique' (*Oeuvres complètes* 1:18–19). For

more on reference versus representation, see Roland Barthes, 'L'effet de réel' and Regalado's *'Effet de réel, Effet du réel.'*

7 Previous discussions of 'La Mort/Repentence Rutebeuf' in the context of Rutebeuf's other repentance poems include Regalado's *Poetic Patterns* 270–82 and Zink's 'De la repentance Rutebeuf à la repentance Théophile.'

8 In these verses, Rutebeuf echoes Gautier's 'D'une amour quoie' closely: 'Amons la rose espanie/ Ou Diex prist *aombrement*' (II Ch 5: 34–5 my emphasis). See Gautier's song editor, Chailley (42–4), and Regalado for more on Gautier's influence on Rutebeuf.

9 Gautier de Coinci uses the example of Mary of Egypt in I Ch 3, 'Amours, qui bien set enchanter,' which begins with an eschewal of the world and secular poetics.

10 For a discussion of Rutebeuf's hagiographical poem in the context of its antecedents and contemporary manifestations, see Nash, Robertson, Cazelle, *The Lady as Saint,* and Gilespie.

11 Faral and Bastin believe these last verses contain a gambling metaphor, which reminds us of the first stanza's conversion of worldly motifs to religious ends: the speaker leaves the game to whomever wishes to continue it (1:578).

12 Faral and Bastin hypothesize that the form's interlinking of rhyme and syntax helped guarantee accurate oral transmission (1:205). Zink elegantly describes the sonorous effects produced in performance: 'le rythme à la fois satisfaisant et dégingandé du tercet coué, avec la surprise attendue du vers bref qui le termine mais ne le clôt pas, puisqu'il reste sur le suspens d'une rime isolée dans l'attente des octosyllabes du tercet suivant, qui eux-mêmes ont besoin de la chute désinvolte, chantante et lasse du vers de quatre pieds, qui à son tour ... les tercets se poussant et s'épaulant ainsi l'un l'autre comme des vagues, sans pouvoir s'arrêter sinon aux prix d'une menue violence métrique' ('Rutebeuf et le cours du poème' 546).

13 Rutebeuf is not the first to use this technique of interweaving the Latin Ave Maria into a French piece. Notably, Gautier de Coinci's 'Entendez tuit ensemble' (II Ch 36) employs the same technique, although differences certainly exist. I believe the differences to be significant enough to dispute Chailley's claim that Rutebeuf's poem is a mere imitation (*décalque*) of Gautier's song (*Les Chansons à la Vierge de Gautier,* 42). See Duys's ingenious reading of Gautier's song as a mnemonic for the Marian psalter (93–9).

14 Jean-Charles Payen includes Rutebeuf among a number of poets whose repentance poems are heavily introspective: 'Jean Bodel, Baude Fastoul, Adam de la Halle et Rutebeuf ne sont pas les poètes des larmes contrites, mais ce sont les poètes de la prise de conscience, de la régénération morale

et spirituelle et, dans la mesure où il nous est permis d'en juger, d'un ferme propos qui est lié à une epreuve (lèpre, exil, pauvreté), laquelle marque la fin définitive d'une époque de frivolité et ouvre une période – troisième ou quatrième âge de l'homme? – de ressaisissement, d'approfondissment intérieur, et de vie religieuse plus intense' (*Le motif du repentir* 589).

15 While these poems seemingly carry us far from the universe of the *grand chant courtois*, Zumthor's analysis of that genre's spatio-temporal dimensions invites us to rethink superficial differences in light of more profound similarities: 'On le voit, l'énoncé se confond ici presque entièrement avec l'énonciation: je, ici, maintenant constituent l'axe auquel se mesure tout ce qui est dit, affirmation sans cesse reprise d'une absence dans la présence' (*Essai* 205). Marian lyric song owes much to the trouvère love song and although these repentance poems seem to stray far from that kind of exchange, these songs still share fundamental elements.

16 One of the more pertinent examples is the parable of the sower recounted in Matt. 13, Mark 4, and Luke 8.

17 In their useful table providing the order in which Rutebeuf's works appear in the different manuscripts, Faral and Bastin list the *Théophile* once in ms. *C*, even if the *Miracle* is excerpted not once, but twice. However, their order of transmission – the 'Repentance' followed by the 'Prière' – helps retain the continuity of the long version.

18 See the 'Miracle de Nostre Dame de Soissons' (II Mir 22: 127–44) and 'Dou chevalier a cui la volonte fu contee por fait' (I Mir 28: 139–54). These instances were identified by Jean-Louis Benoit in his dissertation, 'L'Art Littéraire dans les *Miracles* de Gautier de Coinci: Un Art au service de la foi' (Villeneuve d'Ascq, France, 1999). Other instances include miracles X and XVII of the Gracial of Adgar (c. 1200). I would like to express my gratitude to both Kathryn Duys and Pierre Kunstmann for their help in locating instances of the Virgin overheard speaking to Christ on humanity's behalf.

19 See, for example, Burns, 'The Man Behind the Lady in Troubadour Poetry.'

20 See Regalado's *Poetic Patterns* 213–15 for Rutebeuf's predilection for *annominatio* on 'corde.'

Bibliography

Anthologies, Editions, Facsimilies, Texts

Alfonso el Sabio, *Cantigas de Santa María.* Ed. Walter Nettman. Vol 1. Madrid: Castalia, 1986.

Augustine. *De Doctrina Christiana.* Ed. and trans. R.P.H. Green. Oxford and New York: Clarendon, 1995.

Avril, Joseph, ed. *Les Statuts synodaux français du XIIIe siècle.* Vol. 4, *Les statuts synodaux de l'ancienne province de Reims (Cambrai, Arrus, Noyon, Soissons, et Tournai).* Paris: Editions du Comité des Travaux historiques et scientifiques, 1995.

Bartsch, Karl. *Altfranzösische Romanzen und Pastourellen.* Leipzig: Vogel, 1870.

Beck, Jean. *Les Chansonniers des troubadours et des trouvères. Publiés en Facsimilé et transcrits en notation moderne. Reproduction phototypique du Chansonnier Cangé (Paris, BN, fonds français 846).* Paris: Champion, 1927.

Beck, Jean, and Louise Beck. *Le Manuscrit du Roi.* 2 vols. Philadelphia: U of Pennsylvania P, 1938.

Bédier, Joseph, and Pierre Aubry. *Les Chansons de croisade avec leurs mélodies.* Geneva: Slatkine Reprints, 1974.

Bernard of Clairvaux. 'Epistola CLXXIV (Ad Canonicos Lugdunenses de Conceptione S. Mariae.' *Patrologiae cursus completus. Series Latina.* Ed. J.P. Migne. Paris, 1854. 18: cols 332–6.

– 'De laude novae militiae.' *Éloge de la nouvelle chevalerie; Vie de Saint Malachie; Épitaphe, hymne, lettres.* Intro., trans., notes, and index, Pierre-Yves Emery. Paris: Editions du Cerf 1990.

– *A la Louange de la Vierge Mère (In Laudibus Virginis Matris).* Ed. Marie-Imelda Huille and Joël Regnard. Paris: Editions du Cerf, 1993.

Bianciotto, Gabriel, ed. and trans. *Bestiaires du moyen age.* Paris: Stock, 1980. 117–24.

Boogaard, Nico H.J. van den. *Rondeaux et refrains du XIIe siècle au début du XIVe.* Paris: Klincksieck, 1969.

Bossy, Michel-André, ed. and trans. *Medieval Debate Poetry: Vernacular Works.* New York: Garland, 1987.

Brahney, Kathleen J., ed. and trans. *The Lyrics of Thibaut de Champagne.* New York: Garland, 1989.

Bruckner, Matilda Tomaryn, Laurie Shepard, and Sarah White, eds. *Songs of the Women Troubadours.* New York: Garland, 1995.

Chrétien de Troyes. *Romans suivis des chansons, avec, en appendice, Philomena.* Ed. Michel Zink et al. Paris: La Pochothèque, 1994.

Dante Aligheri. *De Vulgari Eloquentia.* Ed. Bruno Panvini. Palermo: Ando' Editori, 1968.

Dinaux, A.-D. *Les trouvères cambrésiens.* [1836.] Geneva: Slatkine Reprints, 1970.

Doss-Quinby, Eglal, Joan Tasker Grimbert, Wendy Pfeffer, and Elizabeth Aubrey, eds. *Songs of the Women Trouvères.* New Haven and London: Yale UP, 2001.

Dufournet, Jean, trans. *Rutebeuf et les frères mendiants. Poèmes satiriques.* Traductions des classiques français du moyen âge 46. Paris: Champion, 1991.

– ed. and trans. *Rutebeuf. Poèmes de l'infortune et autres poèmes.* Poésie 209. Paris: Gallimard, 1986.

Dyggve, Holger Petersen. *Trouvères et protecteurs de trouvères dans les cours seigneuriales de France: Vieux-Maisons, Membrolles, Mauvoisin, Trie, l'Isle-Adam, Nesle, Harnes.* Helsinki: [n.p.], 1942.

Epstein, Marcia Jenneth, ed. and trans. *'Prions en chantant': Devotional Songs of the Trouvères.* Toronto: U of Toronto P, 1997.

Evergates, Theodore, ed. and trans. *Feudal Society in Medieval France: Documents from the County of Champagne.* Philadelphia: U of Pennsylvania P, 1993.

Faral, Edmond, and Julia Bastin. *Oeuvres complètes de Rutebeuf.* 2 vols. Fondation Singer-Polignac, 1959–60; Paris: Picard, 1977.

Gautier de Coinci. *Les Chansons à la Vierge de Gautier de Coinci.* Ed. Jacques Chailley. Paris: Heugel et Cie, 1959.

Hugh of Saint Victor. *Epistola de virginitate beatae Mariae. Patrologiae cursus completus. Series Latina,* Ed. J.P. Migne. Paris, 1863. 176: col. 857.

Huygens, R.B.C., ed. *Accessus ad auctores, Bernard d'Utrecht, Conrad d'Hirsau, Dialogus super auctores.* Leiden: E.J. Brill, 1970,

Ingnanez, D.M. 'Un dramma della Passione del secolo XX.' *Miscellanea Cassinese* 12 (1936): 7–36.

Järnström, Edward, ed. *Recueil de chansons pieuses du XIIIe siècle.* Vol. 1. Helingsfors, Finland: Imprimerie de la Société de littérature finnoise, 1910.

Järnström, Edward, and Arthur Långfors, eds. *Recueil de chansons pieuses du XIIIe siècle.* Vol. 2. Helsinki: Suomalaisen Tiedeakatemian Toimituksia, 1927.

Jeanroy, Alfred, Pierre Aubry, and Louis Brandin. *Lais et descorts français du XIIIe siècle*. Paris: H. Welter, 1901.

Jerome. 'De Perpetua Virginitate B. Mariae (Adversus Helvidium).' *Patrologia cursus completus. Series Latina*. Ed. J.P. Migne. Paris, 1845. 23: cols. 193–216.

Jubinal, Achille. *Nouveau recueil de contes, dits, fabliaux, et autres pièces inédites des XIIIe, XIVe et XVe siècles*. 1839. 2 vols. Geneva: Slatkine Reprints, 1975.

– *Oeuvres complètes de Rutebeuf: trouvère du XIIIe siècle*. 1874. Nendeln, Lichtenstein: Klaus Reprint: 1970.

Koenig, Frederic, ed. *Les miracles de Nostre Dame par Gautier de Coinci*. 2nd ed. 4 vols. Geneva: Droz, 1966–70.

Kunstmann, Pierre, ed. *Miracles de Notre-Dame tirés du* Rosarius, Paris, ms. B.N.fr. *12483*. Ottawa and Paris: Les Presses de l'Université d'Ottawa, 1991.

Långfors, Arthur. 'Notice du manuscrit français 17068 de la Bibliothèque Nationale.' *Romania* 43 (1914): 21–7.

Marshall, J.H., ed. *The Chansons of Adam de la Halle*. Manchester: Manchester UP, 1971.

Montaiglon, Anatole de, and Gaston Raynaud, eds. *Recueil général et complet des fabliaux des XIIIe et XIVe siècles*. 2 vols. Geneva: Slatkine Reprints, 1973.

Mouskès, Philippe. *Chronique rimée de Philippe Mouskès*. Ed. F.-A.-F-T. Reiffenberg. Collection de Chroniques inédites. 2 vols. Brussels: M. Hayez, 1836–8.

Omont, Henri. *Fabliaux, dits et contes en vers français du 13e siècle: fac-similé du manuscrit français 837 de la Bibliothèque nationale*. 1932. Geneva: Slatkine Reprints, 1973.

Page, Christopher, ed. *Songs of the Trouvères*. Devon, England: Antico Edition, 1995.

Pickens, Rupert T, ed. *The Songs of Jaufré Rudel*. Toronto: Pontifical Institute of Mediaeval Studies, 1978.

Rivière, Jean-Claude, ed. *Les Poésies du Trouvère Jacques de Cambrai*. Geneva: Droz, 1978.

Rosenberg, Samuel N., and Hans Tischler, eds. *Chansons des trouvères*. Paris: Librairie Générale Française, 1995.

Rosenberg, Samuel N., Samuel Danon, and Henrik van der Werf, eds. *The Lyrics and Melodies of Gace Brulé*. New York: Garland, 1985.

Rosketh, Yvonne. *Lamentation de la Vierge au pied de la croix, XIIIe siècle*. Paris: Editions de l'Oiseau Lyre, 1936.

Sandqvist, Sven, ed. *Le Bestiaire et le lapidaire du Rosarius (B.N.F. fr. 12483)*. Lund: Lund UP, 1996.

Savoie, Mary Alberta, ed. *A 'Plantaire' in Honor of the Blessed Virgin Mary Taken from a French Manuscript of the XIVth Century*. Washington, DC: The Catholic University of America, 1933.

Tertullian. 'De cultu feminarum.' *Patrologiae cursus completus. Series Latina.* Ed. J.P. Migne. Paris, 1844. 1: cols 1417–48.

Tischler, Hans, ed. *Trouvère Lyrics with Melodies: Complete Comparative Edition.* 15 vols. Corpus mensurabilis musicae 107. Neuhausen: Hänssler-Verlag' American Institute of Musicology, 1997.

Wallensköld, Axel, ed. *Les Chansons de Thibaut de Champagne, Roi de Navarre. Edition critique.* Paris: Champion, 1925.

Young, Serinity, ed. *An Anthology of Sacred Texts by and about Women.* New York: Crossroad, 1993.

Zetterberg, Anders, and Sven Sandqvist, eds. *Les Propriétés des choses selon le Rosarius (B.N.f. fr. 12483).* Lund, Sweden: Lund UP, 1994.

Zink, Michel, ed. *Rutebeuf. Oeuvres complètes.* 2 vols. Classiques Garnier. Paris: Bordas, 1989–90.

Bibliographies and Reference Works

Doss-Quinby, Eglal. *The Lyrics of the Trouvères: A Research Guide (1970–1990).* New York: Garland, 1994.

Frank, István. *Répertoire métrique de la poésie des troubadours.* 2 vols. Paris. Champion, 1966.

Godefroy, Frédéric. *Dictionnaire de l'ancienne langue française.* 10 vols. Paris, 1883; Kraus Reprint, 1965.

Kibler, William. *An Introduction to Old French.* New York: The Modern Language Association of America, 1984.

Lavis, Georges, and M. Stasse. *Les chansons de Thibaut de Champagne. Concordances et index établis d'après l'édition de A. Wällensköld [sic].* Liège: Publications de l'Institut de Lexicologie Française de l'Université de Liège, 1981.

Linker, Robert White. *A Bibliography of Old French Lyrics.* University, Mississippi : Romance Monographs, 1979.

Ludwig, Friedrich, and Friedrich Gennrich. *Repertorium organorum recentiaris et motetorum retustissimi stili.* Frankfurt: Langen, 1961.

Mölk, Ulrich, and Friedrich Wolfzettel. *Répertoire métrique de la poésie lyrique française des origines à 1350.* Munich: Wilhelm Fink Verlag, 1972.

Raynaud, Gaston. *Bibliographie des chansonniers français des XIIIe et XIVe siècles.* Paris: F. Vieweg, 1844.

Spanke, Hans. *G. Raynauds Bibliographie des altfranzösischen liedes, reu bearbeitet und ergänzt.* Leiden: E.J. Brill, 1955.

Switten, Margaret L. *Music and Poetry in the Middle Ages: A Guide to Research on French and Occitan Song, 1100–1400.* New York: Garland, 1995.

Tobler, Adolf, and Erhard Lommatzsch. *Altfranzösisches Wörterbuch.* Stuttgart: F. Steiner, 1925.

Studies and Secondary Sources

Alpers, Paul. *What is Pastoral?* Chicago and London: U of Chicago P, 1996.

Anglès, Higinio. *Las canciones del rey Teobaldo.* Pamplona: Institución Príncipe de Viana, 1973.

— 'La lírica musical cortesana en Navarra. Teobaldo I, rey de Navarra.' *Historia de la música medieval en Navarra.* Pamplona: Institución Príncipe de Viana, 1970. 79–104.

Ansermet, François, and Marie André. 'Ève dans Marie. L'énigme de la procréation.' *'Ce est li fruis selonc la letre': Mélanges offerts à Charles Méla.* Ed. Olivier Collet, Yasmina Foehr-Janssens, and Sylviane Messerli. Paris: Champion, 2002. 41–68.

Arcangeli Marenzi, Maria Laura. *Forme di discorso medievali.* Padua: Francisci Editore, 1984.

Asperti, Stefano. 'Contrafacta provenzali di modelli francesi.' *Messana* 8 (1991): 5–49.

Aubrey, Elizabeth. 'Forme et formule dans les mélodies des troubadours.' *Actes du Premier Congrès International de l'Association Internationale d'Etudes Occitanes.* Ed. Peter T. Ricketts. London: Assn. Internat. d'Etudes Occitanes, Westfield Coll., U. of London, 1987.

— *The Music of the Troubadours.* Bloomington and Indianapolis: Indiana UP, 1996.

Auerbach, Erich. *Literary Language and Its Public in Late Antiquity and in the Middle Ages.* Trans. Ralph Manheim. Bollingen Series 74. NY: Pantheon Books, 1965.

Balard, Michel. 'La croisade de Thibaud IV de Champagne (1239–1240).' *Les Champenois et la croisade. Actes des quatrièmes journées rémoises, 27–28 novembre 1987.* Ed. Yvonne Bellenger and Danielle Quéruel. Publications du Centre de Recherche sur la Littérature du Moyen Age et de la Renaissance de l'Université de Reims. Paris: Aux Amateurs de Livres, 1989. 85–95.

Baron, Roger. 'La Pensée mariale de Hughes de Saint Victor.' *Revue d'ascétique et de mystique* 31 (1955): 249–71.

Barthes, Roland. 'L'effet de reel.' *Communications* 11 (1968): 84–9.

Baum, Richard. 'Le descort ou l'anti-chanson.' *Mélanges de philologie romane dédiés à la mémoire de Jean Boutière.* Vol. 1. Ed. Irénée Cluzel and François Pirot. Liège: Soledi, 1971. 75–98.

— 'Les troubadours et les lais.' *Zeitschrift für romanische Philologie* 85 (1969): 1–44.

Baumgartner, Emmanuèle. 'Présentation des chansons de Thibaut de Champagne dans les manuscrits de Paris.' *Thibaut de Champagne: Prince et poète au XIIIe siècle.* Ed. Yvonne Bellanger and Danielle Quéruel. Preface Michel Bur. Lyon: La Manufacture, 1987. 35–44.

Baxter, Ron. *Bestiaries and Their Users in the Middle Ages.* Stroud: Sutton; London: Courtauld Institute, 1998.

Bec, Pierre. 'Avoir des enfants ou rester vierge? Une tenson occitane du XIIIe siècle entre femmes.' *Mittelalterstudien: Erich Köhler zum Gedenken.* Ed. Henning Krauss and Dietmar Rieger. Heidelberg: Carl Winter Universitätverlag, 1984. 21–30.

– 'Bernard de Ventadour et Thibaut de Champagne: Essai de bilan comparatif.' *Le Rayonnement des troubadours: Actes du colloque de l'AIEO, Amsterdam, 16–18 octobre 1995.* Ed. Anton Touber. Amsterdam and Atlanta: Rodopi, 1998. 163–71.

– *La Lyrique française au moyen-age (XIIe–XIIIe siècles): Contribution à une typologie des genres poétiques médiévaux.* 2 vols. Paris: Picard, 1977.

– 'Lyrique profane et paraphrase pieuse dans la poésie médiévale (XIIe–XIIIe s.).' *Jean Misrahi Memorial Volume: Studies in Medieval Literature.* Ed. Hans R. Runte, Henri Niedzielski, and William L. Hendrickson. Colombia, SC: French Literature Publications Company, 1977. 229–46.

Beebee, Thomas O. *The Ideology of Genre: A Comparative Study of Generic Instability.* University Park, PA: Pennsylvania State UP, 1994.

Beer, Jeannette. *Beasts of Love: Richard de Fournival's* Bestiaire d'amour *and a* Woman's Response. Toronto: U of Toronto P, 2003.

Bellanger, Yvonne, and Danielle Quéruel, eds. *Thibaut de Champagne. Prince et poète au XIIIe siècle.* Lyons: La Manufacture, 1987.

Benoit, Jean-Louis. 'L'Art litteraire dans les Miracles de Gautier de Coinci: Un Art au service de la foi.' PhD dissertation. Villeneuve d'Ascq, France: Presses Universitaires du Septentrion, 1999.

Benton, John F. 'The Court of Champagne as a Literary Center.' *Speculum* 36 (1961): 551–91.

Berger, Roger. *Littérature et société arrageoises au XIIIe siècle: Les chansons et les dits artésiens.* Arras: Commission Départementale des Monuments Historiques du Pas-de-Calais, 1981.

– *Le Nécrologe de la confrérie des jongleurs et des bourgeois d'Arras (1194–1361).* 2 vols. Arras: Commission Départementale des Monuments Historiques du Pas-de-Calais, 1963–70.

Berthelot, Anne. 'Anti-miracle et anti-fabliau: La subversion des genres.' *Romania* 106 (1985): 399–419.

Billy, Dominique. '*Lai* et *descort*: La théorie des genres comme volonté et comme représentation.' *Actes du Premier Congres International de l'Association Internationale d'Etudes Occitanes.* Ed. Peter T. Ricketts. London: Assn. Internat. d'Etudes Occitanes, Westfield Coll., U of London, 1987. 95–117.

Black, Nancy B. 'Woman as Savior: The Virgin Mary and the Empress of Rome in Gautier de Coinci's *Miracles.*' *Romanic Review* 88 (1997): 503–17.

Blakeslee, Merritt R. 'Apostrophe, Dialogue, and the Generic Conventions of the Troubadour Canso.' *The Spirit of the Court: Selected Proceedings of the Fourth Congress of the International Courtly Literature Society (Toronto 1983).* Ed. Glyn S. Burgess and Robert A. Taylor. Cambridge: D.S. Brewer, 1985. 41–51.

Bonifacio, Mariella Vianello. 'Temi e motivi nelle *chansons* di Gautier de Conci.' *Studi Francesi* 27 (1983): 458–70.

Boogaard, Nico van den. *Rondeaux et refrains du XIIe siècle au début du XIVe.* Bibliothèque Française et Romane Série D, 3. Paris: Klincksieck, 1969.

Boss, Sarah Jane. *Empress and Handmaid: On Nature and Gender in the Cult of the Virgin Mary.* London: Cassell, 2000.

Boulton, Maureen Barry McCann. *The Song in the Story: Lyric Insertions in French Narrative Fiction, 1200–1400.* Philadelphia: U of Pennsylvania P, 1993.

Boynton, Susan. 'Women's Performance of Lyric before 1500.' *Medieval Woman's Song: Cross-Cultural Approches.* Ed. Anne L. Klinck and Ann Marie Rasmussen. Philadelphia: U of Pennsylvania P, 2002. 47–65.

Brackelmann, J. 'Die altfranzösische Liederhandschaft Nr 389 der Stadtbilbiothek zu Bern.' *Archiv* 41 (1867): 339–76; 42–3 (1868): 47–8, 73–82, 241–392.

Brucker, Charles. 'Conventions, variations et innovations stylistiques dans la poésie lyrique du XIIIe siècle: Thibaut de Champagne.' *Le génie de la forme. Mélanges de langue et littérature offerts à Jean Mourot.* Nancy: Presses Universitaires de Nancy, 1982. 27–40.

– 'Le temps grammatical et le temps vécu dans la poésie lyrique courtoise: de Thibaut de Champagne à Guillaume de Machaut.' *Verbum* 13 (1990): 13–26.

Bruckner, Matilda Tomaryn. 'Fictions of the Female Voice: The Women Troubadours.' *Speculum* 67 (1992): 865–91 (reprinted in Klinck and Rasmussen, *Medieval Woman's Song*, 127–51).

– 'Jaufré Rudel and Lyric Reception: The Problem of Abusive Generalization.' *Style* 20 (1986): 203–19.

– 'Na Castelloza, *Trobairitz*, and Troubadour Lyric.' *Romance Notes* 25 (1985): 239–53.

– *Narrative Invention in Twelfth-Century Romance: The Convention of Hospitality (1160–1200).* Lexington: French Forum, 1980.

Brunn, Emilie Zum, and Georgette Epiney-Burgard. *Women Mystics in Medieval Europe.* New York: Paragon House, 1989.

Brusegan, Rosanna. 'Culte de la Vierge et origine des puys et confréries en France au Moyen Age.' *Revue des langues romanes* 95 (1991): 31–58.

Bugge, John. *Virginitas: An Essay in the History of a Medieval Ideal.* The Hague: Martinus Nijhoff, 1975.

Burkard, Richard. '"Comme musars bien m'amusai": The Frustrated Yearning of

Gautier de Coincy's Theophilus Figure.' *Romanische Forschungen* 97 (1985): 402–11.

Burke, Kenneth. *The Rhetoric of Religion: Studies in Logology*. Boston: Beacon P, 1961.

Burns, E. Jane. *Bodytalk: When Women Speak in Old French Literature*. Philadelphia: U of Pennsylvania P, 1993.

– 'The Man Behind the Lady in Troubadour Poetry.' *Romance Notes* 25 (1985): 254–70.

– 'Sewing Like a Girl: Working Women in the *Chansons de toile*.' In Klinck and Rasmussen, *Medieval Woman's Song*, 99–126.

Butler, Johanna. 'The Lover and the Unicorn: The Integration of Natural, Magical, Psychological, Allegorical Perspectives in a Medieval Lyric Image.' *Studies in Medieval Culture* 11 (1977): 95–102.

Butterfield, Ardis. *Poetry and Music in Medieval France*. Cambridge: Cambridge UP, 2002.

Calin, William. 'On the Nature of Christian Poetry: From the Courtly to the Sacred and the Functioning of *Contrafactum* in Gautier de Coinci.' *Studia in honorem prof. M. de Riquer*. Ed. Jaume Vallcorba. Madrid: Quaderns Crema, 1986. 385–94.

Carpenter, Dwayne E. 'The Portrayal of the Jew in Alfonso the Learned's *Cantigas de Santa Maria*.' *In Iberia and Beyond: Hispanic Jews between Cultures*. Ed. Bernard Dov Cooperman. Newark: U of Delaware P, 1998. 15–42.

– 'A Sorcerer Defends the Virgin: Merlin in the *Cantigas de Santa Maria*.' *Bulletin of the Cantigueiros de Santa Maria* 5 (1993): 5–24.

Carruthers, Mary. *The Book of Memory: A Study of Memory in Medieval Culture*. Cambridge and New York : Cambridge UP, 1990.

Cazelles, Brigitte. *La Faiblesse chez Gautier de Coinci*. Saratoga: Anma Libri, 1978.

– 'Un Héros fatigué: Sens et fonction du mot *las* dans les *Miracles de Nostre Dame* de Gautier de Coinci.' *Romance Philology* 30 (1977): 616–22.

– '"Jeter puer." Le traitement de la "fuite du monde" dans les *Miracles* de Gautier de Coinci.' *Le Moyen Age* 83 (1977): 255–65.

– *The Lady as Saint: A Collection of French Hagiographic Romances of the Thirteenth Century*. Philadelphia: U of Pennsylvania P, 1991.

– 'Souvenez-vous.' *Poétique* 60 (1984): 395–410.

Chambers, Frank M. 'Imitation of Form in the Old Provençal Lyric.' *Romance Philology* 6 (1953): 104–20.

Chartier, M. 'Cambrai.' *Dictionnaire d'histoire et de géographie ecclésiastiques*. Ed. Alfred Baudrillart, Albert de Meyer, and Roger Aubert. Vol. 11. Paris: Letouzey et Ané, 1938. Cols. 547–65.

Cingolani, Stefano Maria. 'Gautier de Coincy e Guittone d'Arezzo.' *Miscellanea di studi in onore di Aurelio Roncaglia*. Vol. 2. Modena: Mucchi, 1989. 451–4.

Colombani, Dominique. 'La liturgie dans *Les Miracles de Nostre Dame* Gautier de Coinci.' *Mosaic* 12 (1979): 33–54.

– 'La Prière du coeur dans *Les Miracles de Nostre Dame* de Gautier de Coinci.' *La Prière au Moyen Age*. Aix-en-Provence: Centre Universitaire d'Etudes et de Recherche Médiévales d'Aix; 1981. 75–90.

Copeland, Rita. *Rhetoric, Hermeneutics, and Translation in the Middle Ages: Academic Traditions and Vernacular Texts*. Cambridge: Cambridge UP, 1991.

Dane, Joseph. 'Parody and Satire in the Literature of Thirteenth-Century Arras, Parts I and II.' *Studies in Philology* 81 (1984): 1–27 and 119–44.

Derrida, Jacques. *Marges de la philosophie*. Paris: Les Editions de Minuit, 1972.

Diehl, Patrick S. *The Medieval European Lyric: An Ars Poetica*. Berkeley and Los Angeles: U of California P, 1985.

Dijkstra, Cathyrnke. *La Chanson de croisade: Etude thématique d'un genre hybride*. Amsterdam: Schiphouwer en Brinkman, 1995.

– 'Troubadours, Trouvères, and Crusade Lyrics.' *Le Rayonnement des troubadours: Actes du colloque de l'AIEO, Amsterdam, 16–18 octobre 1995*. Ed. Anton Touber. Amsterdam and Atlanta: Rodopi, 1998. 173–84.

Dolly, Martha, and Raymond Cormier. 'Aimer, souvenir, souffrir: Les chansons d'amour chez Thibaut de Champagne.' *Romania* 99 (1978): 311– 46.

Donovan, Peter. *Religious Language*. London: Sheldon P, 1976.

Dragonetti, Roger. 'Rutebeuf: Les poèmes de la "griesche."' *'La Musique et les lettres': Etudes de littérature médiévale*. Geneva: Librairie Droz, 1986.

– *La Technique poétique des trouvères dans la chanson courtoise: Contribution à l'étude de la rhétorique médiévale*. Brugge: De Tempel, 1960; Geneva: Slaktine Reprints, 1979.

Dronke, Peter. *The Medieval Lyric*. 3rd ed. Cambridge: D.S. Brewer, 1996.

Drzewicka, Anna. 'La Fonction des emprunts à la poésie profane dans les chansons mariales de Gautier de Coinci.' *Le Moyen Age* 91 (1985): 33–51 and 179–200.

– 'Le livre ou la voix? Le moi poétique dans les *Miracles de Nostre Dame* de Gautier de Coinci.' *Le Moyen Age* 96 (1990): 245–63.

Dubrow, Heather. *Genre*. The Critical Idiom 42. London and New York: Methuen, 1982.

Ducrot-Granderye, Arlette P. *Etudes sur les* Miracles Nostre Dame *de Gautier de Coinci*. 1932. Geneva: Slatkine Reprints, 1980.

Dufeil, Michel-Marie. *Guillaume de Saint-Amour et la polémique universitaire parisienne, 1250–1259*. Paris: Picard, 1972.

– 'L'Oeuvre d'une vie rythmée: Chronographie de Rutebeuf.' *Musique, littérature et société au moyen âge*. Ed. Danielle Buschinger and André Crépin. Paris: Champion, 1980. 279–94.

Dufournet, Jean. 'Deux poètes du Moyen Age en face de la mort: Rutebeuf et

Villon.' *Dies Illa: Death in the Middle Ages* (Proceedings of the 1983 Manchester Colloquium). Ed. Jane H.M. Taylor. Liverpool: Francis Cairns, 1984.

– 'Rutebeuf et la Vierge.' *Bien dire et bien aprandre* 5 (1987): 7–25.

– 'Rutebeuf et les moines mendiants.' *Neuphilologische Mitteilungen* 85 (1984): 152–68.

Duys, Kathryn A. 'Books Shaped by Song: Early Literary Literacy in the *Miracles de Nostre Dame* of *Gautier de Coinci.*' PhD diss. New York U, 1997.

Eden, Kathy. *Hermeneutics and the Rhetorical Tradition: Chapters in the Ancient Legacy and its Humanist Reception.* New Haven and London: Yale UP, 1997.

Edwards, Robert. *The Montecassino Passion and the Poetics of Medieval Drama.* Berkeley and Los Angeles: U of California P, 1977.

Faure, Marcel. '"Aussi com l'unicorne sui" ou le désir d'amour et le désir de mort dans une chanson de Thibaut de Champagne.' *Revue des Langues Romanes* 88 (1984): 15–21.

Fawcett, Thomas. *The Symbolic Language of Religion: An Introductory Study.* London: SCM P, 1970.

Ferrand, Françoise. 'Les nombres dans l'espace-temps poétique des trouvères.' *Le nombre du temps. En hommage à Paul Zumthor.* Ed. Emmanuèle Baumgartner. Paris: Champion, 1988. 73–85.

– 'Thibaut de Champagne, de l'obsession du mal à la mort du chant.' In *Thibaut de Champagne: Prince et poète au XIIIe siècle.* Ed. Yvonne Bellenger and Danielle Quéruel. Lyons: La Manufacture, 1987. 77–87.

Finke, Laurie. *Feminist Theory, Women's Writing.* Ithaca, NY: Cornell UP, 1992.

Fletcher, Anne. *Allegory: The Theory of a Symbolic Mode.* Ithaca, NY: Cornell UP, 1964.

Flory, David A. *Marian Representations in the Miracle Tales of Thirteenth-Century Spain and France.* Washington, DC: The Catholic U of America P, 2000.

Fraise, Nathalie. *L'Anorexie mentale et le jeûne mystique du Moyen Age: Faim, foi, et pouvoir.* Paris: Harmattan, 2000.

Frappier, Jean. 'D'amors, par amors.' *Romania* 88 (1967): 433–74.

– 'Rutebeuf et la Vierge.' *Bien dire et bien aprandre* 5 (1987): 7–25.

Frye, Northrop. *Anatomy of Criticism: Four Essays.* Princeton: Princeton UP, 1957.

Furlong, Monica. *Visions and Longings: Medieval Women Mystics.* Boston and New York: Shambhala, 1996.

Gadamer, Hans-Georg. *Hermeneutics, Religion, and Ethics.* Trans. Joel Weinsheimer. New Haven and London: Yale UP, 1999.

– *The Relevance of the Beautiful and Other Essays.* Ed. Robert Bernasconi. Trans. Nicholas Walker. Cambridge: Cambridge UP, 1986.

– *Truth and Method.* Trans. Joel Weinsheimer and Donald G. Marshall. 2nd ed., rev. New York: Continuum, 1989.

– *Wahrheit und Methode.* 3rd ed. Tübingen: J.C.B. Mohr, 1972.

Gardner, Helen. *Religion and Literature*. London: Faber and Faber, 1971.

Garnier, Annette. 'Autour de la mort: Temps de la dilation et purgatoire dans les *Miracles de Nostre Dame* de Gautier de Coinci.' *Le Moyen Age* 94 (1988): 183–202.

– 'Deux *Miracles de Nostre Dame* de Gautier de Coinci. Essai d'analyse.' *Romania* 106 (1985): 341–98.

Gaunt, Simon. *Gender and Genre in Medieval French Literature*. Cambridge: Cambridge UP, 1995.

Gégou, Fabienne. 'La langue du poète Adam de la Halle dans ses chansons courtoises.' *Mélanges de philologie et de littératures romanes offerts à Jeanne Wathelet-Willem*. Liège: Cahiers de l'Association des Romanistes de l'Université de Liège, 1978. 175–88.

– 'Les Trouvères artésiens et la cour d'Angleterre de 1263 à 1306.' *Mélanges de langue et littérature françaises du Moyen Age et de la Renaissance offerts a Monsieur Charles Foulon*. Vol. 1. Rennes: Institut de Français, Université de Haute-Bretagne, 1980.

Gennrich, F. *Die Kontrafaktur im Liedschaffen des Mittelalters*. Frankfurt: Langen bei Frankfurt, 1965.

Gilespie, Maureen. '"De tut changea cele vie": Religious Conversion in French Medieval Saints' Lives.' PhD diss., New York U, 1995.

Gold, Penny Schinne. *The Lady and the Virgin: Image, Attitude, and Experience in Twelfth-Century France*. Chicago: U of Chicago P, 1985.

Grimbert, Joan. 'Songs by Women and Women's Songs: How Useful Is the Concept of Register?' *The Court Reconvenes*. Ed. Chantal Phan, Barbara Altmann, and Carleton Carroll. Cambridge: D.S. Brewer, 2003.

Gros, Gérard. 'Au Jardin des images mariales: Aspect du plantaire moralisé dans la poésie religieuse du XIVe siècle.' *Vergers et jardins dans l'univers médiéval*. Aix-en-Provence: Centre Universitaire d'Etudes et de Recherche Médiévales d'Aix, 1990. 141–53.

– *Le Poème du Puy marial: étude sur le servantois et le chant royal du XIVe siècle à la Renaissance*. Paris: Klincksieck, 1996.

– *Le Poète, la Vierge, et le Prince du Puy: Etude sur les Puys marials de la France du Nord du XIVe siècle à la Renaissance*. Paris: Editions Klincksieck, 1992.

– 'Préférer la Vierge à l'autre Marie (Etude sur le *Miracle XXIII* de Jean le Marchant).' *Le 'Cuer' au moyen age*. Ed. Margaret Bertrand. Aix-en-Provence: Centre Universitaire d'Etudes et de Recherche Médiévales d'Aix, 1991. 147–60.

– 'La *semblance* de la *verrine*: Description et interprétation d'une image mariale.' *Le Moyen Age* 97 (1991): 217–57.

Grossel, Marie-Geneviève. 'La poétique du mot chez Thibaut de Champagne.' *Etudes Champenoises* 5 (1986): 11–17.

– 'Le temps dans la chanson de trouvère: l'exemple de Thibaut de Champagne.' *Le temps et la durée dans la littérature au Moyen Age et à la Renaissance. Actes du colloque organisé par le Centre de Recherche sur la Littérature du Moyen Age et de la Renaissance de l'Université de Reims (novembre 1984)*. Ed. Yvonne Bellenger. Paris: Nizet, 1986. 71–83.

Grundmann, Herbert. *Religious Movements in the Middle Ages: The Historical Links between Heresy, the Mendicant Orders, and the Women's Religious Movement in the Twelfth and Thirteenth Century, with the Historical Foundations of German Mysticism*. Trans. Steven Rowan. Intro. Robert E. Lerner. Notre Dame, IN: U of Notre Dame P, 1995.

Hassig, Debra, ed. *The Mark of the Beast: The Medieval Bestiary in Art, Life, and Literature*. New York: Garland, 1999.

Heider, Andrew B. *The Blessed Virgin Mary in Early Christian Latin Poetry*. Washington, DC: Catholic U of America P, 1918.

Hinnebusch, William A. *The History of the Dominican Order*. Staten Island, NY: Alba House, 1966.

Hofmann, K. 'Altfranzösische Pastourelle aus der Berner Handschrift nr 389.' *Sitzungsberichte der königlichen bayerischen Akademie der Wissenschaft*, Munich 2, 1865. 301–40.

– 'Eine Anzahl altfranzösische lyrischer Gedichte aus Berner Codex 389' *Sitzungsberichte der königlichen bayerischen Akademie der Wissenschaft*, Munich 2, 1867. 486–527.

Huot, Sylvia. 'A Book Made for a Queen: The Shaping of a Late Medieval Anthology Manuscript (B. N. fr. 24429).' *The Whole Book: Cultural Perspectives on the Medieval Miscellany*. Ed. and intro. Stephen G. Nichols and Siegfried Wenzel. Ann Arbor, MI: U of Michigan P, 1996. 123–43.

– *From Song to Book: The Poetics of Writing in Old French Lyric and Lyrical Narrative Poetry*. Ithaca and London: Cornell UP, 1987.

– Review of Doss-Quinby, E., et al. *Songs of the Women Trouvères. Speculum*. 78 (2003): 873–4.

– 'Transformations of Lyric Voice in the Songs, Motets, and Plays of Adam de la Halle.' *Romanic Review* 78 (1987): 148–64.

Jauss, Hans-Robert. *Aesthetic Experience and Literary Hermeneutics*. Trans. Michael Shaw. Intro. Wlad Godzich. Minneapolis: U of Minnesota P, 1982.

– 'Littérature médiévale et théorie des genres.' *Poétique* 1 (1970): 79–101.

Jeanroy, Alfred. 'Les chansons pieuses du ms. fr. 12483 de la Bibliothèque Nationale.' *Mélanges de philologie romane et d'histoire littéraires: offerts à Maurice Wilmotte à l'occasion de son 25ᵉ anniversaire d'enseignement*. Paris: Champion, 1910.

Jones, Valerie. 'The Phoenix and the Resurrection.' *The Mark of the Beast: The*

Medieval Bestiary in Art, Life, and Literature. Ed. Debra Hassig. New York: Garland, 1999. 99–115.

Joris, Pierre-Marie. 'L'esloignance dans le jeu d'amour: Thibaut de Champagne, autour de la chanson IX.' *Thibaut de Champagne. Prince et poète au XIIIe siècle.* Ed. Yvonne Bellenger and Danielle Quéruel. Lyons: La Manufacture, 1987. 99–106.

Karp, Theodore. 'Interrelationships between Poetic and Musical Form in *Trouvère* Song.' *A Musical Offering: Essays in Honor of Martin Bernstein.* Ed. Edward H. Clinkscale and Claire Brook. New York: Pendragon P, 1977.

Kay, Sarah. *Subjectivity in Troubadour Poetry.* Cambridge: Cambridge UP, 1990.

Kelly, Douglas. *The Arts of Poetry and Prose.* Turnhout, Belgium: Brepols, 1991.

Klinck, Anne Ligard, and Ann Marie Rasmussen, eds. *Medieval Woman's Song: Cross-Cultural Approaches.* Philadelphia: U of Pennsylvania P, 2002.

Koenig, Frederic. 'Sur une prétendue reverdie de Gautier de Coinci.' *Romania* 99 (1978): 255–63.

Köhler, Erich. 'Deliberations on a Theory of the Genre of the Old Provençal *Descort.*' *Italian Literature: Roots and Branches. Essays in Honor of Thomas Goodard Bergin.* Ed. Giose Rimanelli and Kenneth John Atchity. London and New Haven: Yale UP, 1976.

Kuhs, Elisabeth. *Buchstabendichtung: zur gattungskonstituierenden Funktion von Buchstabenformationem in der französischen Litertatur vom Mittelalter bis zum Ende des 19. Jahrhunderts.* Studia Romanica 49. Heidelberg: Carl Winter, 1982.

Lacy, Norris. 'Fabliaux and the Question of Genre.' *Reading Medieval Studies: Annual Proceedings of the Graduate Centre for Medieval Studies in the University of Reading* 13 (1987): 25–34.

Långfors, Arthur. 'La Belette buveuse d'huile. Un motif de folk-lore chez Gautier de Coinci.' *Romania* 64 (1938): 523–5.

– 'Mots rares chez Gautier de Coinci.' *Romania* 59 (1933): 481–96.

Larmat, Jean. 'Les métaphores dans quatre éloges de Notre-Dame du XIIIe siècle ou de la liberté du poète.' *Hommage à Jean Richer.* Annales de la Faculté des Lettres et Sciences Humaines de Nice 51. Paris: Les Belles Lettres, 1985. 273–86.

Leclercq, Jean. *L'Amour vu par les moines au XIIe siècle.* Paris: Editions du Cerf, 1983.

– *Bernard of Clairvaux and the Cistercian Spirit.* Kalamazoo, MI: Cistercia Publications, 1976.

– *The Love of Learning and the Desire for God.* Trans. Catharine Misrahi. New York: Fordham UP, 1982.

Leclereque, Jean, François Vandenbroucke, and Louis Bouyer. *La Spiritualité du moyen age.* Paris: Editions Montaigne, 1961.

Lefay-Toury, Marie-Noëlle. 'Les masques du *je* amoureux chez Thibaut de Champagne.' *Court and Poet: Selected Proceedings of the Third Congress of the International Courtly Literature Society (Liverpool)*. Ed. Glyn Burgess. ARCA Classical and Medieval Texts, Papers and Monographs 5. Liverpool: Francis Cairns, 1981. 241–8.

Lemaire, Jacques. 'Les motifs de l'eau et du feu chez trois trouvères du XIIIe siècle (Thibaut de Champagne, Colin Muset, Rutebeuf).' *Les quatre éléments dans la culture médiévale*. Ed. Danielle Buschinger and André Crépin. Göppinger: Kümmerle, 1983. 171–83.

Maillard, Jean. *Evolution et esthétique du lai lyrique des origines à la fin du XIVème siècle*. Paris: Centre de documentation universitaire, 1961.

– 'Variantes mélodiques dans les chansons de trouvères.' *Musique, littérature, et société au moyen âge*. Ed. Danielle Buschinger and André Crépin. Paris: Champion, 1980. 159–70.

Malaxecheverria, Ignacio. 'Notes sur le pélican au moyen âge.' *Neophilologus* 63 (1979): 491–7.

Malizia, Uberto. 'Gautier de Coinci e la *chanson* medievale.' *Quaderni di Filologia e Lingue Romanze* [3rd ser., 2] (1987): 61–75.

– 'Gautier de Coinci: la volontà [*sic*] di rinnovare la musica lirica ne *Les Miracles de Nostre Dame*.' *La lengua y la literatura en tiempos de Alfonso X. Actas del Congreso Internacional. Murcia, 5–10 marzo 1984*. Ed. Fernando Carmona and Francisco Flores. Murcia: Departamento de Literaturas Romanicas, Facultad de Letras, Universidad de Murcia, 1985. 319–32.

– 'Intorno al lessico tecnico-musicale ne *Les Miracles de Nostre Dame* di Gautier de Coinci.' *Actes du XVIIIe Congrès International de Linguistique et de Philologie Romanes*. Ed. Dieter Kremer. Vol. 6. Tübingen: Niemeyer, 1988. 405–17.

Malkiel, Yakov. 'The Derivation of Old French *Servantois*, Old Provençal *Sirventes*.' *Medium Aevum* 54 (1985): 272–4.

Marshall, J.H. 'The *descort* of Albertet and Its Old French Imitations.' *Zeitschrift für Romanische Philologie* 95 (1979): 290–306.

– 'Gautier de Coinci imitateur de Guilhem de Cabestanh.' *Romania* 98 (1977): 245–9.

– 'Pour l'étude des *contrafacta* dans la poésie des troubadours.' *Romania* 101 (1980): 289–335.

Martel, Pierre. 'Etude sémantique et essai de structuration lexicale du vocabulaire de l'habitation dans l'oeuvre de Rutebeuf.' *Bulletin des Jeunes Romanistes* 16 (1970): 12–32.

McAlpine, Fiona Wylie. 'A Hard Look at Trouvère Melodic Style.' *Songs of the Dove and the Nightingale: Sacred and Secular Music c. 900–1600*. Ed. Greta Mary Hair and Robyn E. Smith. Basel, Switzerland; New York: Gordon and Breach, 1995.

McAvoy, Jane Elle. *The Satisfied Life: Medieval Women Mystics on Atonement*. Cleveland, OH: Pilgrim P, 2000.

McNamara, Jo Ann Kay. *Sisters in Arms: Catholic Nuns through Two Milennia*. Cambridge, MA: Harvard UP, 1996.

Ménard, Philippe. 'Le Dieu d'Amour, figure poétique du trouble et du désir dans les poesies de Thibaut de Champagne.' *Thibaut de Champagne. Prince et poète au XIIIe siècle*. Ed. Yvonne Bellenger and Danielle Quéruel. Lyons: La Manufacture, 1987. 65–75.

Miyazaki, Mariko. 'Misericord Owls and Medieval Anti-Semitism.' *The Mark of the Beast: The Medieval Bestiary in Art, Life, and Literature*. Ed. Debra Hassig. New York: Garland, 1999. 23–49.

Mohrmann, Christine. 'Observations sur la langue et le style de Saint Bernard.' *Sancti Bernardi Opera*. Ed. J. Leclercq and H. Rochais. Vol. 2. Rome: Editiones Cistercienses, 1958. ii–xxxiii.

Moreau, E. de. 'Belgique' *Dictionnaire d'histoire et de géographie ecclésiastiques*. Ed. Alfred Baudrillart, Albert de Meyer, and Roger Aubert. Vol. 7. Paris: Letouzey et Ané, 1912. Cols 520–726.

Moreno, Paola. '3: C Bern, Burgerbibliothek 389.' *'Intavulare': Tables de chansonniers romans. Vol. 2, Chansonniers français (série coordonnée par Madeleine Tyssens)*. Documenta et instrumenta, 3. Liège: Université de Liège, Bibliothèque de la Faculté de Philosophie et Lettres, 1999.

Mustanoja, Tauno F. '*Les neuf joies Nostre Dame,' a Poem Attributed to Rutebeuf*. Helsinki, 1952.

Nash, Suzanne. 'Rutebeuf's Contribution to the Saint Mary the Egyptian Legend.' *The French Review* 44 (1971): 695–705.

O'Sullivan, Daniel E. 'Old French Refrains in Song, Verse, and Prose: A Case Study.' Forthcoming.

– 'Reading Children in Gautier de Coinci's *Miracles de Nostre Dame*.' *Neophilologus* 89 (2005): 201–19.

– 'Revisiting *Mouvance* and Medieval Lyric Performance.' *Romance Language Annual* 12 (2001): 83–8.

– 'Text and Melody in Early Trouvère Song: The Example of Chrétien de Troyes's "D'Amors qui m'a tolu a moi."' *TEXT: An Interdisciplinary Annual of Textual Studies*. 15 (2003): 97–119.

Page, Christopher. *Discarding Images: Reflections on Music and Culture in Medieval France*. Oxford: Clarendon P, 1993.

– *The Owl and the Nightingale: Musical Life and Ideas in France 1100–1300*. Berkeley and Los Angeles: U of California P, 1990.

Palazzo, Russo, ed. *Marie: le culte de la Vierge dans la société médiévale*. Paris: Beauchesne, 1996.

Parker, Ian. 'The Performance of Troubadour and Trouvère Songs: Some Facts and Conjectures.' *Early Music* 5 (1977): 184–207.

Payen, Jean-Charles. 'Le "je" chez Rutebeuf, ou les fausses confidences d'un auteur en quête de personnage.' *Mittelalterstudien. Erich Köhler zum Gedenken.* Ed. Hennig Krauss and Dietmar Rieger. Studia Romanica 55. Heidelberg: Carl Winter, 1984. 229–40.

– *Le motif du repentir dans la littérature française médiévale des origines à 1230.* Geneva: Droz, 1967.

Pfeffer, Wendy. *The Change of Philomel: The Nightingale in Medieval Literature.* New York: Peter Lang, 1985.

– '"Mourir comme le rossignol": A Secular Motif in a Religious Context.' *Revue de l'Universite d'Ottawa/University of Ottawa Quarterly* 50 (1980): 209–14.

Pierrard, Pierre. *Les Diocèses de Cambrai et de Lille.* Paris: Editions Beauchesne, 1978.

Pintarič, Miha. 'Rutebeuf entre le temps de l'église et le temps du marchand.' *Acta Neophilologica* 27 (1994): 17–22.

Planche, Alice. 'La double licorne ou le chasseur chassé.' *Marche Romane* 30 (1980): 237–46.

Pouchelle, Marie-Christine. 'Mots, fluides et vertiges: Les fêtes orales de la mystique chez Gautier de Coinci.' *Annales: Economies, Sociétés, Civilisations* 42 (1987): 1209–30.

Quain, Edwin A. 'The Medieval *Accessus ad auctores.' Traditio* 3 (1945): 215–64.

Regalado, Nancy Freeman. '*Effet de réel, Effet du réel*: Representation and Reference in Villon's *Testament.' Yale French Studies* 70 (1987): 63–77.

– *Poetic Patterns in Rutebeuf: A Study in Noncourtly Poetic Modes of the Thirteenth Century.* New Haven: Yale UP, 1970.

Ricoeur, Paul. *Le Conflit des interprétations: Essais d'hermeneutique.* Ed. Don Ihde. Paris: Editions du Seuil, 1969.

– *The Conflict of Interpretations.* Evanston, IL: Northwestern UP, 1974.

– *From Text to Action: Essays in Hermeneutics, II.* Trans. Kathleen Blamey and John B. Thompson. Evanston, IL: Northwestern UP, 1991.

– *Interpretation Theory: Discourse and the Surplus of Meaning.* Fort Worth: The Texas Christian UP, 1976.

– *La Métaphore vive.* Paris: Editions du Seuil, 1975.

– 'Philosophical Hermeneutics and Biblical Hermeneutics.' *From Text to Action: Essays in Hermeneutics, II*, trans. Kathleen Blamey and John B. Thompson. Evanston, IL: Northwestern UP, 1991. 89–101.

– *The Philosophy of Paul Ricoeur: An Anthology of His Work.* Ed. Charles E. Reagan and David Stewart. Boston: Beacon, 1978.

– *A Ricoeur Reader: Reflection and Imagination.* Ed. Mario J. Valdés. Toronto: U of Toronto P, 1991.

– *The Rule of Metaphor*. Trans. Robert Czerny with Kathleen McLaughlin and John Costello. Toronto: U of Toronto P, 1977.

Rivière, Jean-Claude. *Pastourelles: Introduction à l'étude formelle des pastourelles anonymes françaises des XIIe et XIIIe siècles*. Geneva: Droz, 1974–5.

Robertson, Duncan. *The Medieval Saints' Lives: Spiritual Renewal and Old French Literature*. Lexington, KY: French Forum, 1995.

Rosmarin, Adena. *The Power of Genre*. Minneapolis: U of Minnesota P, 1985.

Rossi, Luciano, and Agostino Ziino. 'Mout m'alegra douza vos per boscaje.' *Cultura Neolatina* 39 (1979): 69–80.

Rousse, Michel. 'Le *Mariage Rutebeuf* et la fête des Fous.' *Le Moyen Age* 88 (1982): 435–49.

Roussel, Henri. 'Notes sur la littérature arrageoise du XIIIe siècle.' *Revue des sciences humaines* 87 (1957): 249–86.

Schillebeeckx, Edward. *Marriage: Human Reality and Saving Mystery*. Trans. N.D. Smith. London: Sheed and Ward, 1976.

Schinz, Albert. 'L'Art dans les *contes dévots* de Gautier de Coincy.' *PMLA* 22 (1907): 465–520.

Schutz, Richard A. 'The Unedited Poems of Codex 389 of the Municipal Library of Berne, Switzerland.' PhD diss., Indiana U, 1976.

Secor, John R. 'The *Planctus Mariae* in Provençal Literature: A Subtle Blend of Courtly and Religious Traditions.' *The Spirit of the Court: Selected Proceedings of the Fourth Congress of the International Courtly Literature Society (Toronto 1983)*. Cambridge: D.S. Brewer, 1985. 321–6.

– '*Planctus Mariae*: The Laments of Mary as Influenced by Courtly Literature.' PhD diss., U of North Carolina-Chapel Hill, 1985.

Serper, Arié. *La manière satirique de Rutebeuf: Le ton et le style*. Romanica Neapolitana 7. Naples: Liguori, 1972.

– *Rutebeuf, poète satirique*. Paris: Klincksieck, 1969.

Siberry, Elizabeth. 'Troubadours, trouvères, minnesangers and the crusades.' *Studi Medievali* (Spoleto) 29 (1988): 19–43.

Spanke, Hans. 'Sequenz und Lai.' *Studi Medievali* 11 (1938): 12–63.

Spencer, Richard. 'Sin and Retribution, and the Hope of Salvation, in Rutebeuf's Lyrical Works.' *Rewards and Punishments in the Arthurian Romances and Lyric Poetry of Mediaeval France: Essays Presented to Kenneth Varty on the Occasion of His Sixtieth Birthday*. Ed. Peter V. Davies and Angus J. Kennedy. Cambridge: D.S. Brewer, 1987.

Stadtmüller, M.A. 'Die Marienlieder des Gautier de Coincy.' *Zeitschrift für französische Sprache und Literatur* 54 (1931): 481–510.

Sticca, Sandro. *Il Planctus Mariae nella tradizione drammatica del Medio Evo*. Sulmona: Teatro Club, 1984.

Strayer, Joseph. *The Albigensian Crusades*. New York: Dial, 1971.

Strubel, Armand. 'L'Allegorisation du verger courtois.' *Vergers et jardins dans l'univers médiéval.* Aix-en-Provence: Centre Universitaire d'Etudes et de Recherche Médiévales d'Aix, 1990. 345–57.

Switten, Margaret L. 'Modèle et variation: Saint-Martial de Limoges et les troubadours.' *Contacts de langues, de civilisations et intertextualité: IIIeme Congrès international de l'Association internationale d'études occitanes (Montpellier, 20–26 septembre 1990).* Montpellier: Centre d'études occitanes de l'Université de Montpellier, 1992. 679–96.

Taylor, Steven. 'God's Queen: Chess Imagery in the Poetry of Gautier de Coinci.' *Fifteenth-Century Studies* 17 (1990): 403–19.

Todorov, Tzvetan. 'The Origin of Genres.' Trans. Richard M. Barrong. *New Literary History: A Journal of Theory and Interpretation* 8 (1976): 159–70.

Tracy, David. *The Analogical Imagination: Christian Theology and the Culture of Pluralism.* New York: Crossroad, 1981.

– *Plurality and Ambiguity: Hermeneutics, Religion, Hope.* San Fransisco: Harper and Row, 1987.

Treitler, Leo. 'Once More, Music and Language in Medieval Song.' *Essays on Medieval Music in Honor of David G. Hughes.* Ed. Graeme M. Boone. Isham Library Papers 4. Cambridge, MA: Harvard Department of Music, 1995.

Verrier, Paul. 'La "chanson de Notre Dame" de Gautier de Coinci.' *Romania* 59 (1933): 497–519.

Wackernagel, W. *Altfranzösische Lieder und Leiche.* Basel, 1846.

Wardropper, Bruce W. *Historia de la poesia lírica a lo divino en la Cristiandad occidental.* Madrid: Revista de Occidente, 1958.

Warner, Marina. *Alone of All Her Sex: The Myth and Cult of the Virgin Mary.* New York: Knopf, 1976.

Yates, Frances Amelia. *The Art of Memory.* Chicago: U of Chicago P, 1966.

Yedlicka, Leo Charles. *Expressions of the Linguistic Area of Repentance and Remorse in Old French.* Washington, DC: The Catholic U of America P, 1945.

Yllera, A. 'Ensayo de estilistica medieval: Rutebeuf, goliardo y "syntaxier."' *Filología Moderna* 14 (1973): 65–102.

Zaganelli, Gioia. 'Donne e amore nella poesia di Arras dei secoli XII e XIII.' *Spicilegio Moderno* 4 (1975): 9–25.

Zink, Michel. 'Bonheurs de l'inconséquence dans le texte de Rutebeuf.' *L'Esprit Créateur* 27 (1987): 79–89.

– 'De la repentance Rutebeuf à la repentance Théophile.' *Littératures* 15 (1986): 19–24.

– 'Rutebeuf et le cours du poème.' *Romania* 107 (1986): 546–51.

– *La Subjectivité littéraire.* Paris: Presses universitaires de France, 1985

Zorzi, Diego. *Valori religiosi nella letteratura provenzale: La Spiritualità trinitaria.*
    Milan: Società Editrice Vita e Pensiero, 1954.
Zumthor, Paul. *Essai de poétique médiévale.* Paris: Seuil, 1972.
– 'Intertextualité et *mouvance.*' *Littérature* 41 (1981): 8–16.
– 'Le texte-fragment.' *Langue française* 40 (1978): 75–82.

Index

Adam (de la Bassée), 81–2
aesthetic consciousness, 53
aesthetic play, 53
Alfonso X (the Wise), 58–9
All Alone of Her Sex (Warner), 68
allegory, 43, 115
anaphora, 18
annominatio, 18–19, 23, 24, 26–7, 93,
    100–1, 103–5, 112–13
apostrophe, 18, 21, 23, 25, 87, 102
application, 6
appropriation, 6, 74–6, 79
Aristotle, 226n30
Assumption of Mary, the, 14–15
Aubrey, Pierre, 50
Augustine, Saint, bishop of Hippo, 5
Ave Maria, 39–40, 97–8
'*Ave Maria, j'aim* tant,' 55, 63, 66–8
Avril, Joseph, 233n1

Bartsch, Karl, 233n1
Bastin, Julia, 93, 106
Baumgartner, Emmanuèle, 227n1
Baxter, Ron, 83
Bec, Pierre, 3–4, 7, 44, 55, 75
Bedier, Joseph, 44–5
Benoit, Jean-Louis, 238n18

Bernard de Clairvaux, 45, 82
bestiaries, 43, 56, 83–6
Billy, Dominique, 51
Blanche (de Castille), 54
Blondel (de Nesles), 17–18, 19, 80
Boss, Sarah Jane, 223n6
Boynton, Susan, 57
Brahney, Kathleen, 33
Bruckner, Matilda, 57
Brulé, Gace, 78
Brunetto Latini, 34
Bugge, John, 224n12
Burns, E. Jane, 57

canso, 17, 231n7
Cantigas de Santa Maria (Alfonso),
    58–9
Carruthers, Mary, 18
Chailley, Jacques, 28
chanson avec des refrains, 17
chanson d'ami, 54–5, 57
chanson de femme, 17–18, 19
chanson de toile, 231n7
chant royal, 91
'Chanter m'estuet de la virge
    puchele' (RS 611a), 55, 57–9
coblas doblas, 78, 83

coblas unisonnans, 78
conductus, 81–2
congés, 95
contrafactum, 8, 28, 40, 74, 78–9, 85,
    90, 92, 114–15
contrafacture, 8, 75, 90, 115
conversio, 27
cross-voicings, 56–7
crusade songs, 47, 49, 106

débat, 34–5
De Doctrina Christiana (Augustine), 5
Devil, the, 42–6, 107
Diehl, Patrick S., 18
Dijkstra, Cathyrnke, 221n4
distinctive traditionalism, 9
Dominic, Saint, 66–7
Dominicans (*jacobins* and *jacobines*),
    63–8
Doss-Quinby, Eglal, 55
Drzewicka, Anna, 4
Ducrot-Graderye, Arlette P., 224n9
*'Du dous Jhesu souvent devons chanter et
    lire'* (RS 1195), 55, 59–62
Dufeil, Michel-Marie, 236n6
Dufournet, Jean, 235n4
Duys, Kathryn A., 17–18
Dyggve, Holger Peterson, 227n34

Edwards, Robert, 68
Epstein, Marcia Jenneth, 4

familiar strangeness, 11
Faral, Edmond, 93, 106
Faure, Marcel, 83
Ferri, Lambert, 91
fin'amors, 14
fole amor, 16
forme chanson, 17, 22, 24
Frank, István, 8

Frederick II, Emperor, 35

Gadamer, Hans-Georg, 6, 32, 53, 115
Gauthier d'Espinal, 78–9
Gautier (de Coinci), 4–6, 8, 11–32,
    36–9, 50–1, 53, 54, 79, 94, 99, 107,
    113, 114–15; Songs: 'Amours, qui
    bien set enchanter' (RS 851),
    19–24, 50–1; 'D'une amour quoie
    et serie' (RS 1212), 19, 27–31; 'Ja
    pour yver, pour noif ne pour gelee'
    (RS 520), 17; 'Roÿne celestre' (RS
    1903), 19, 24–7, 36, 50
generic hybridity, 35
genre, 74
Gilles (de Vieux Maisons), 19, 28–31,
    82
Gobius, Johannes, 58
grand chant courtois, 17
Gregory IX, Pope, 35
Gros, Gérard, 91

Hassig, Debra, 83
Hélinand de Froimond, 95
hermeneutics, 5–6, 32, 49, 90
Hermeneutics, Religion, and Ethics
    (Weinsheimer), 115
Herolt, Johannes, 58
Holy Land, the, 47
Hugh of Saint Victor, 224n6
Hult, David, 227n33
Huot, Sylvia, 93, 106, 229n2

Incarnation, mystery of, 14–15, 26, 36,
    38–40, 75–6, 84–5, 95, 103, 110
Isidore of Seville, 56

Jacques (de Cambrai), 6, 9, 37, 74–92,
    113, 114; Songs: 'Grant talent ai k'a
    chanteir me retraie' (RS 114), 77;

'Haute dame, com rose et lis' (RS
  1563), 76–8, 83–6, 91; 'Kant je plus
  pens a commencier chanson' (RS
  1856), 76–8, 82; 'Loeir m'estuet la
  roïne Marie' (RS 1178), 79–80;
  'Meire, douce creature' (RS 2091),
  76–7, 81; 'O Dame, ke Deu portais'
  (RS 380, 197a), 77, 87; 'Retrowange
  novelle' (RS 602), 76–7, 87–90
Järnström, Edward, 230n10
Jeanroy, Alfred, 229nn10, 12
Jehan (de Maisons), 82–3
jeu-parti, 34, 40
Jones, Valerie, 86
Joris, Pierre-Marie, 35–6
Judgment Day, 45–6

kaleidoscopic contrafacta, 9, 74, 82,
  86
Kuhs, Elizabeth, 228n4

lai, 17, 24–5, 36, 49–52, 68–9, 72
lai religieux, 33, 36, 40
Långfors, Arthur, 230n6, 233n20
'*Lasse, que devendrai gié,*' (RS 1093),
  55, 68–73
Lefay-Toury, Marie-Noëlle, 37
Leocadia, Saint, 13
Leocadia sequence (Gautier de
  Coinci), 13–14, 19–20, 113
'*Li debonnaires Dieus m'a mis en sa
  prison*' (RS 1646), 55, 63–8
'*Li solaus qui en moy luist est mes deduis*'
  (RS 1936a, 2076), 55, 57, 59–62

Maillard, Jean, 229n11
mala canso, 28, 30, 82
manuscripts: Bern, Stadtbibliothek
  389, 74–5, 79, 106–7; Paris, Bibliothèque de l'Arsenal 3517, 58; Paris,
Bibliothèque de l'Arsenal 5198, 41;
  Paris, BnF fr. 837, 93, 106–7; Paris,
  BnF fr. 844, 34–5, 42; Paris, BnF
  fr. 845, 33, 35; Paris, BnF fr. 1593,
  93; Paris, BnF fr. 1635, 93; Paris,
  BnF fr. 12483, 56; Paris, BnF fr.
  12581, 34, 42; Paris, BnF fr. 12615,
  33, 35
Mary: Assumption of, 14–15; as *mediatrix*, 16, 19, 24, 41–4, 46, 50–1, 58,
  72, 75, 95; perpetual virginity of,
  71–2, 95, 97
Mary (of Egypt), 95–6, 98
Mary (of Magdala), 95–8
maternity, 15–16, 50, 59
McNamara, Jo Ann Kay, 63–4
melody, 7–8, 25, 28–9, 69–72, 93
metaphor, 18–19, 25–6, 27–8, 31,
  49–51, 102–3, 107–8, 109, 115
metonymy, 49
Mettman, Walter, 231n9
Miracles de Nostre Dame (Gautier de
  Coinci), 8, 11–31, 32, 53, 107, 114
misericords, 86
Miyazaki, Mariko, 86
model, lyric, 74
Mölk, Ulrich, 8
Monty Python, 115
motif, 74
mouvance, 87
Mustanoja, Tauna F., 235n4

Notre Dame school, the, 18

octave species, 69

Page, Christopher, 231n7
Palazzo, Russo, 223n6
papelardie, papelarde, 66–7
Passion, of Jesus, 68, 75–6, 84–5, 88

pastourelle, 18, 34, 74
Payen, Jean-Charles, 237n14
pelican, 86
phoenix, 86
Physiologus, the, 85
Pierre (de Gand), 83–6, 91
pitch nomenclature, 226n27
planctus Mariae, 68, 108
Pliny, 56
puy, 91–2

refrains, 78
Regaldo, Nancy Freeman, 225n21,
   236n5
Renart, 66, 96
Ricoeur, Paul, 6, 27–8, 31, 115
Rivière, Jean-Claude, 233n1
Robert le Bougre, 233n1
roman du graal, 34
rondet de carole, 231n7
Rosarius (Paris, BnF fr. 12483), 9, 56,
   60, 63, 69, 85
rubric, rubrication, 74–5, 77, 107–8
Rudolf (von Fenis), 80
Rutebeuf, 8, 9, 92, 93–113, 114;
   works: 'L' *Ave Maria* Rustebeuf,' 94,
   97–8; 'C'est de Notre Dame' (RS
   1998), 93–4; *Le Miracle de Théophile*,
   98, 105, 107–8; 'Prière Théophile,'
   98–9, 102–8; 'La Repentance Rutebeuf,' 94–6; 'Repentance Théophile,' 98–102, 105–8; 'Un dist de
   Nostre Dame,' 108–12

salamander, 84–5
Savoie, Mary Alberta, 230n6
Schillebeeckx, Edward, 224n6
Secor, John R., 232n18
serventois, 91–2
Siberry, Elizabeth, 228n6

Simeon, 70
sirventois, 34
Songs of the Women Trouvères (Doss-
   Quinby et al.), 54–5
Spanke, Hans, 50–2
Strayer, Joseph, 234n5
strophe d'Hélinand, 95, 102
Svenqvist, Sven, 56
Switten, Margaret, 221n1

theme, 74
Theophilus, 13, 27, 98–108
Theotókos, 68
Thibaut (de Blason), 36; songs:
   'Amors, que porra devenir' (RS
   1402), 36
Thibaut (de Champagne), 4, 6, 8,
   33–53, 54, 75, 78, 83–6, 113, 114;
   songs: 'Ausi conme unicorne sui'
   (RS 2075), 77, 83–4; 'Commencerai
   a fere un lai' (RS 84, 73a), 34,
   49–53; 'Dame, einsi est qu'il m'en
   couveient aler' (RS 757), 47–9; 'De
   chanter ne me puis tenir' (RS
   1475), 36–7, 39, 75; 'De grant travail' (RS 1843), 42–4; 'Dex est ensi
   comne li pellicans' (RS 273), 35, 86;
   'Dou tres douz non a la virge Marie'
   (RS 1181), 36, 38–9; 'Mauvez arbres
   ne puet florir' (RS 1410), 40–2; 'Seignor, sachiés qui or ne s'en ira' (RS
   6), 45–7, 49, 75; 'Tant ai amors
   servie longuement,' (RS 711, 1067),
   35–6; 'Tuit mi desir et tuit mi grief
   torment' (RS 741, 991), 77
Tischler, Hans, 51

unicorn, 83–4

vilannie/vilains, 29–31

Vincent de Beauvais, 58
virelai, 17
voice, women's vs. men's, 56–7

Wallensköld, Axel, 33, 35–6
Warner, Marina, 68
Weinsheimer, Joel, 115
Wolfzettel, Friedrich, 8

women's songs, 9, 114

Yates, Frances, 18
Yvain (Chrétien de Troyes), 29

Zetterberg, Anders, 230n4
Zink, Michel, 99, 106–7